IMAGES
of America

FORT WORTH PARKS

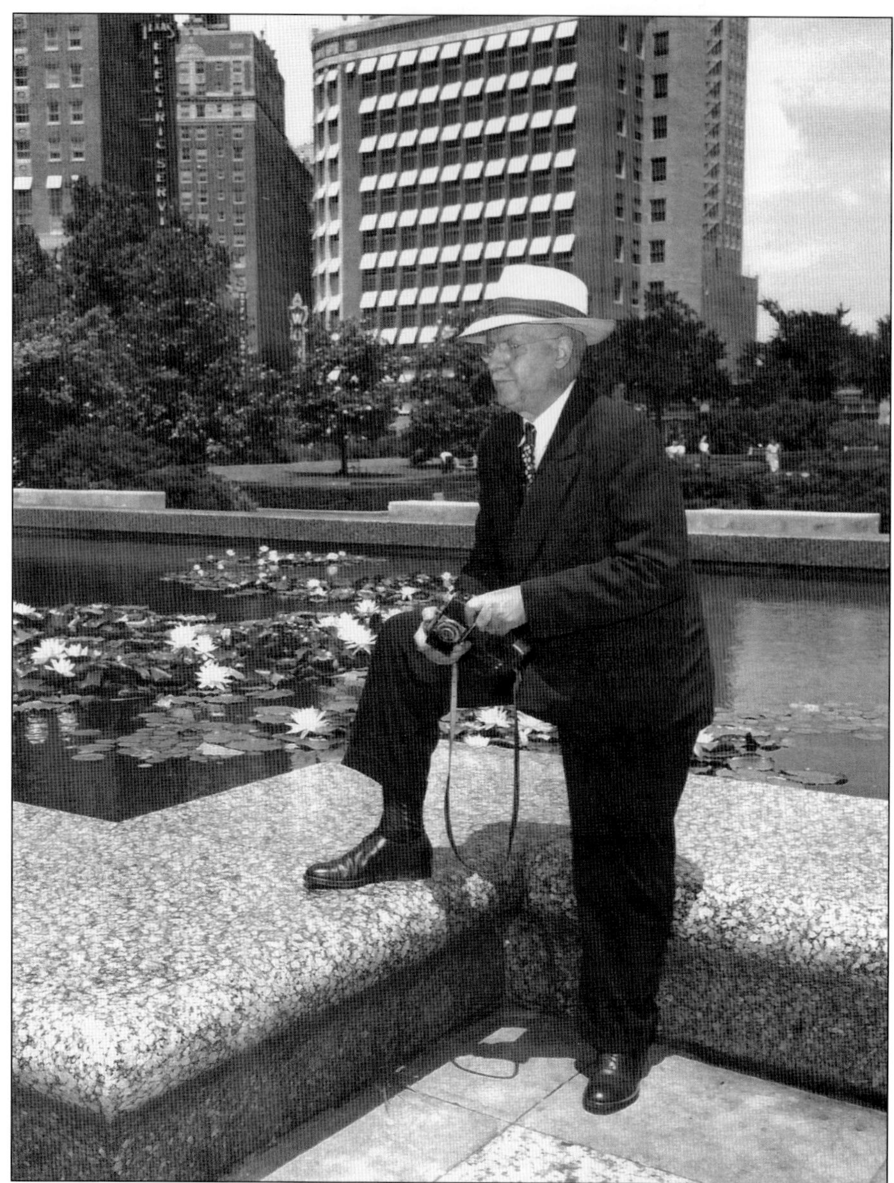

S. Herbert Hare of the famed landscape architecture firm of Hare and Hare of Kansas City, Missouri, became Fort Worth's park consultant in 1925. During the next 35 years, the firm was responsible for the design of nearly 60 park projects in the city. Here Hare is pictured in 1950 at one of his favorite projects—Burnett Park in downtown Fort Worth. (*Fort Worth Star-Telegram* Collections, the University of Texas at Arlington Library, Arlington, Texas [FWSTC/SCUTA].)

On the Cover: Around 1941, Farm Security Administration–Office of War Information photographer Alfred T. Palmer captured this idyllic scene at the Fort Worth Botanic Garden. The Office of War Information used this image in a montage of photographs to represent the ideal of "Freedom from Fear" made famous in Franklin Delano Roosevelt's "Four Freedoms" speech of 1941. (Library of Congress, Washington, D.C.)

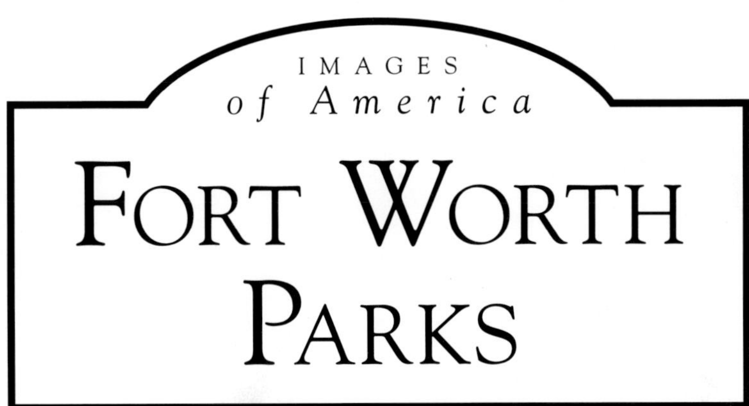

Susan Allen Kline and the
Fort Worth Parks and
Community Services Department

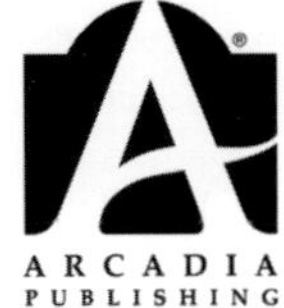

ISBN 978-0-7385-7866-8

Published by Arcadia Publishing
Charleston SC, Chicago IL, Portsmouth NH, San Francisco CA

Printed in the United States of America

Library of Congress Control Number: 2009930173

For all general information contact Arcadia Publishing at:
Telephone 843-853-2070
Fax 843-853-0044
E-mail sales@arcadiapublishing.com
For customer service and orders:
Toll-Free 1-888-313-2665

Visit us on the Internet at www.arcadiapublishing.com

Dedicated to the citizens of Fort Worth
for their tireless support of our park system,
which ensures a quality of life legacy for future generations.

Contents

Acknowledgments

Besides the individuals and institutions acknowledged elsewhere in this book, the following also deserve credit for sharing information or pointing us toward that next great photograph: the staff of the Genealogy, History, and Archives Unit, Fort Worth Library; the staff of Special Collections, University of Texas at Arlington Library; Historic Fort Worth, Inc.; Ana Briseno; Summer Burke; Bob Crow; Juliet George; Shirley Lewis; Remekca Owens; Carol Roark; Clara Ruddell; Rick Selcer; Susie Pritchett; Hollace Ava Weiner; and Alexis Wilson. Steve Kline provided invaluable assistance, love, and encouragement. Many thanks also go to the Allen clan and friends.

Tom Kellam, archivist at the Genealogy, History, and Archives Unit, Fort Worth Library; Cathleen Spitzenberger, photograph librarian at Special Collections, University of Texas at Arlington Library; and Kathleen Cook, Fort Worth Botanic Garden, cheerfully answered numerous search requests and scanned many of the images used in this book. We express our thanks to Arcadia Publishing and our editors, Kristie Kelly for her early and enthusiastic support of this project and Hannah Carney for expertly guiding it through to completion.

Parks and Community Services Department staff assisting with this book include Richard Zavala Jr. (director), Sandra Youngblood, Kelli Pickard, Cindy Brooks, Judy Bauereisen, Rena Lawrence, Melody Mitchell, Ivette Ray, and Suzanne Tuttle. We are also grateful to the organizations that have supported the department over the years. They include Streams and Valleys, Mayfest, Trinity River Steering Committee, Fort Worth Botanical Society, Fort Worth Garden Club, Outriders, Youth Sports Council, Log Cabin Heritage Foundation, Friends of the Van Zandt Cottage, Sports Advisory Council, Friends of the Nature Center, Community Action Partners Council, and Cowboy Santas.

The Texas State Historical Association's Cecilia Steinfeldt Fellowship provided the means to conduct research in the Hare and Hare Collection at the Western Historical Manuscript Collection, University of Missouri–Kansas City.

Many of the images in this volume appear courtesy of the Genealogy, History, and Archives Unit, Fort Worth Library (FWL); *Fort Worth Star-Telegram* Collections, the University of Texas at Arlington Library, Arlington, Texas (FWSTC/SCUTA); Fort Worth Botanic Garden (FWBG); and the Parks and Community Services Department (PACS).

INTRODUCTION

There is a way in Fort Worth that is unique to the people of the place we call Cowtown. It is guided by a set of community values established upon the spirit of the frontier. It is the spirit of determination, a hard work ethic, a commitment to the community, and a respect for one's neighbor. This is the way in Fort Worth, and these are the values that guided our citizens who collectively helped to establish, nurture, grow, and preserve our park system.

In 1908, a group of interested citizens working under the auspices of the Fort Worth Park League recommended that Kansas City landscape architect George E. Kessler be engaged to prepare a park plan for Fort Worth. It was the community volunteers of the park league who recognized the importance of parks to the city of Fort Worth and the need for a plan to guide in the acquisition and development of the park system. As Kessler observed, "In the competition of cities for new and desirable population, no other element of advertisement is worth so much as an ample and attractive park system, making a pleasant city in which to live comfortably." Kessler and the members of the park league understood the need for parks. In order for a Board of Park Commissioners to have the power of acquiring property for parks, the Fort Worth City Charter would have to be changed. In 1909, the state legislature approved an amendment that provided monetary powers, including an ad valorem levy of 10¢ "for the use and benefit of the park fund." On April 20, 1909, when the amendment became effective, the Fort Worth park system was officially established. Were it not for this group of civic-minded preservationists and their forward thinking and sense of urgency, the foundation of our park system would most likely be different today. Fortunately for the generations that followed, and those that will follow the generation of today, the people of Fort Worth 100 years ago gave of themselves for the betterment of the community and set the standard of a philanthropic park legacy that still exists today.

In 1930, the firm of Hare and Hare, City Planners–Landscape Architects completed a study commissioned by the Board of Park Commissioners that resulted in the park system's second plan, entitled "A Comprehensive Park System for Fort Worth, Texas." The 1930 plan helped to address the rapid growth that Fort Worth had experienced in the 1920s and served as a guide for the development of the park system through the Great Depression, World War II, and the baby boom growth period of the early and mid-1950s. The plan stated, "Besides paying dividends in the increased happiness and health of citizens, such parks have an even more tangible value in increasing adjacent land values," as well as "the publicity value of beauty." Twenty-seven years later, the Hare and Hare firm conducted a second review of the park system, which resulted in the publication of a new plan, entitled "A Master Park Plan for Fort Worth, Texas." This plan positioned the city to effectively address the rapid growth occurring in both the city's population and land area.

In 1978, an amendment to the City of Fort Worth Sub Division Ordinance was passed requiring that residential developers set aside park land to address population growth. For more than 30 years, the Park Land Dedication Policy has ensured the presence of neighborhood parks in each community. In 1992, the park and recreation board and city council adopted the Strategic Plan for the Fort Worth Park and Recreation Department to guide in the effective and efficient management of department resources. In 1998, the city council adopted by resolution the Park, Recreation, and Open Space Master Plan that built upon the planning and stewardship legacy of the community. The Park, Recreation, and Open Space Master Plan was updated and endorsed by the Parks and Community Services Advisory Board in 2004, adopted by the city council, and incorporated into the City of Fort Worth Comprehensive Plan.

In the first few years of the 21st century, the exploration and extraction of natural gas began in the Fort Worth area. The Barnett Shale play has provided the City of Fort Worth park system with the resources necessary to rebuild an aging infrastructure and address some of its critical capital improvement needs. Early on in the era of leasing mineral rights from under the park land (from off-site locations as a result of horizontal drilling processes), community leaders had the foresight and vision to establish a prudent financial management strategy that will maximize the impact of this windfall for both the present and the future. With the establishment of the Fort Worth Permanent Fund–Park System Endowment Fund, the community is ensuring that the financial benefits of the present will last into the future.

The Fort Worth parks and open space system serves as the foundation of the community's greatest asset—its quality of life. Built upon this base of open space are many quality recreational, historical, environmental, and educational amenities. The pillars of the system that have been acquired and developed during the last 100 years include the Fort Worth Botanic Garden; the Fort Worth Zoo; the Log Cabin Village; the Fort Worth Nature Center and Refuge; Trinity, Forest, Marine, and Sycamore Parks; and the Trinity River corridor and trail system. Collectively these treasures ensure what is most important to our community—our quality of life.

During the last 100 years, it has been the people of Fort Worth who helped build and preserve our park system. Today (and, with all certainty, tomorrow) they continue to be stalwart in their stewardship duty.

Our park system is likely the greatest legacy that our foremothers and forefathers built for us, and it will surely be the greatest legacy the people of today will leave for the community of tomorrow. In the end, it is the people who make a park system. And the people of Fort Worth have done a very good job building and preserving ours. It is "the Fort Worth Way."

—Richard Zavala Jr.
Director, Parks and Community Services Department

One

The Early Years 1873 to 1919

Fort Worth's namesake military outpost was established at the confluence of the Clear and West Forks of the Trinity River in north central Texas in 1849. Its physical setting with high bluffs above the river was considered of strategic importance for the defense of the frontier. Such physical attributes would be of prime importance in the future planning of a park system.

After the fort was abandoned, the community that had grown up around it became the seat of government for Tarrant County in 1856 and was incorporated in 1873. That same year, the Jennings family donated to the city a small tract of land in the heart of the business district for use as a park. Hyde Park became Fort Worth's first, and now its oldest, public park.

Fort Worth's second park was acquired in 1892 when the city purchased 50 acres straddling the Clear Fork of the Trinity River. Approximately 31 acres on the west side was designated for park use, known simply as City Park. Improvements to it were slow in coming. Management of the park fell to the City Federation of Women's Clubs. It was through their efforts, as well as men such as Sam Davidson and A. W. Grant, that a Park League was formed in 1908. The Park League advocated the creation of more parks and the development of a park master plan. The league secured the services of George E. Kessler, a landscape architect of national renown. Kessler first visited Fort Worth in November 1908, and the following month, the city commission voted to pay him $1,500 to develop a park plan. His recommendations included the creation of a comprehensive system of parks and connecting boulevards as well as a park board. The latter was realized in 1909, giving the city an official park department.

Over the next decade, the park board aggressively bought land for park use. City Park became Trinity Park, and its acreage was increased. Other parks created during this time were Forest (including its zoo), Sycamore, Capps, Hillside, Paddock, and Burnett.

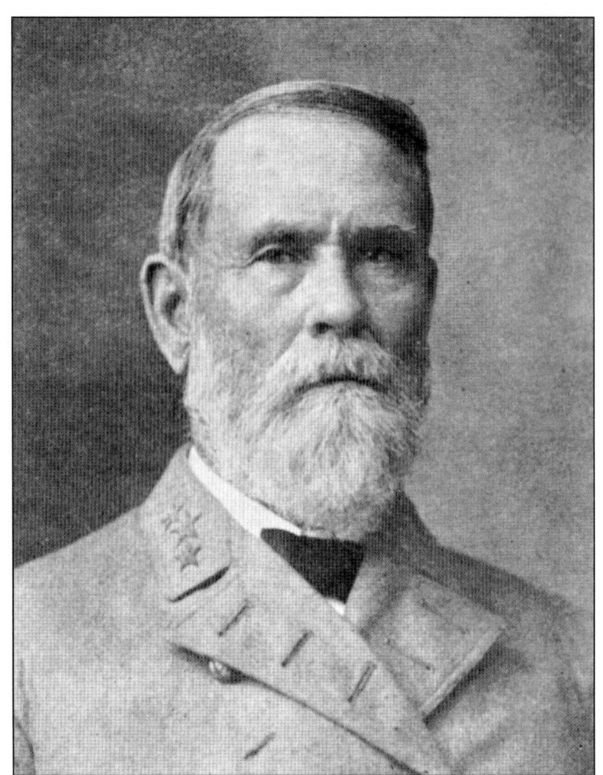

Maj. K. M. Van Zandt (1836–1930) arrived in Fort Worth in 1865 after a career as a lawyer in Marshall, Texas, and service in Company D, 7th Texas Infantry, during the Civil War. A successful merchant, cattleman, and town leader, he acquired land along the west bank of the Clear Fork of the Trinity River, which became the sites of City (later Trinity) Park and the Fort Worth Botanic Garden. (FWL.)

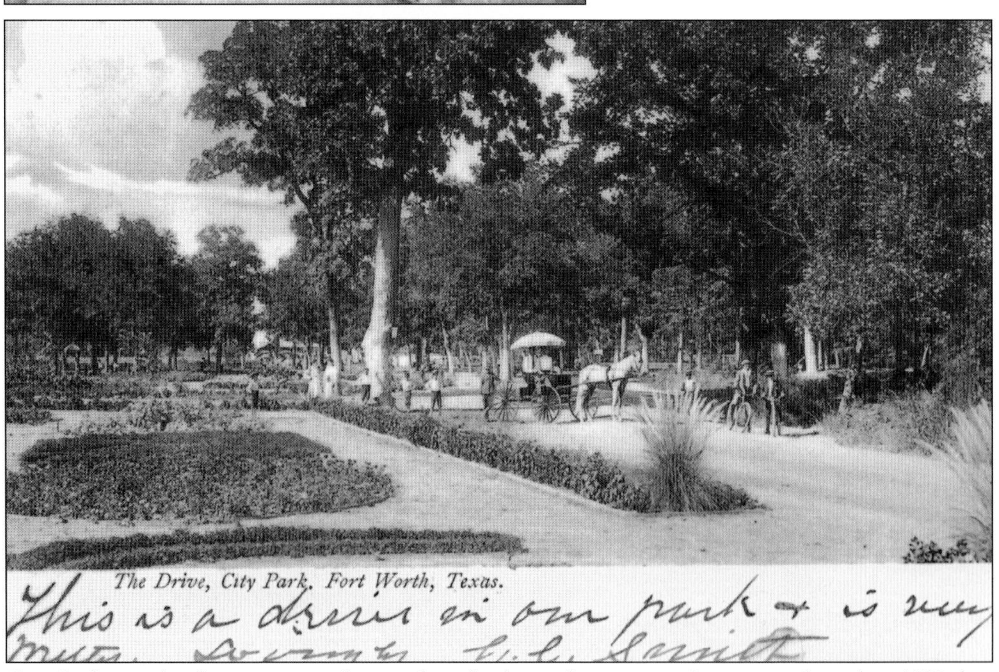

City Park was the first property the city bought for park purposes. It was purchased in 1892, but even prior to that, it was a favorite gathering spot for picnics and outings when owned by Major Van Zandt. The gardens shown in this image were some of the early improvements made in the park after it became city property. (FWL.)

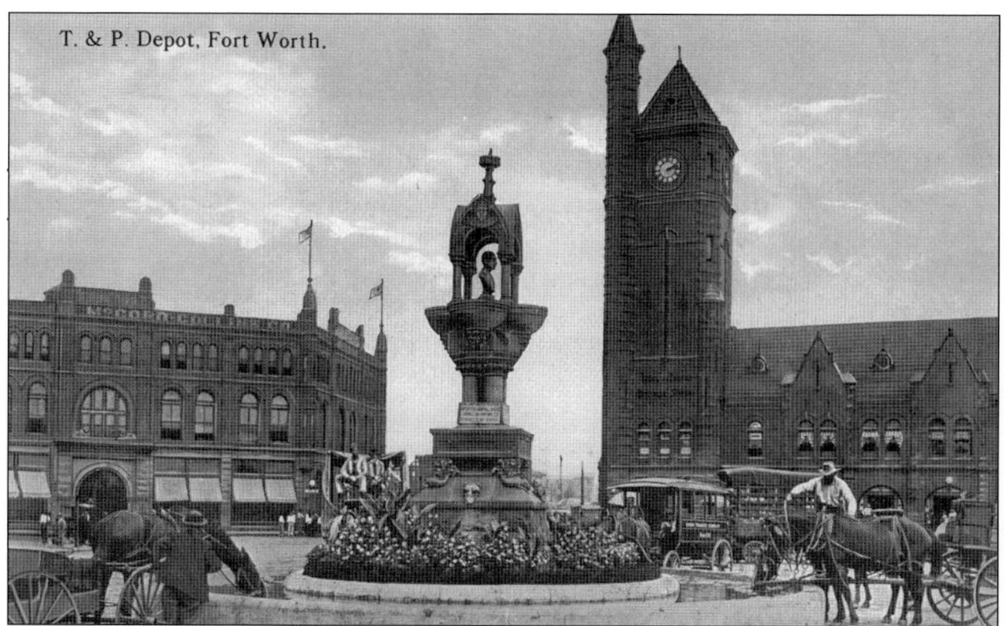

Now located near the intersection of Lancaster Avenue and Main Street, the Al Hayne monument memorializes the heroic actions of its namesake. When the nearby Texas Spring Palace burned in May 1890, Hayne rescued many people but ironically was the fire's only fatality. This horse fountain was erected in 1893 and became part of the park system in 1916. (Larry Schuessler.)

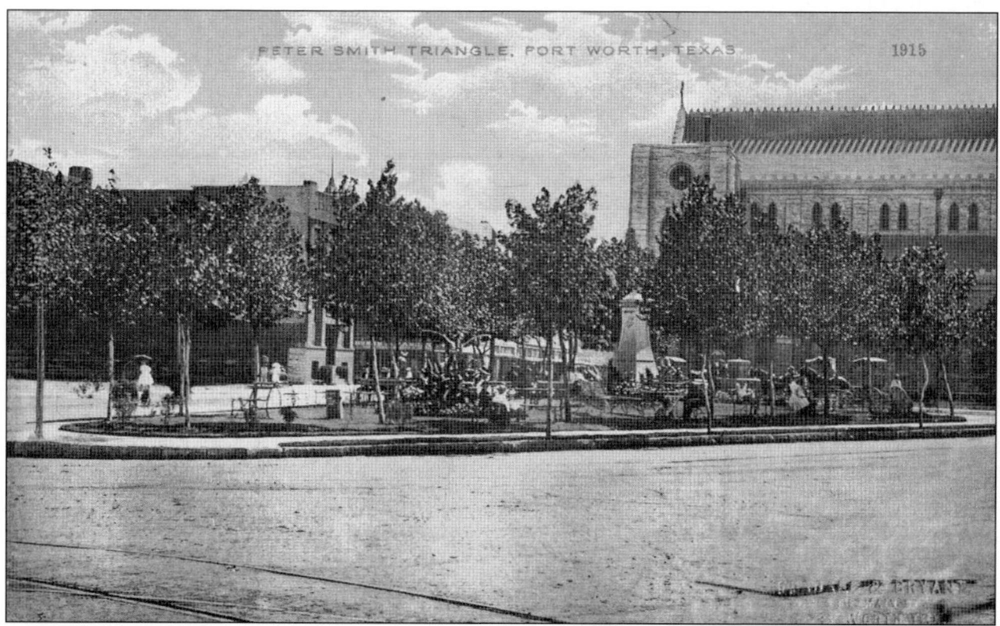

In 1906, a monument to city pioneer John Peter Smith (1831–1901) was erected downtown on a small triangle at Jennings Avenue and Throckmorton Street. Peter Smith opened the town's first school in 1854. A self-taught lawyer, he had numerous business and real estate dealings. His civic accomplishments included several terms as mayor. Funding for the monument was raised through public subscription. (Dalton Hoffman.)

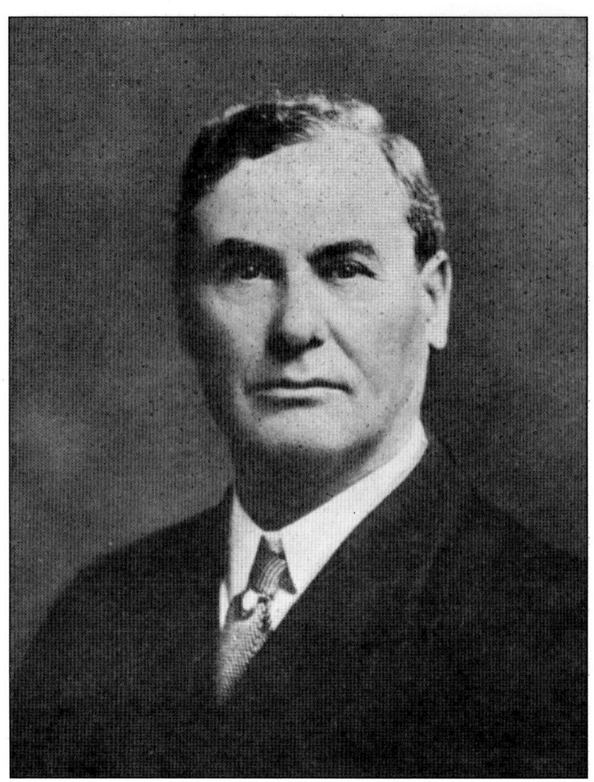

Sam Davidson (1855–1924), a Jewish immigrant from Prussia, was a prominent businessman and cattleman when he was elected to the city commission in 1907. As commissioner of streets and public grounds, he became a driving force behind the creation of the Park League in 1908. Officers of that organization were A. W. Grant, president; Ida Caldwell Saunders, first vice president; and Belle Burney, secretary. (FWL.)

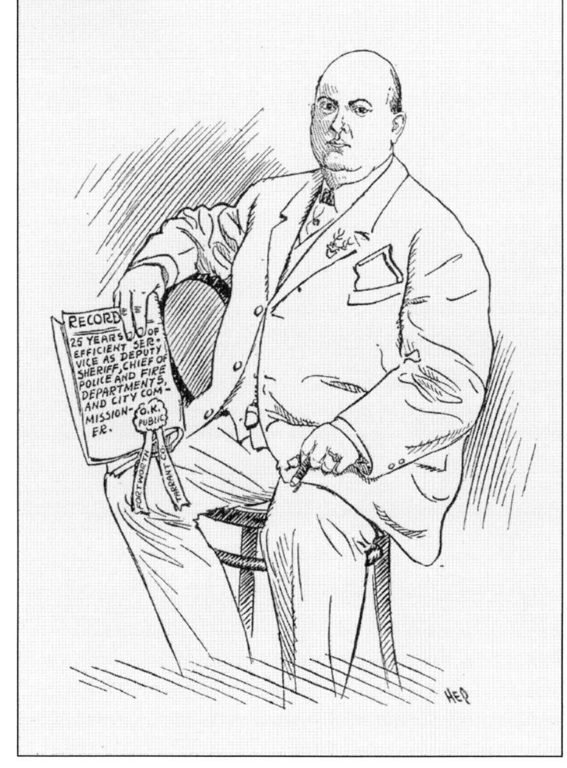

By virtue of his position as commissioner of streets and public grounds, J. H. Maddox became the park board's first chairman when that body was organized in 1909. In 1912, the park board named a new park on Gould Avenue on Fort Worth's Northside in his honor at the request of the Hill Crest Civic League, a woman's organization in that section of the city. (FWL.)

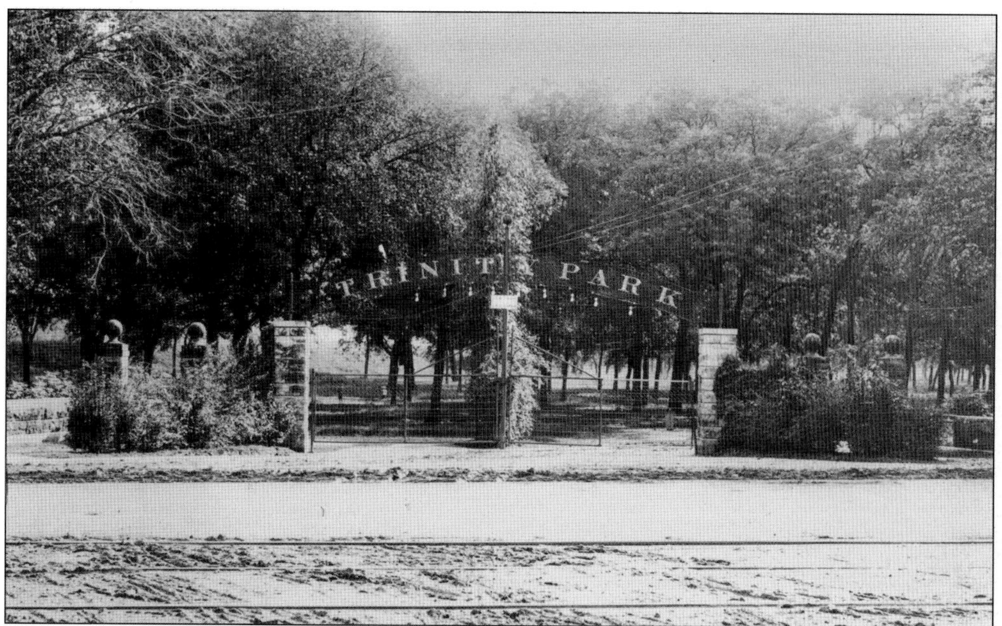

Prior to the establishment of a city park department in 1909, the City Federation of Women's Clubs managed improvements made in City Park. In 1908, the federation contracted for the erection of an iron gate for the park. In June 1910, the park board's secretary was directed to have the name sign changed to reflect the park's new name—Trinity Park. The entrance was also widened at that time. (FWL.)

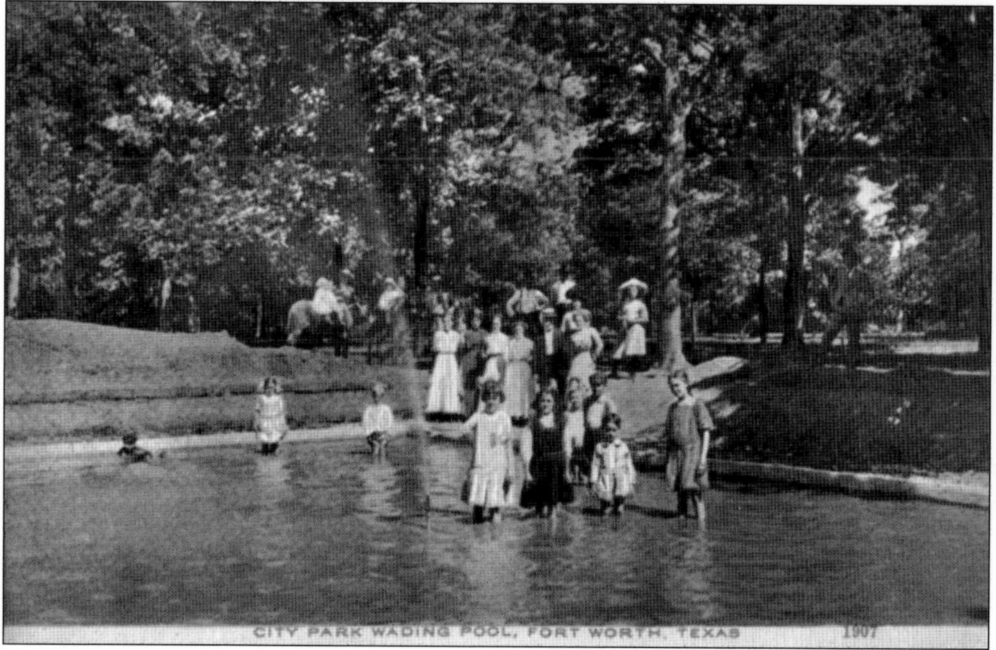

Based on a photograph that appeared in the *Fort Worth Star-Telegram* on June 2, 1910, this postcard image shows a group of youngsters trying out the new wading pool in Trinity Park. They are as nearly well dressed as the adults standing behind them. Those on the burros in the background may have found the pool a pleasant place to cool off after a ride. (Larry Schuessler.)

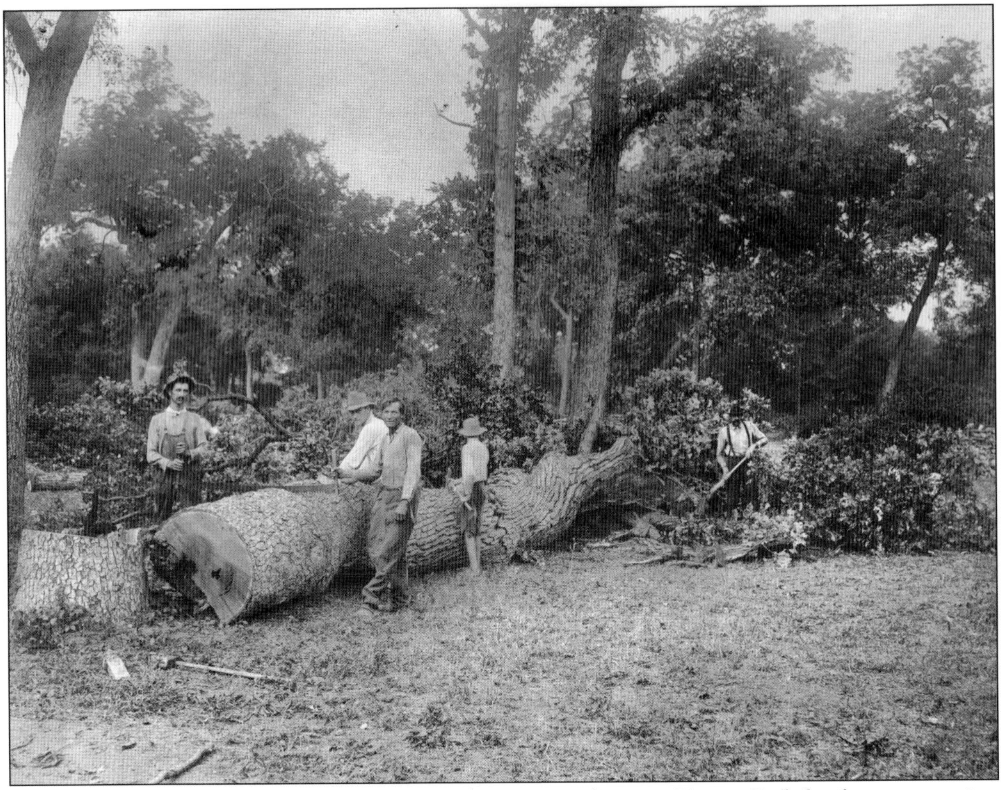

In the summer of 1910, controversy arose over the cutting of trees in Trinity Park for the construction of levees along the Trinity River. The Drainage District Commission (levee board) authorized what was termed the "denuding" of the park over the objections of citizens and the park board. As a compromise, the levee board gave the park board 42 acres from the Van Zandt tract adjoining the park. (FWL.)

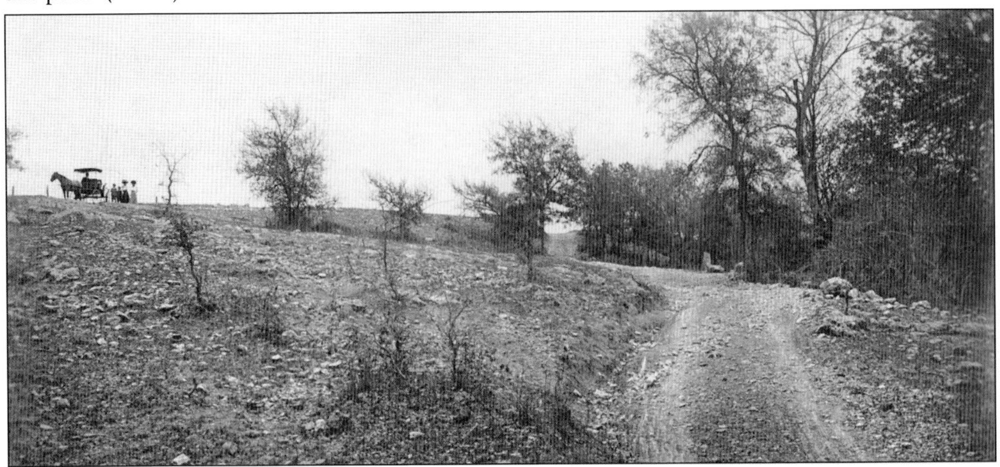

Upon the advice of George E. Kessler, park consultant for the city, the newly formed park board acquired the first 74.73 acres of Forest Park in October 1909. Kessler envisioned this park, originally called Southwest Park, as one of four that would surround the city. As shown in this photograph from November 1909, the park was valued for its rolling terrain and native trees offset by large open areas. (FWL.)

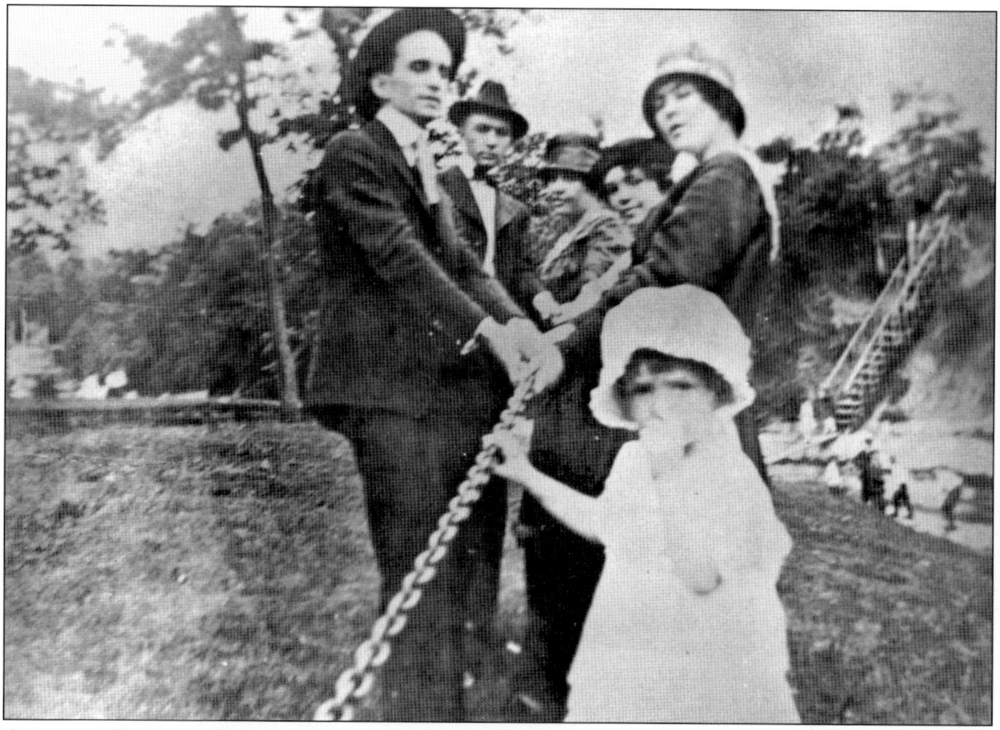

A visit to Forest or Trinity Park was considered a special occasion, and park patrons dressed appropriately. Once the streetcar line to Texas Christian University was completed in 1912, access to Forest Park was made easier for residents. After disembarking from the streetcar, visitors could enter the park by descending the stairs shown on the right in this photograph. (Mike McDermott.)

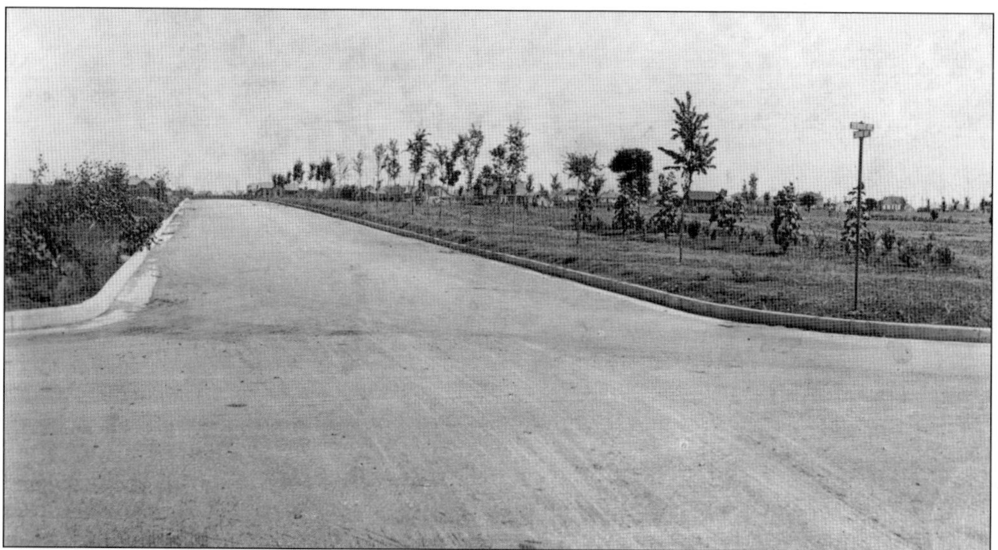

William Capps, a prominent attorney, newspaper publisher, and real estate developer, offered a block situated between Devitt Street and what is now Berry Street for use as a city park in exchange for the city paving the streets around it. The park board officially accepted the offer in June 1909. This photograph may have been taken in 1910 after the board appropriated $75 for the planting of trees. (FWL.)

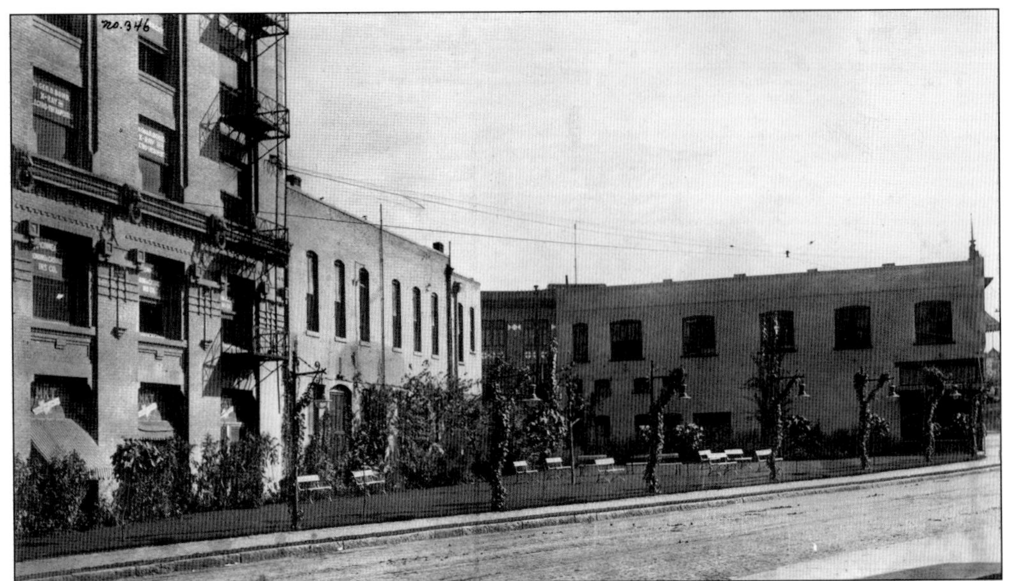

Downtown's Hyde Park, located adjacent to the Flatiron Building (left) and fronting Jennings Avenue, was a gift to the city from the Jennings family in 1873, making it the city's oldest park. In 1910, it was beautified with flower beds, trellises to hide advertising on adjacent walls, benches, and trees. In November of that year, the Fort Worth Gas Company donated ornamental lamps that were placed along the street. (FWL.)

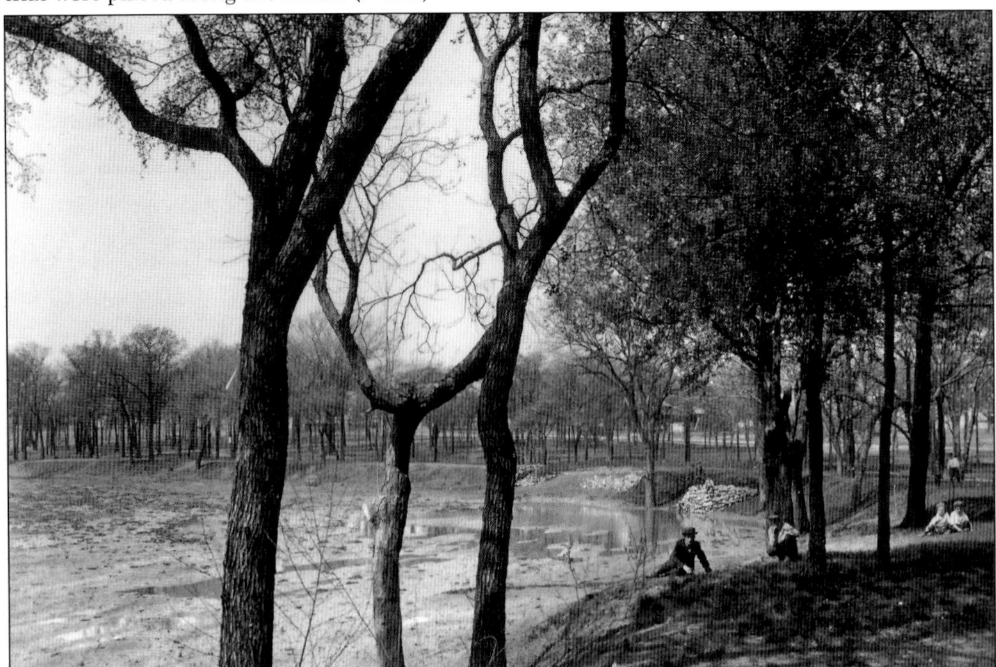

Marine Park was a popular picnic spot for north-siders before North Fort Worth was annexed into Fort Worth in 1909. That same year, the park board approved the construction of a lake in the park. It was completed in 1910, but as shown in this photograph from April 1911, patrons were still waiting for rains to completely fill it. The lake was drained after neighbors complained it was a breeding ground for mosquitoes. (FWL.)

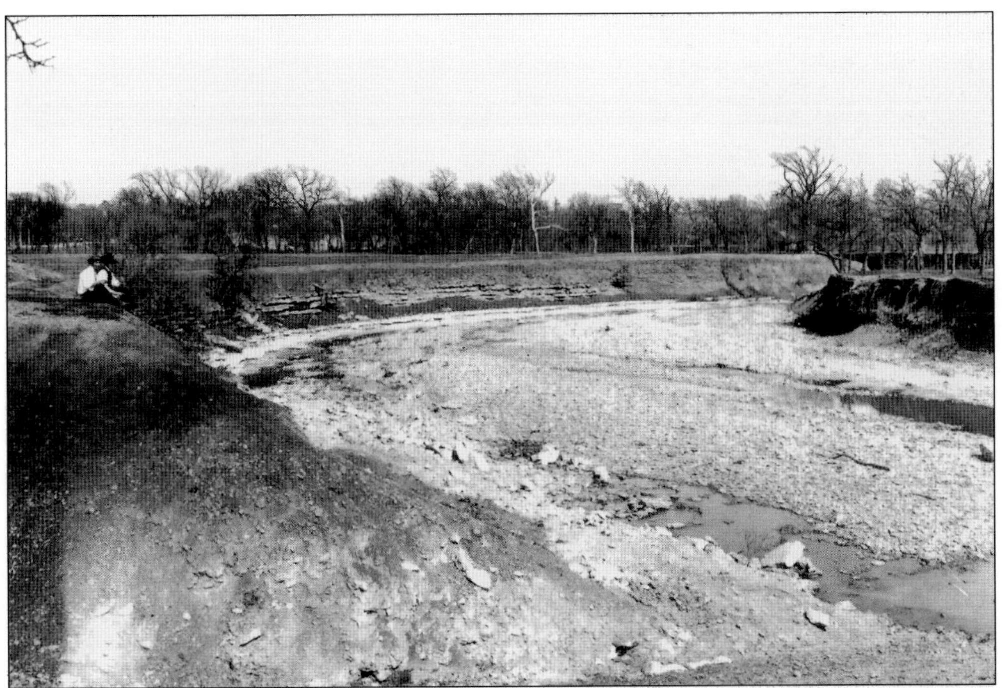

Under Kessler's plan, Glenwood Park, located in East Fort Worth, was to become an athletic field with a variety of recreational amenities. The above photograph was taken in 1910 before many improvements had been made. By May 1911, it was being proclaimed as the city's favorite playground, with swing sets for different age groups, a merry-go-round, baseball diamonds, and running tracks. The photograph below from that year shows the swings (far left) and the band shelter (far right). To avoid confusion with another area on the east side, the park's name was changed to Sycamore in July 1911. (Both, FWL.)

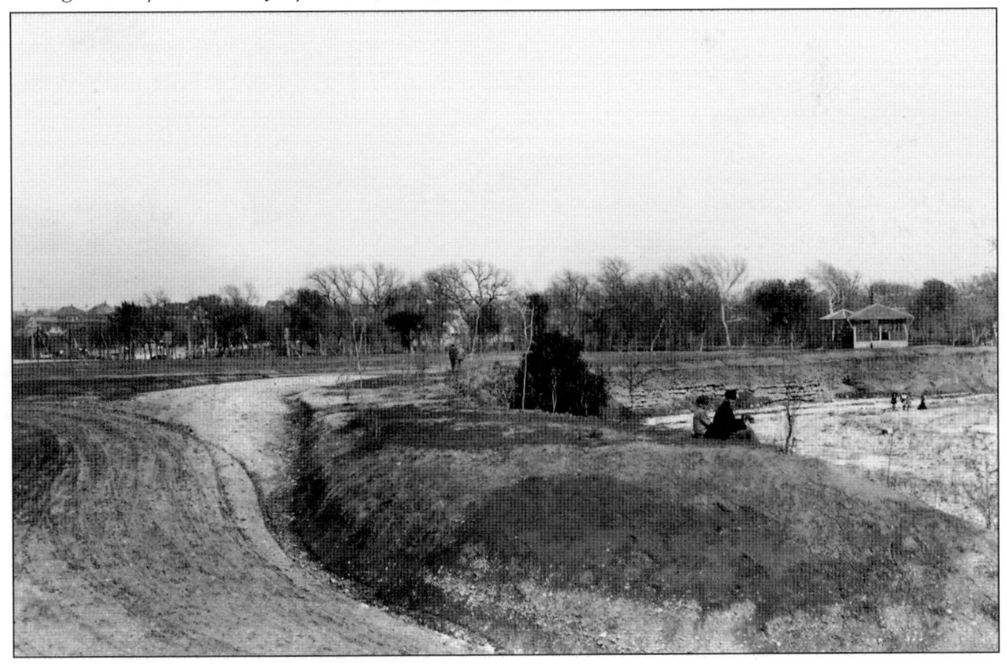

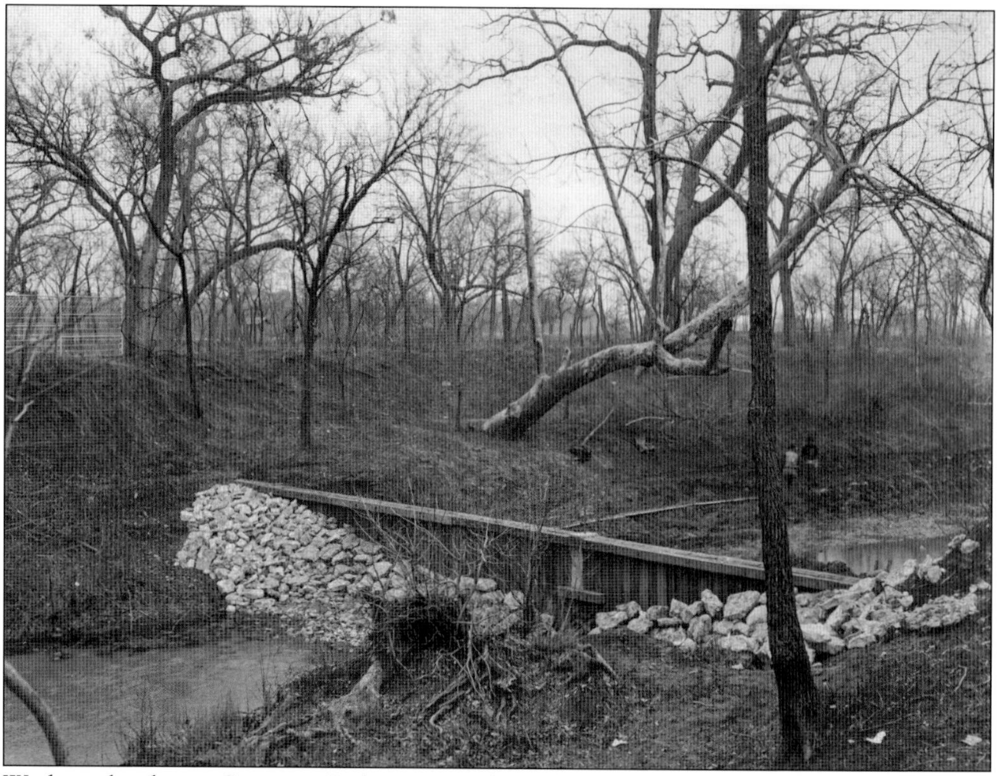

Work on this dam in Sycamore Park was started in February 1912. The structure was 7 feet high and 80 feet long. It was envisioned that impounding Sycamore Creek would create a lagoon large enough to accommodate wading, swimming, and boating. This photograph was taken on March 8, 1912. Two weeks later, heavy rains did extensive damage to the rock filling, but the dam itself withstood the deluge. (FWL.)

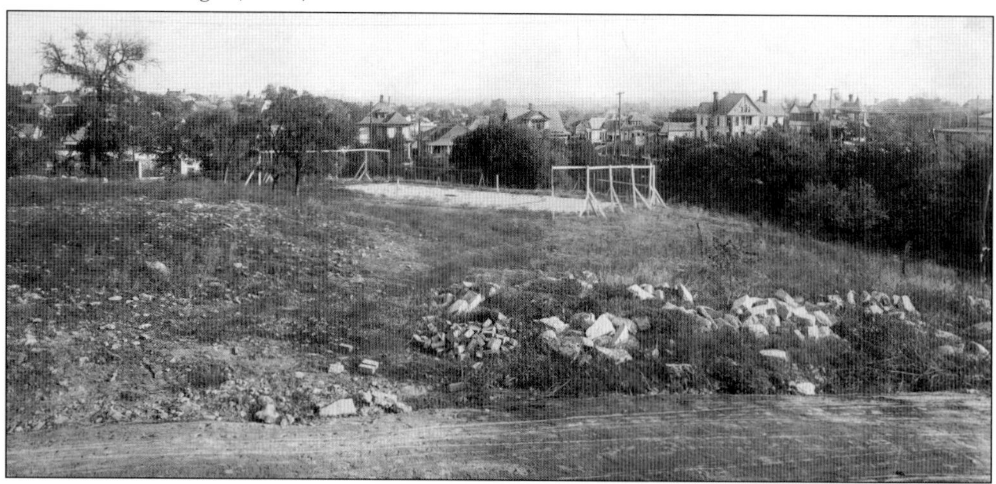

Although near downtown, the steep topography of this parcel made it difficult to develop. This is how it looked in 1912 when the park board purchased it. Named Grant Park in honor of A. W. Grant, a prominent figure in Fort Worth's park movement, it remained largely unimproved until the Rotary Club came to its rescue in 1916. That year, the name was changed to Rotary Park with Grant's approval. (FWL.)

George E. Vinnedge, a consulting landscape engineer who twice served as park superintendent, made this plaster layout of the proposed improvements to Rotary Park. The model included replicas of the swimming pools, bathhouse, bandstand, and the streetcar rails on West Seventh Street and Summit Avenue. Tufts of sponges dyed green were used for the tree foliage. (FWL.)

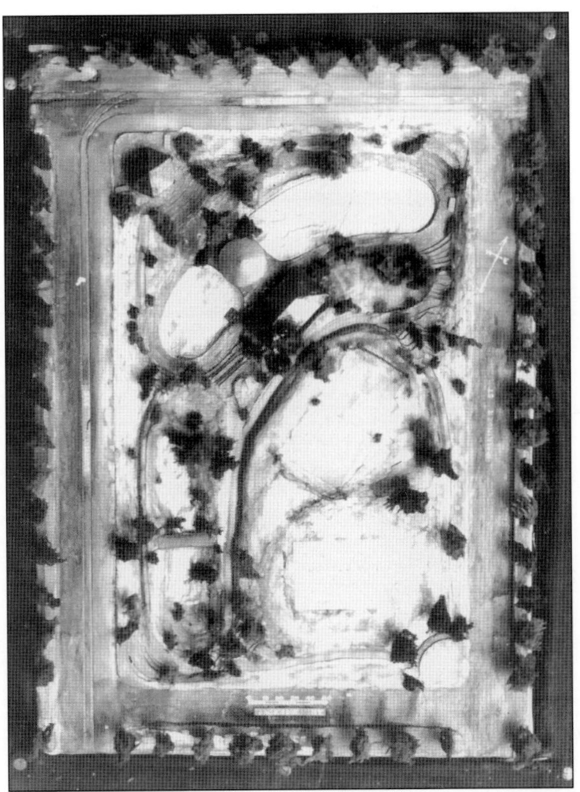

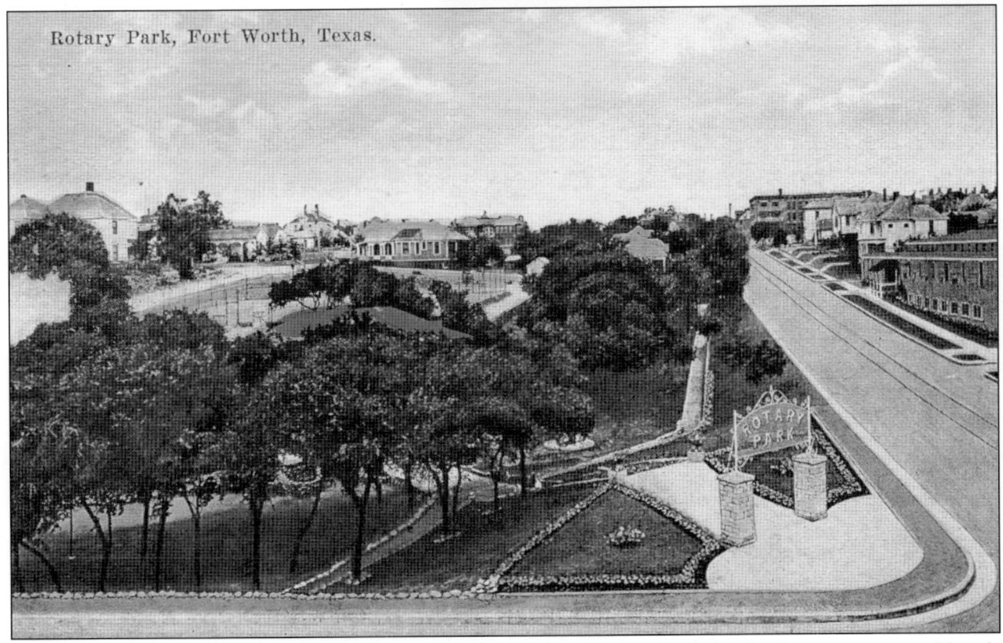

This postcard view depicts the improvements made to Rotary Park with the assistance of funds from the Rotary Club. The park department's headquarters were moved to this location in 1924. When Rotary Park was sold in 1955, the park offices were moved to the Fort Worth Botanic Garden. (Jennifer Harnish.)

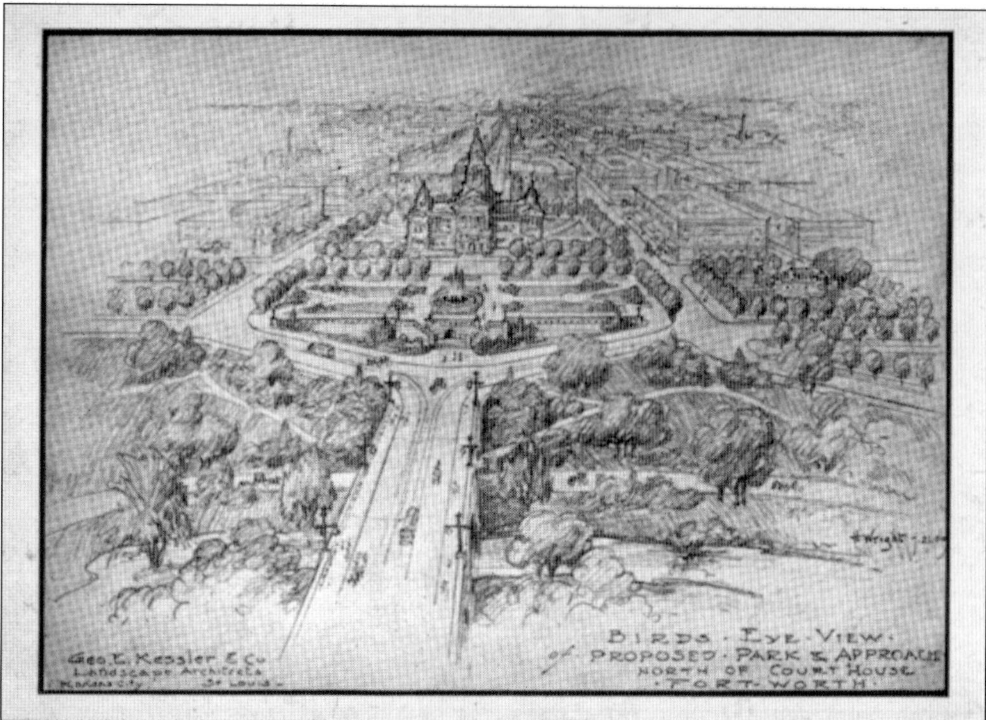

In late 1912, proponents of Kessler's concept for a stately approach to the Tarrant County Courthouse produced this postcard to garner support for the plan. Implementation would require the removal of the county jail and several small commercial buildings north of the courthouse. Although the plan was not adopted, later parks such as Paddock and Heritage Park along the bluff now provide a more appropriate setting for the grand building. (Larry Schuessler.)

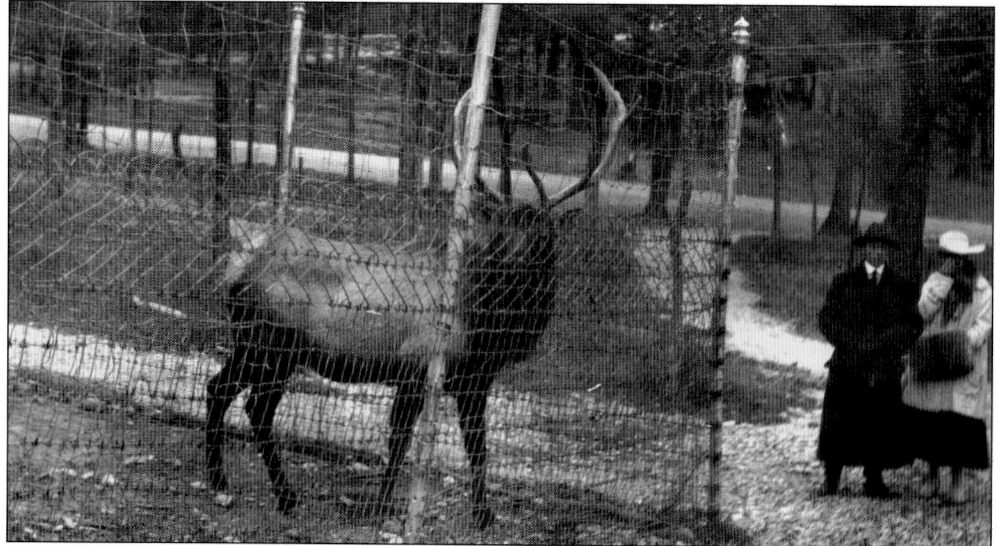

Forest Park Zoo received its first pair of elk in 1914 as a gift of the local Elks organization. The animals were captured at Yellowstone National Park. To the right of the pen are Arthur and Stella Paddock. Many of the early animals at the zoo were acquired through donations or funds raised for the purchase of a specific specimen. (Dorothy Paddock Dixson.)

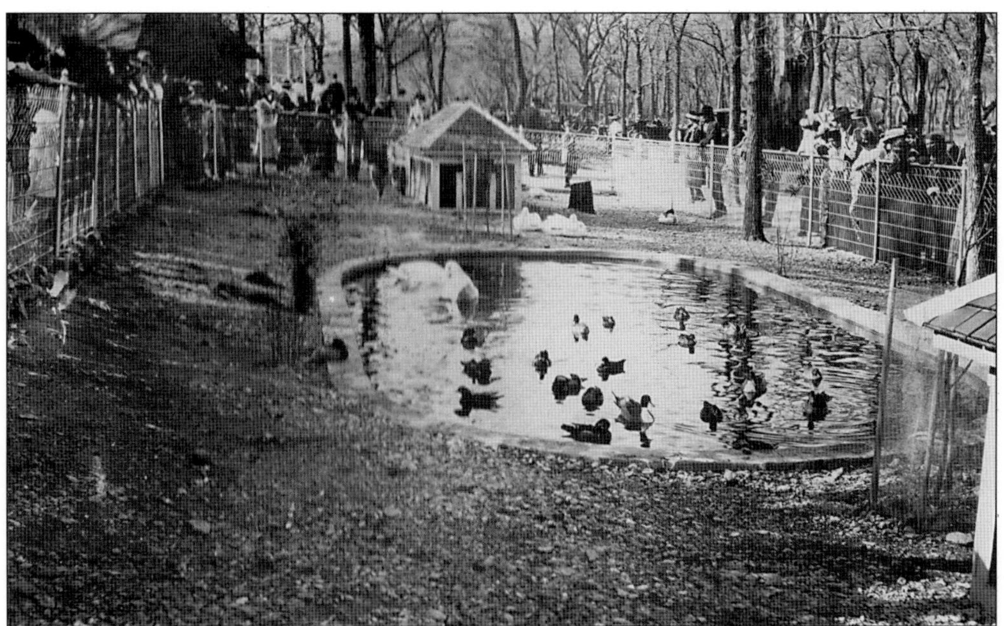

Water fowl were among the animals donated by residents to increase the zoo's inventory. A 113-pound turtle found at Lake Worth became an early resident. Other easily acquired animals included rabbits, squirrels, bears, raccoons, wolves, prairie dogs, a coyote, and badgers. Here onlookers watch ducks and swans swim in their own pool. (Dorothy Paddock Dixson.)

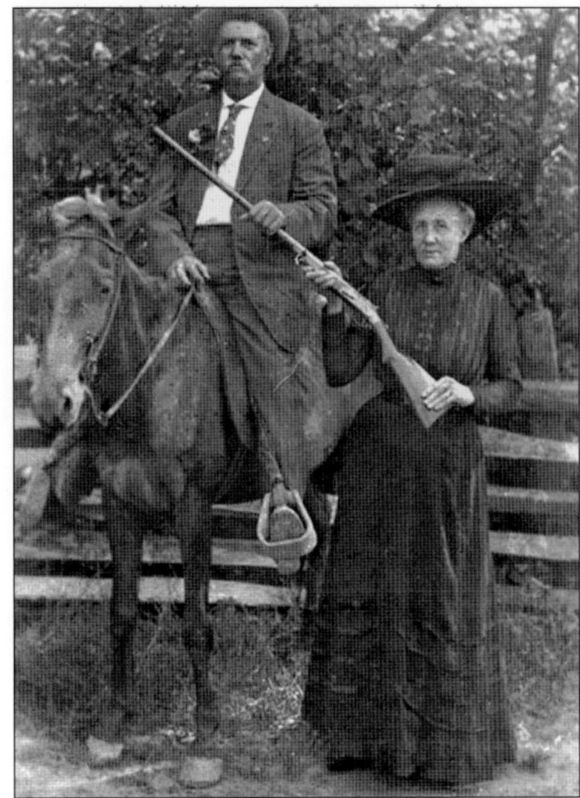

For seven years, John Franklin Dollins served as a police officer patrolling Trinity and Forest Parks on horseback. Family members recalled driving around the curve close to the zoo in Forest Park at night to scare him. Here he poses on his horse with his rifle and his wife, Sarah, in one of the parks. (Carol Dean Crabtree Peacock and the late Thelma Lucille Dollins Crabtree.)

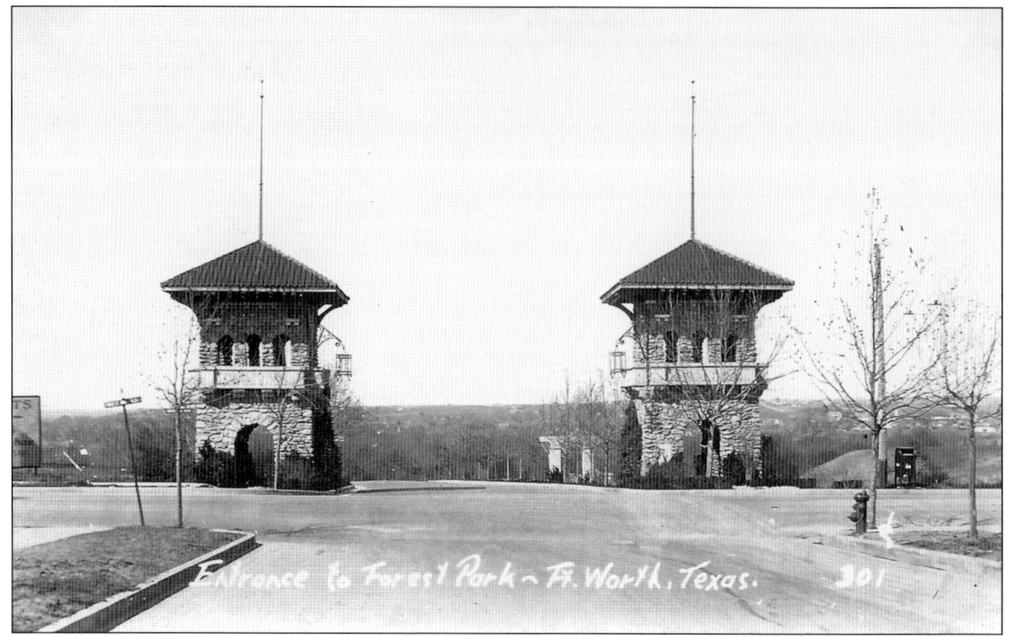

Constructed of native limestone rubble, these striking towers provide a grand entrance to Forest Park. They were designed by local architect John Pollard and were erected by the Bryce Building Company around 1918. The north tower originally contained the cornerstone. It was removed years later under mysterious circumstances. (Larry Schuessler.)

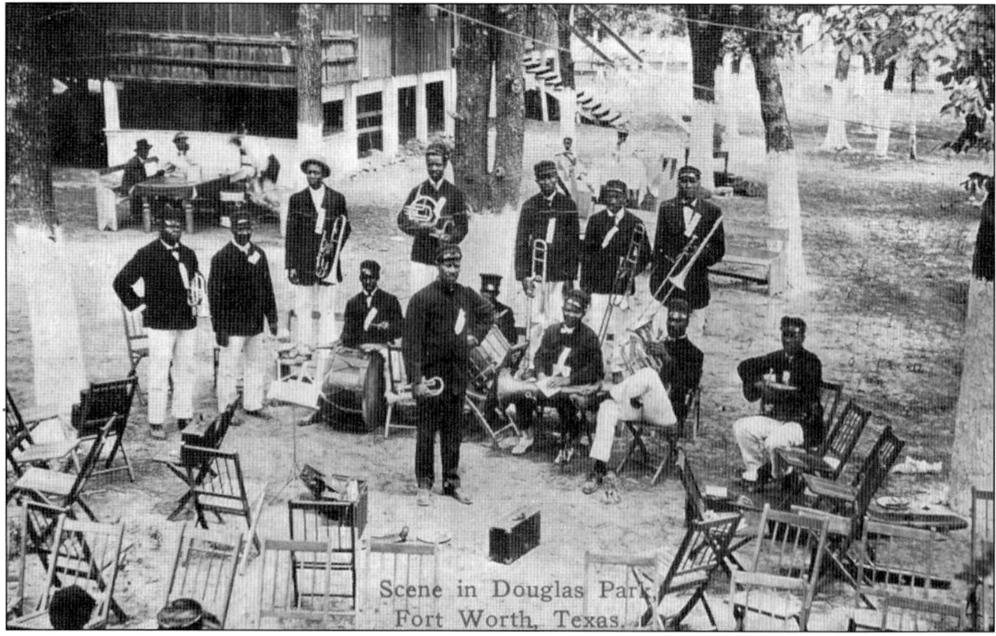

Fort Worth's first park for African Americans began as a private park. Black entrepreneur Thomas Mason and two partners purchased land along the Trinity River bottoms in 1895. It was named Douglas Park in honor of Frederick Douglass, a former slave and abolitionist. It became city property in 1918, was sold, and then was repurchased. Prone to flooding, the land was finally sold to a utility company. (Dalton Hoffman.)

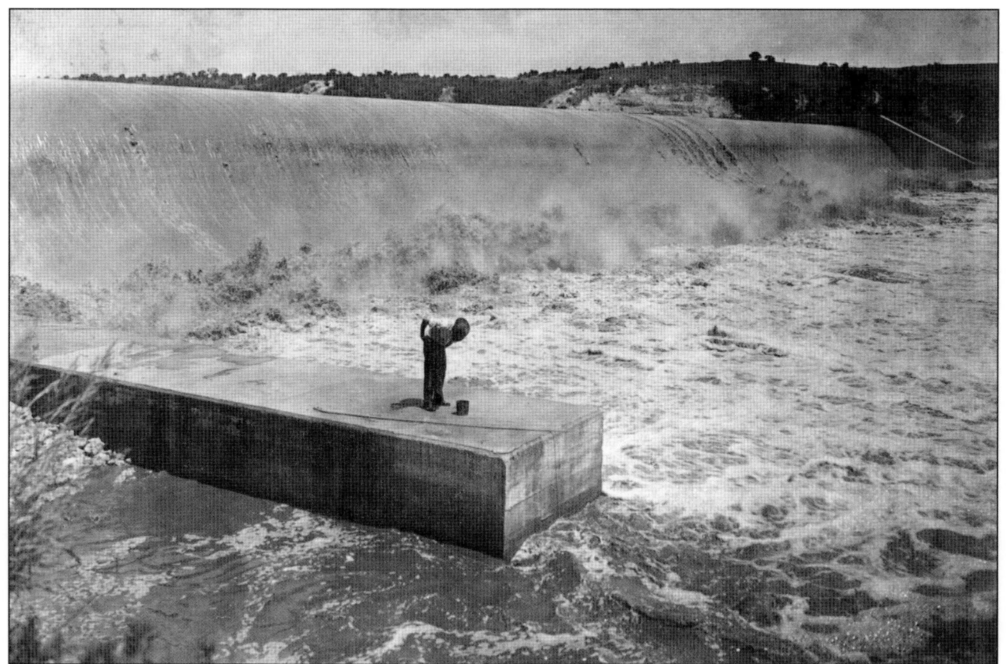

After the Lake Worth dam was completed in 1914 and the lake filled with water, city officials seized the opportunity to make the lake a recreational destination. The city sold or leased land for summer cottages, camps, and lodge sites. A swimming area was also provided. This image of a lone fisherman below the dam appeared in the March 1918 issue of *American City* magazine. (FWL.)

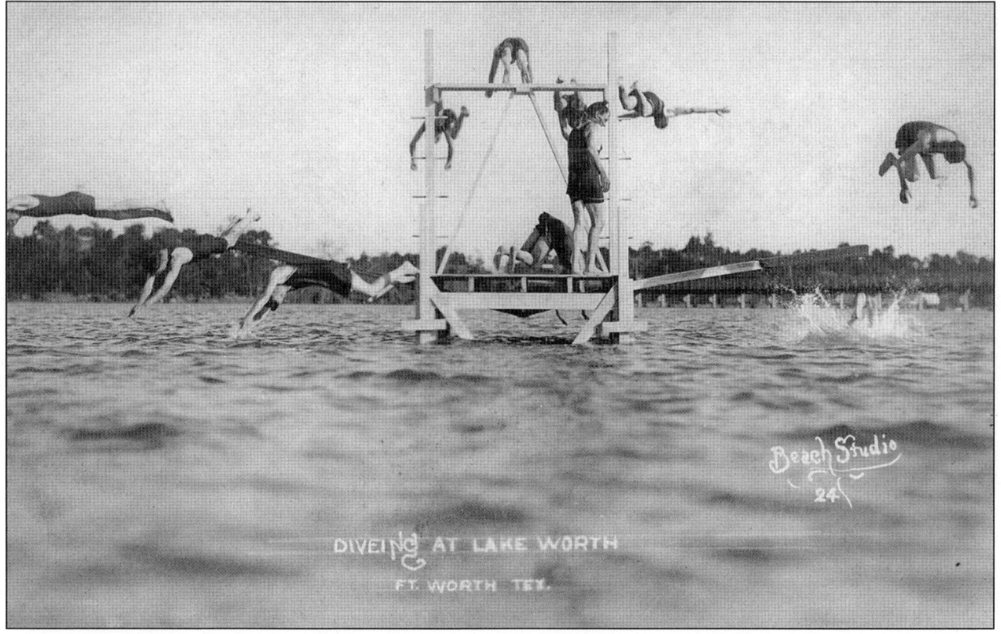

Before the construction of public swimming pools in city parks, Lake Worth was a favorite destination for swimmers and onlookers alike. It was not uncommon for thousands to visit the municipal beach on sweltering summer days. This well-timed photograph caught multiple divers in midair as they enjoyed a day at the lake. (Larry Schuessler.)

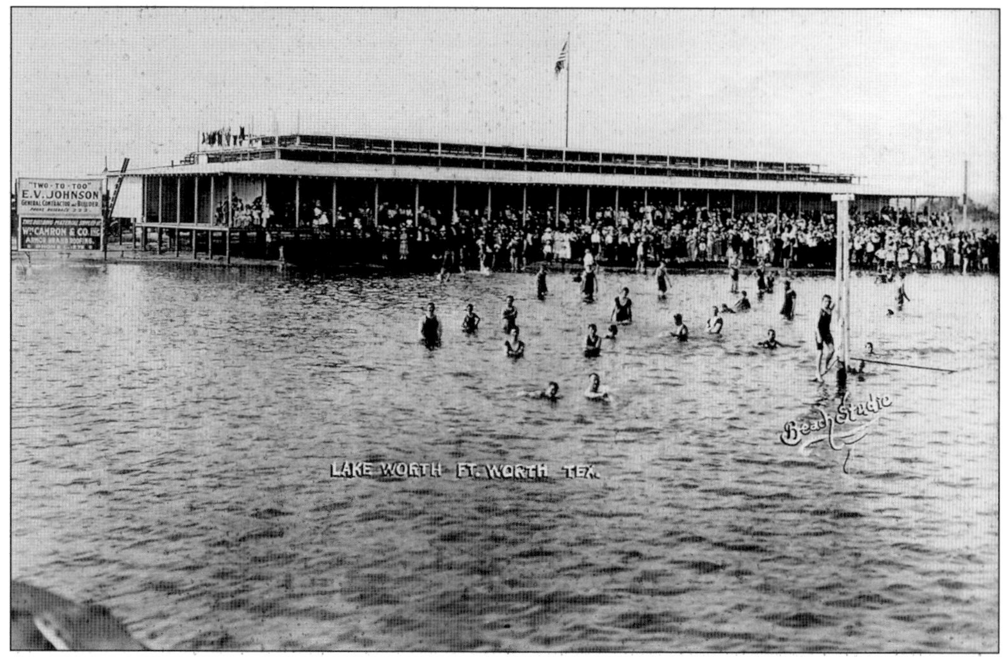

Those not adventurous enough for a swim could watch the action from the veranda of the city-owned bathhouse. Constructed by E. V. Johnson and opened in June 1917, the bathhouse was 208 feet long and 64 feet wide. A portion of it jutted out over the lake. All visitors to the beach had to pass through the structure to get to the water. Spectators could watch for free, but those going for a swim paid 25¢ whether they brought their own bathing suits or used one furnished by the city. Note the bathing suits drying on the line above the bathhouse's roof. (Above, Dalton Hoffman; below, Larry Schuessler.)

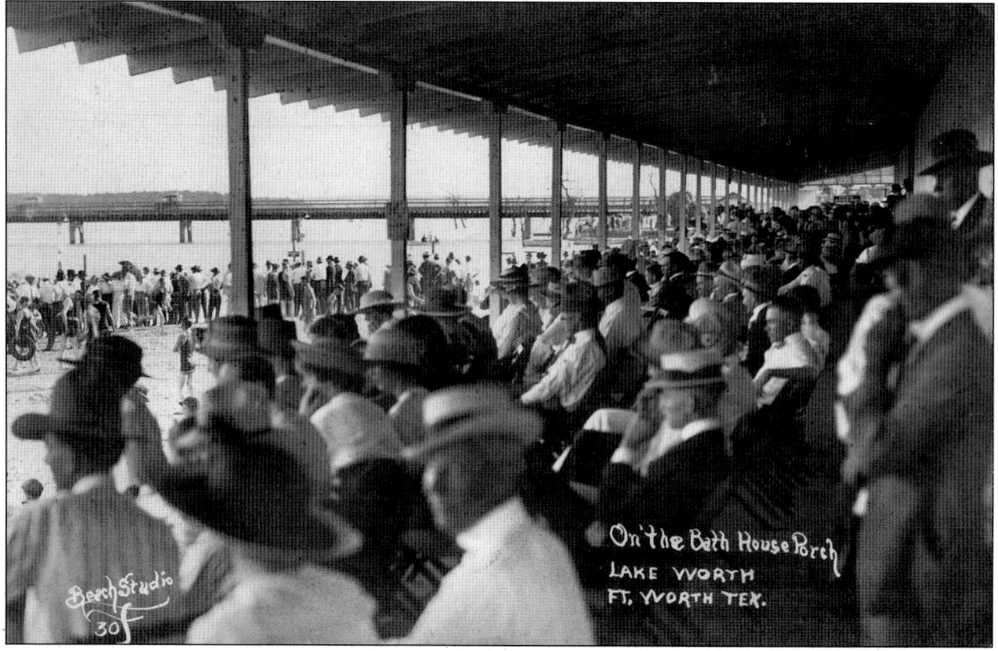

Two

Recreation Comes of Age
1920 to 1929

The 1920s was a decade of tremendous growth for Fort Worth. In 1920, the city had a population of 106,482, and by 1930, that number had increased almost 50 percent to equal 154,847 residents. Some of this growth was the result of the annexation of eight suburbs in 1922 and the influx of residents associated with the petroleum industry. As the city's boundaries expanded and the number of residents increased, so did the park department's quest for more parkland. Parks acquired during this decade included Cobb, Sylvania, Greenway, Rockwood, Glenwood, Oakland Lake, Rosemont, Trail Drivers, Buck Sansom, and Z. Boaz Parks. Some criticized the department's emphasis on creating new parks at the expense of improving existing parks.

After George E. Kessler's death in 1923, the park board hired the father-son landscape architecture team of Hare and Hare of Kansas City, Missouri, to be the city's park consultant in 1925. One of the firm's earliest charges was to update the park system's master plan. Most of this work fell to the son, S. Herbert Hare. The master plan was completed in 1930, but little of it was implemented until the creation of Franklin Delano Roosevelt's New Deal programs a few years later.

In 1922, the city charter was changed to allow for the creation of a separate recreation department with its own board of commissioners. Programs and facilities such as playground supervision, athletic competitions, public swimming pools, golf courses, and outdoor events such as summer concerts came under its purview. By 1926, the department had under its jurisdiction six swimming pools, one beach, a municipal golf course, and the supervision of 15 playgrounds. In 1927, a Recreation Building was constructed to serve as the administrative headquarters for the department. Located just south of the Central Business District, it also included an auditorium that accommodated two basketball courts, a stage, locker rooms, and handball courts. Its design was considered to be innovative, and it served as the city's primary recreation center for 20 years.

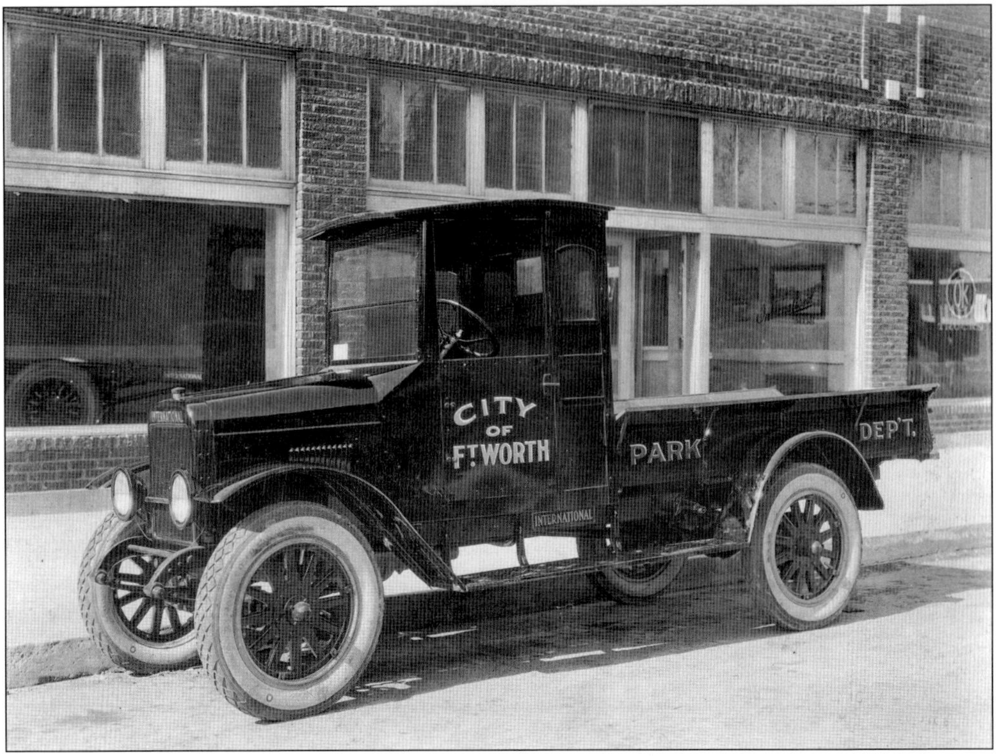

In 1910, park superintendent George E. Vinnedge requested $900 from the park department's budget for the purchase of an automobile. Considering the distances between parks, he argued that this mode of transportation would be a time-saver instead of depending on horse and buggy or streetcars. City departments were relying less and less on horses and streetcars by the time this *c.* 1921 International truck was put into service. (FWL.)

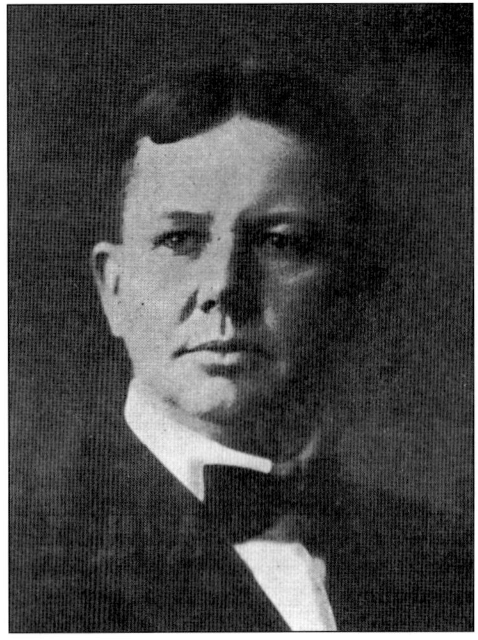

George C. Clarke was appointed superintendent of parks in 1921 and served in that position until 1929. During Clarke's tenure, a $500,000 bond issue for park beautification was passed in 1925. This act enabled the park board to hire the landscape architecture firm of Hare and Hare of Kansas City, Missouri, to develop a second park master plan. The firm remained the city's primary park consultant until 1960. (FWL.)

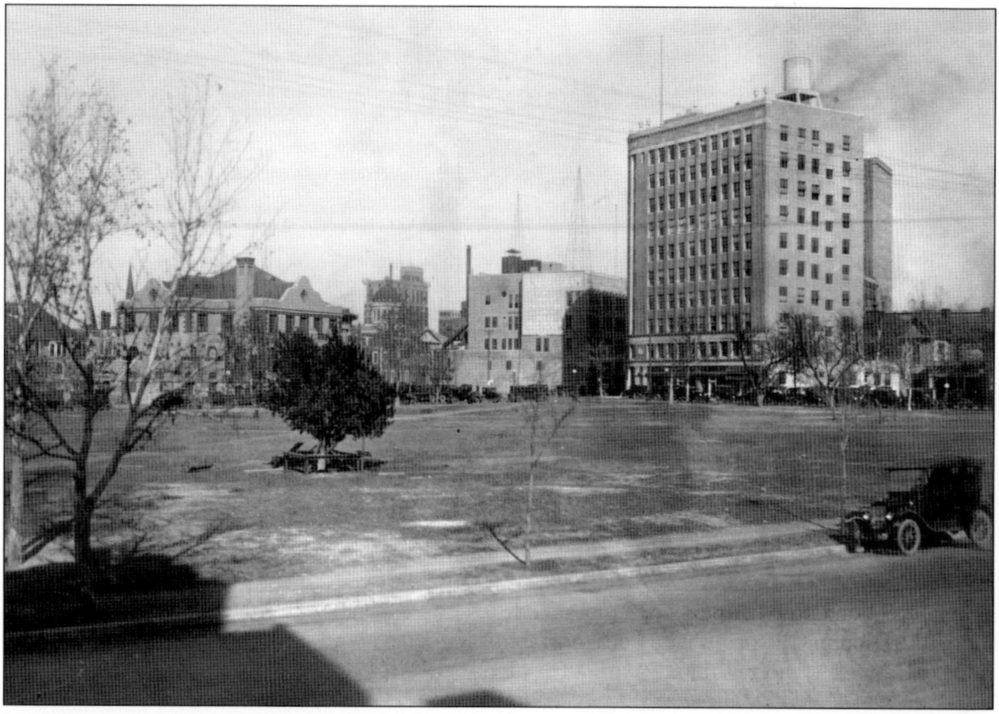

In 1919, Samuel Burk Burnett deeded most of this downtown tract to the city for use as a park in honor of his children. But with his death in 1922 and Kessler's death in 1923, the completion of the park would be left to Hare and Hare (using Kessler's design) with financial support from Burnett's estate. This view of the largely unimproved park is toward the northeast. (FWSTC/SCUTA.)

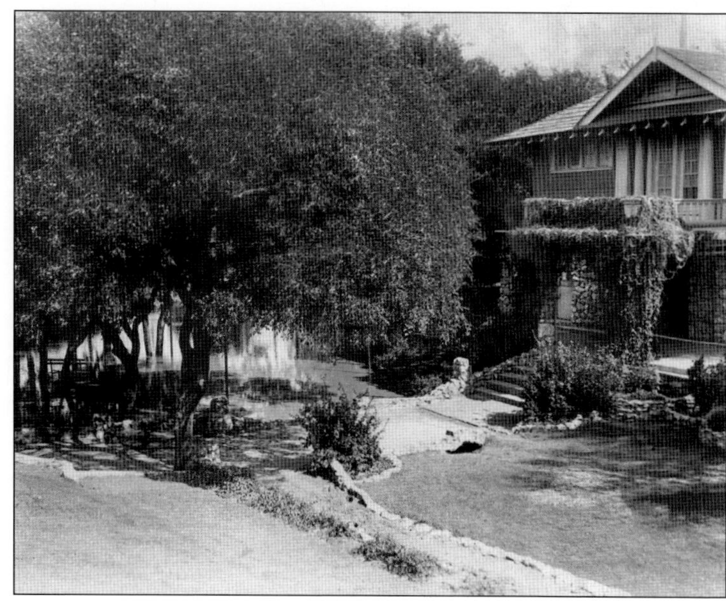

The construction of this quaint bathhouse was a part of the improvements supported by the Rotary Club in its namesake park. This view depicts the building in a more mature landscape with a reflecting pond and garden paths nearby. Other improvements included a small rose garden and tennis courts. (FWSTC/SCUTA.)

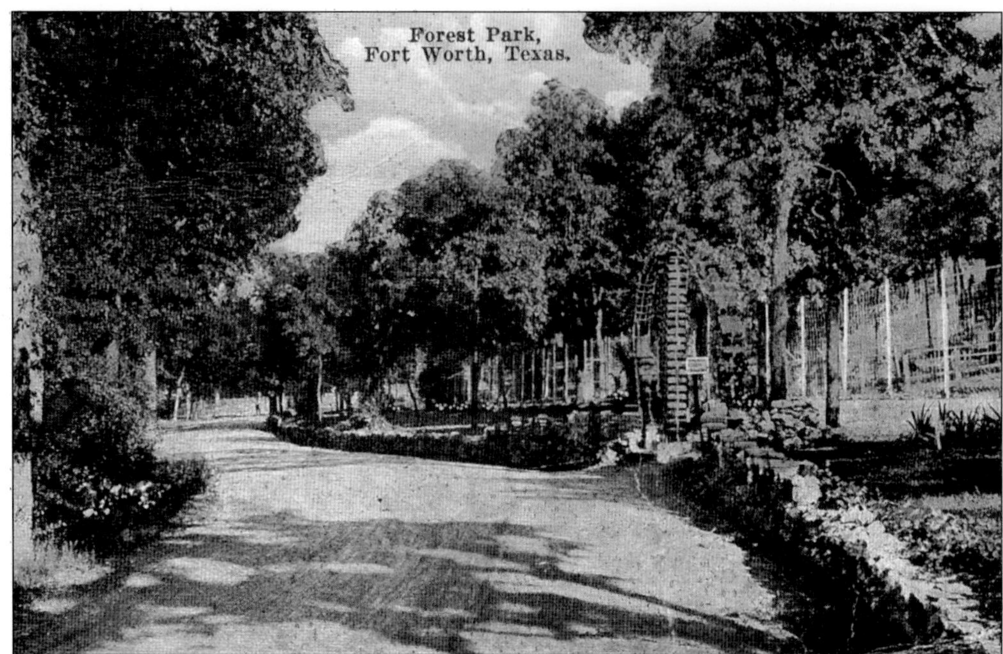

This postcard from the early 1920s shows an unpaved drive winding past the animal pens at the zoo in Forest Park. S. Herbert Hare created the zoo's first master plan and advocated that it be moved to a location such as Lake Worth where expansion would be easier. Public outcry kept the zoo in Forest Park, where it remains today. (Jennifer Harnish.)

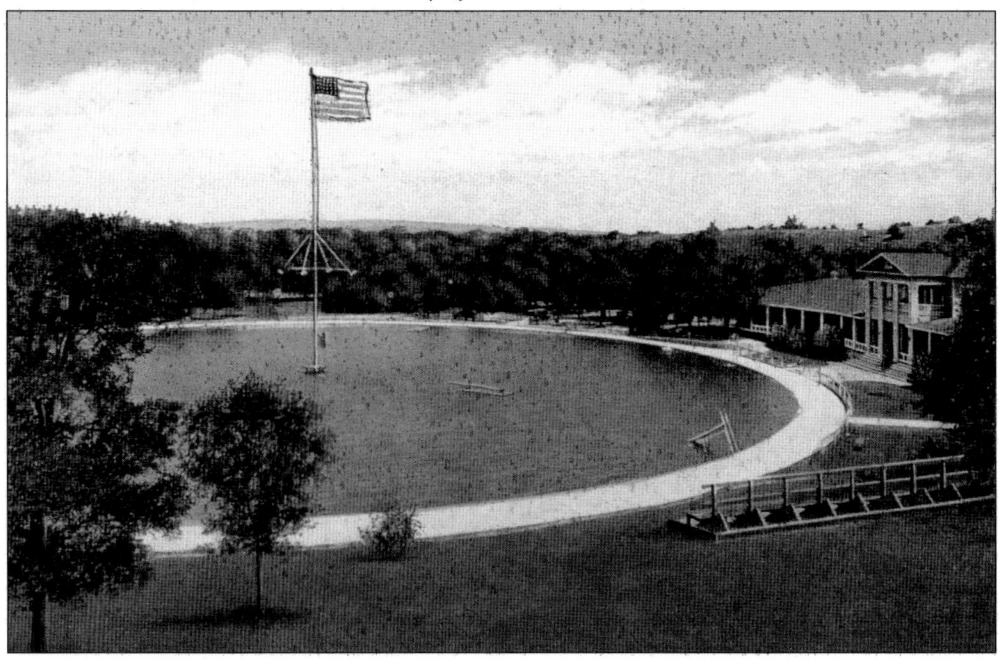

City engineer S. D. Lewis designed the circular all-concrete Forest Park swimming pool. Its depth ranged from 1 to 9 feet, and it had a diameter of 250 feet. The pool's contractor, J. F. Wills, donated an 80-foot flagpole for its center. As the speeches ended at its dedication on June 16, 1922, a total of 250 kids jumped into the water nearly simultaneously. (Jennifer Harnish.)

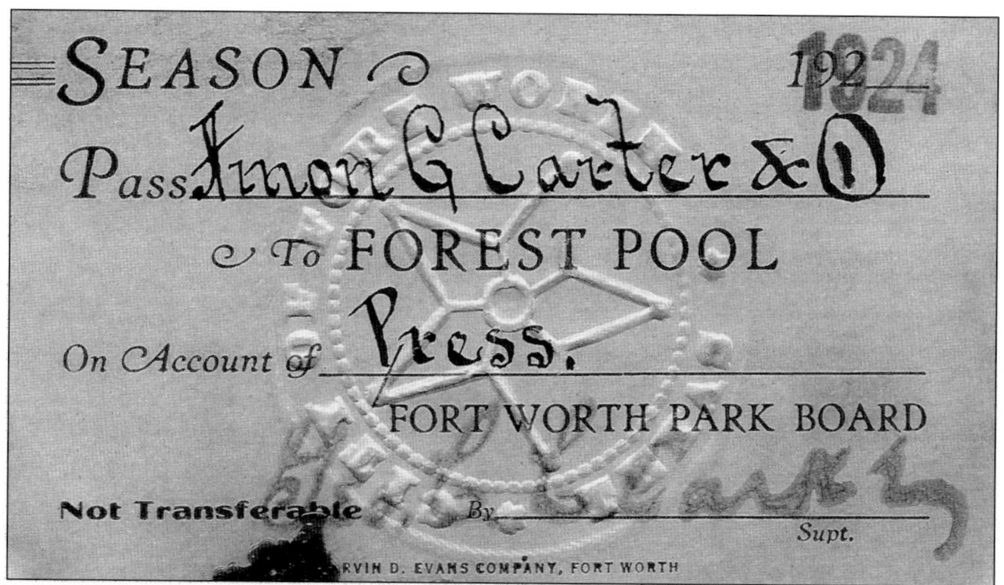

SEASON 192 1924

Pass Amon G Carter & (1)

To FOREST POOL

On Account of Press.

FORT WORTH PARK BOARD

Not Transferable By ________ Supt.

RVIN D. EVANS COMPANY, FORT WORTH

Amon G. Carter Sr. (1879–1955) was publisher and president of the *Fort Worth Star-Telegram* when he was issued this pass to the Forest Park swimming pool in 1924. As a newspaperman, entrepreneur, and philanthropist, Carter became the city's foremost booster, and many institutions were beneficiaries of his largess. Today the Amon G. Carter Foundation provides vital support to Fort Worth's parks and recreational facilities. (Larry Schuessler.)

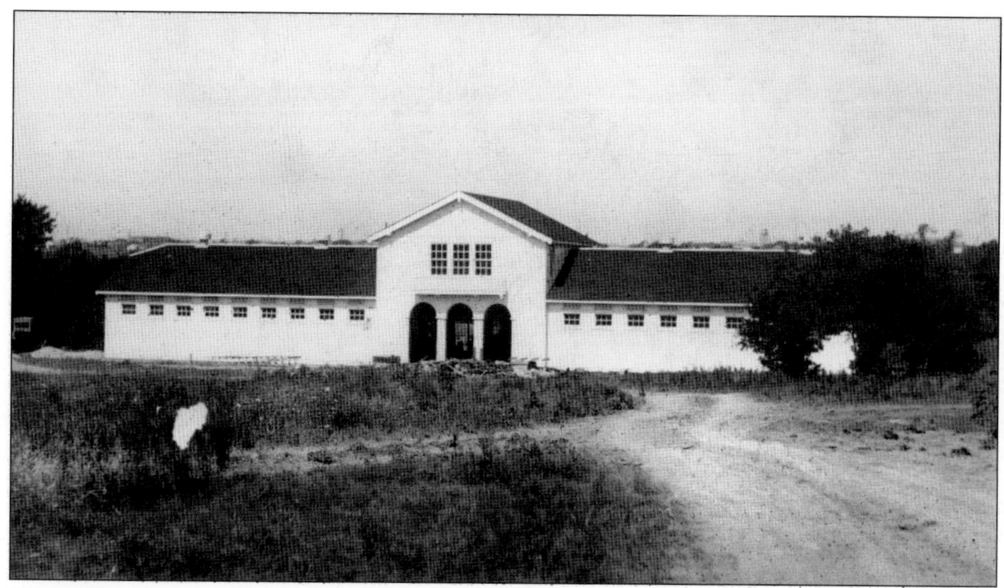

Two public swimming pools were constructed in 1926—one in the north side's Marine Park and one in the east side's Sycamore Park. That same year, the city purchased Dixie Park, an amusement park with a swimming pool for African Americans. This beautiful bathhouse was constructed for the Sycamore Park pool. (FWSTC/SCUTA.)

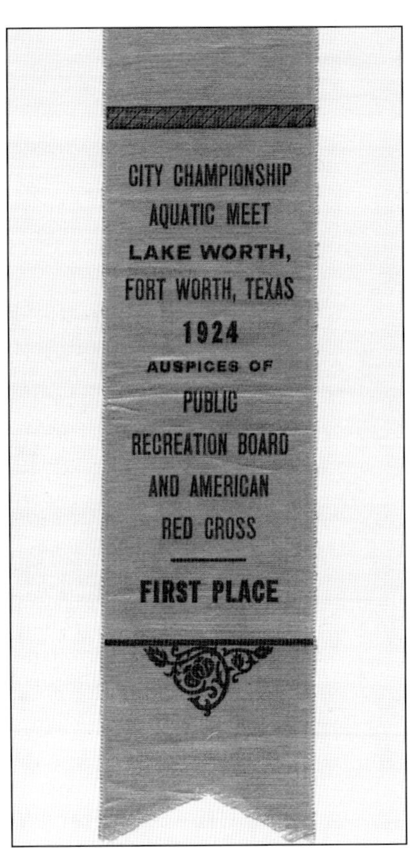

Athletic competitions were a program of the recreation department. An annual track meet at Sycamore Park attracted 1,000 children and 12,000 spectators. Aquatic competitions were popular events also sponsored by the department. Some lucky winner received this ribbon for taking first place at a Lake Worth meet sponsored by the recreation board and the American Red Cross in 1924. (Dalton Hoffman.)

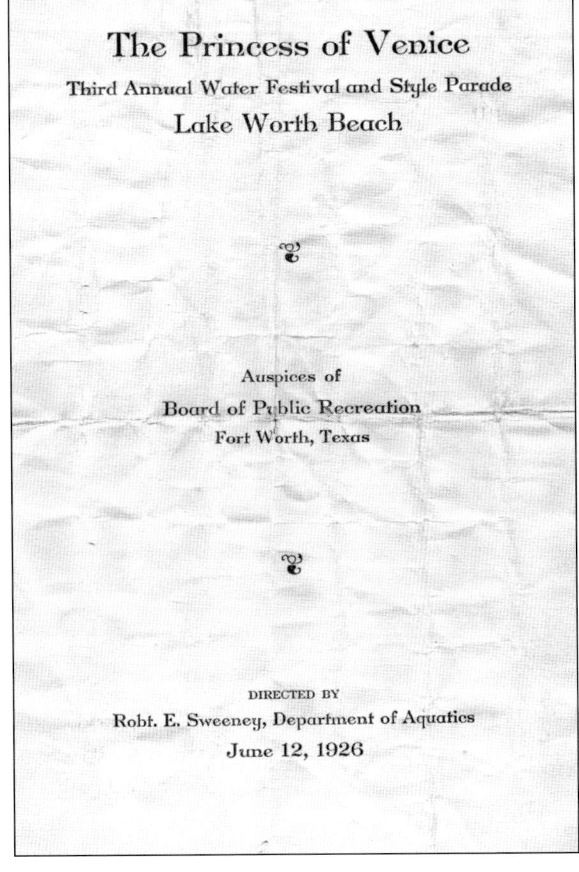

The Princess of Venice

Third Annual Water Festival and Style Parade

Lake Worth Beach

Auspices of

Board of Public Recreation

Fort Worth, Texas

DIRECTED BY

Robt. E. Sweeney, Department of Aquatics

June 12, 1926

The recreation department sponsored four water pageants in 1926 with an attendance of 30,000 spectators. A pageant at Lake Worth offered a style parade and the musical pageant *Princess of Venice* with a cast of adults and children alike. The style parade featured girls modeling clothes from local department stores Meachams, Monnigs, Montgomery Ward, and Weixels. The store winning the most points was presented a loving cup. (Dalton Hoffman.)

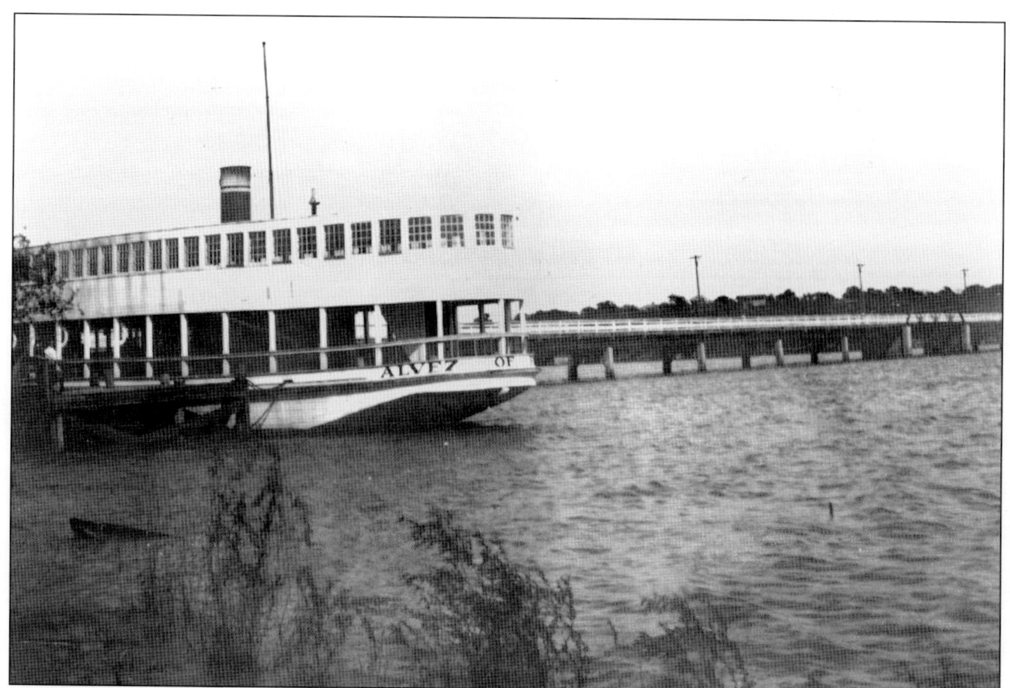

Commercial pleasure boats were permitted to operate on Lake Worth. The *Alvez* was 130 feet long and had the capacity to carry 600 people. Capt. B. R. Dalehite of Galveston was the owner and pilot. Its maiden voyage was on May 28, 1925, with 150 city and county officials on board. The ship burned in 1928 and sank below Mosque Point. Here it is shown by the Nine-Mile Bridge. (FWL.)

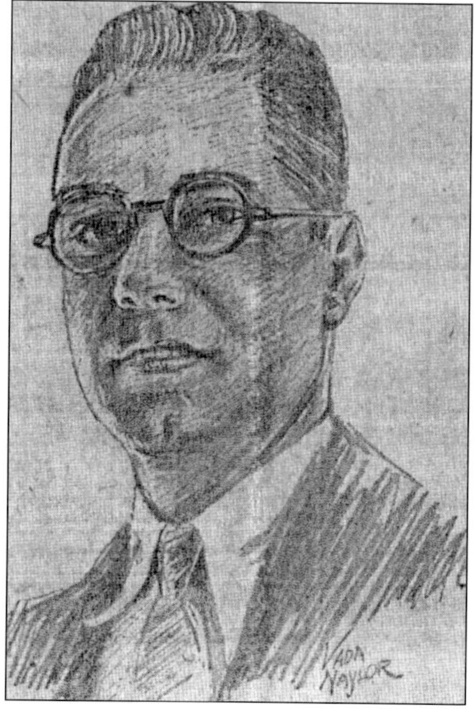

Raymond C. Morrison became the city's first forester in 1926. Morrison's duties quickly expanded beyond caring for the city's trees. He worked closely with S. Herbert Hare on the planning for the Fort Worth Botanic Garden and the school playground improvement program of the 1930s. He was an accomplished photographer, author, and advocate for parks and good landscape design. (*Fort Worth Press*, May 20, 1932.)

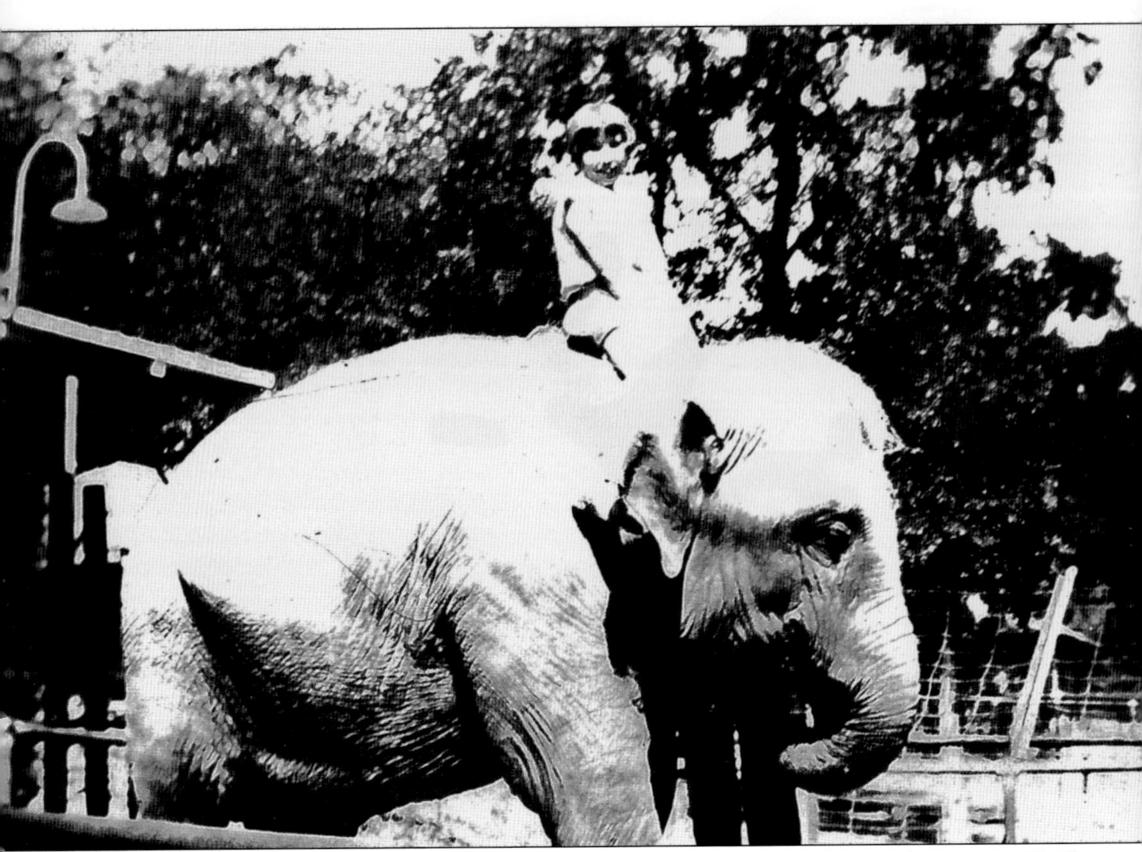

The Forest Park Zoo acquired the elephant Queen Tut in 1923 when she was three years old. She became an immediate sensation and favorite of visitors of all ages. It was not uncommon for her handlers to allow zoo patrons to ride on her back or to take her on strolls through neighborhood streets. Here 10-year-old Doris Louise Hardy (later Adams) smiles at the camera during her ride in 1926. For many years, Queen Tut's birthday parties were much-anticipated and well-attended events. Many stories associated with her have become legend. One of the best known occurred in 1940. When another elephant trampled an attendant named Jim Brown, Queen Tut held her at bay and stood guard over the severely injured man until help arrived. Fortunately, Brown recovered and credited the huge beast with his survival. (Robert G. Adams.)

Constructed near Inspiration Point and overlooking Lake Worth, this shelter was one of three built by the Board of Park Commissioners after Hare and Hare became its consultant. Among Hare and Hare's early designs, the structure featured native stone columns and a pyramidal roof. Other improvements from this era included open-air stoves and concrete-topped picnic tables. Today only the foundation of the shelter remains. (FWBG.)

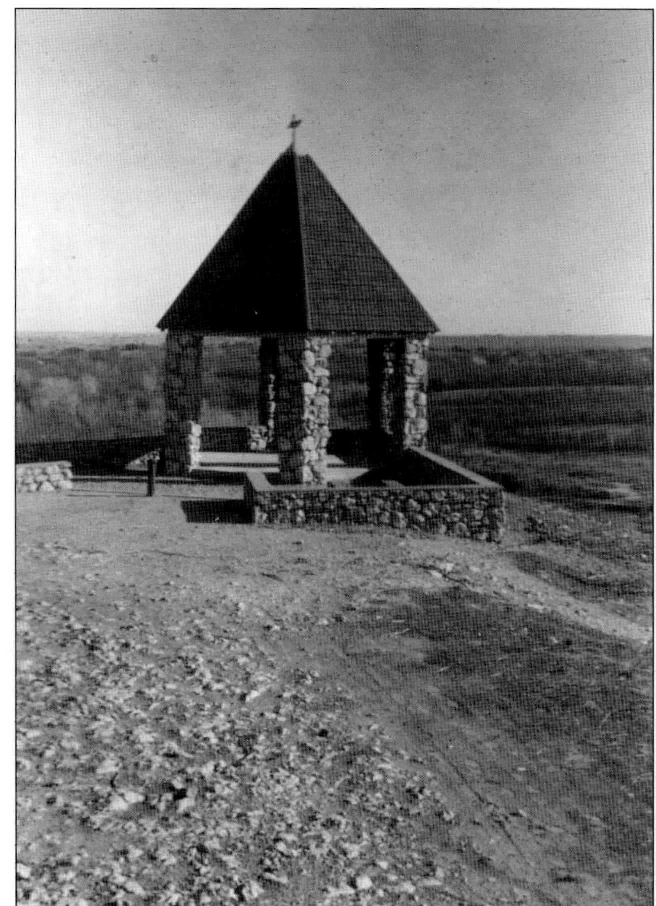

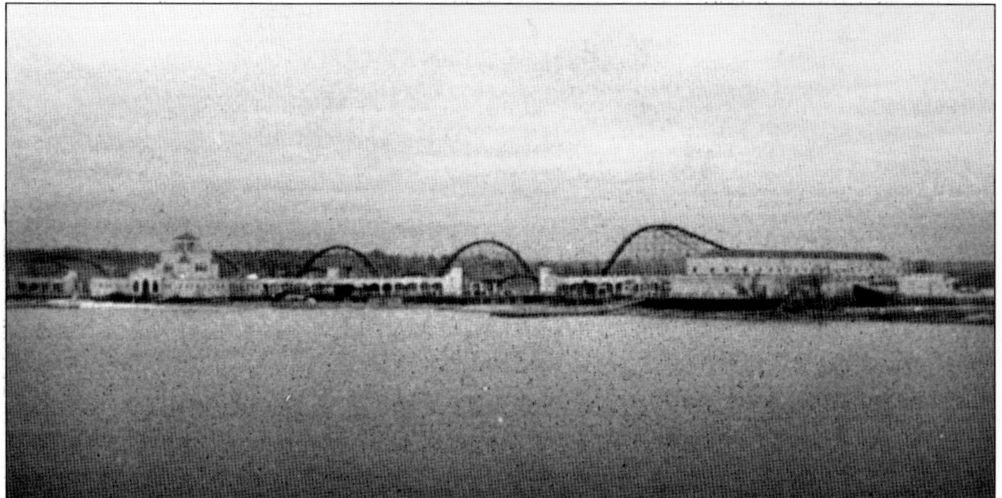

Taking advantage of its popularity as a recreation destination, A. J. Miller and Company from Bellafontaine, Ohio, constructed Casino Park on the shores of Lake Worth in 1927. The park consisted of a midway, rides, a boardwalk, a bathhouse and swimming area, and a dance pavilion or ballroom. Among its attractions was "The Thriller," the largest roller coaster in the Southwest. (FWL.)

CASINO PARK

FORT WORTH

GOOD ONLY FOR SEASON 1928

We reserve the right to revoke the privilege granted by this ticket by refunding the purchase price. Not responsible for accidents

216555 | ONE DANCE 5c

WELDON, WILLIAMS & LICK, FT. SMITH, ARK.

The original Casino Ballroom was described as a handsome wooden structure with an unusual, beautiful ceiling and fine dance floor. Tickets such as this one entitled the holder to a spin around the dance floor. A major part of the Casino Park burned in the summer of 1929, including the ballroom, a bathhouse, and 25 to 30 concessions. The replacement ballroom remained a lively venue during the big band era. As musical tastes changed, it fell into disrepair and was demolished in 1973. (Dalton Hoffman.)

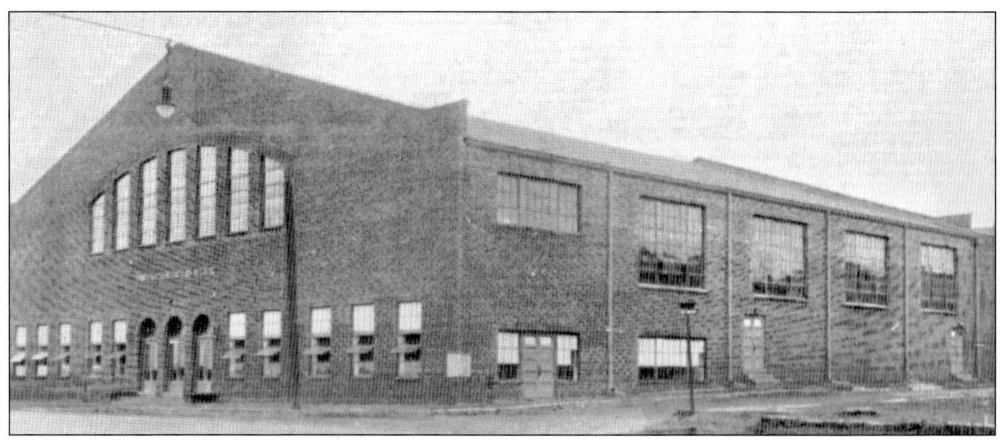

The recreation department constructed its headquarters building in 1927 just south of downtown. Designed by E. W. Van Slyke and Company, the combination auditorium and gymnasium could seat 3,000 people. The stage was flanked by handball courts, and underneath the auditorium's bleachers were department offices, club rooms, locker rooms, and public showers. The innovative building received attention from across the country. (Dalton Hoffman.)

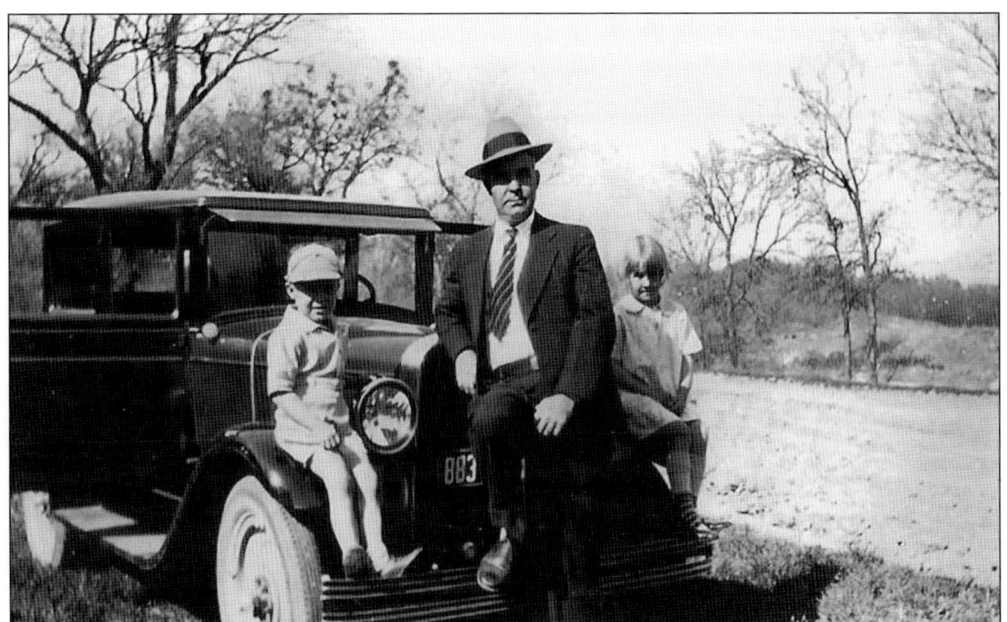

Edmond Maxon (center) and his children, Ed Jr. (left) and Dorothy, enjoyed a springtime outing in Trinity Park in 1928. That same year, Maxon transferred from the city's public health department to the park department to become superintendent at Lake Worth. By 1930, he was assistant superintendent for the park department and remained there until his death in 1940. (Jim Cushman.)

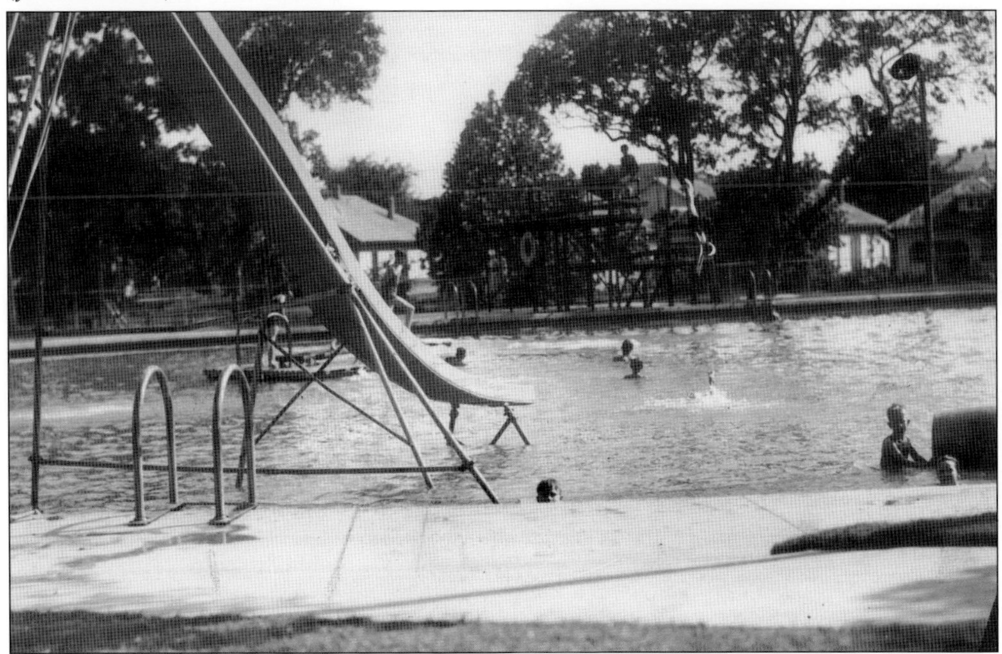

More than 3,000 people attended the dedication of the Marine Park swimming pool in August 1926. Entertainment included a performance by the vaudeville diver Miss Ideal, a children's revue, and lifeguard contests. A more typical experience is represented by this photograph from 1929. (FWSTC/SCUTA.)

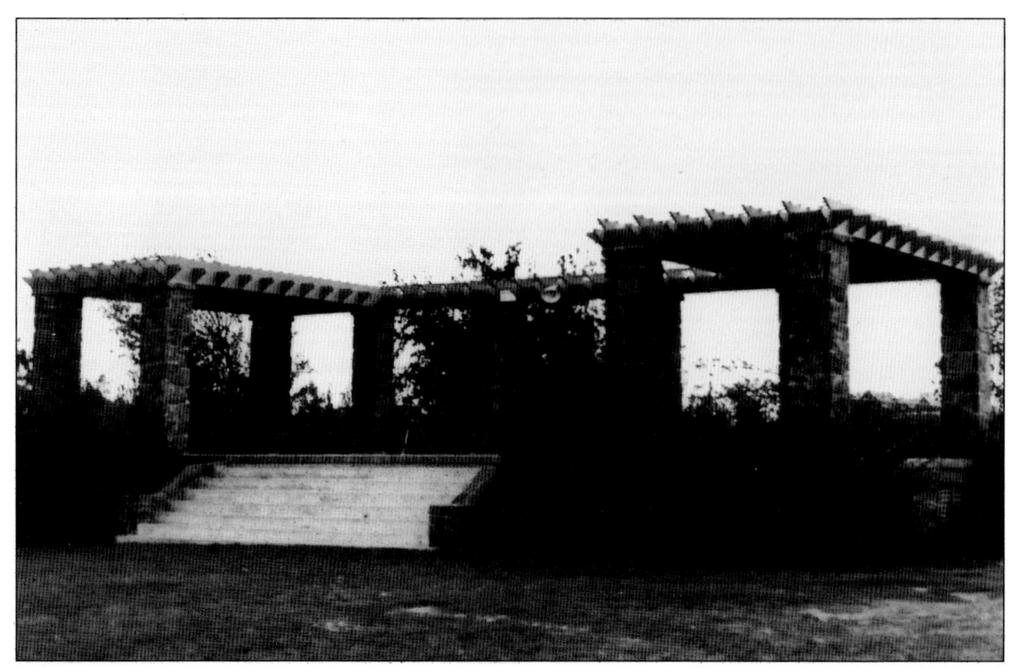

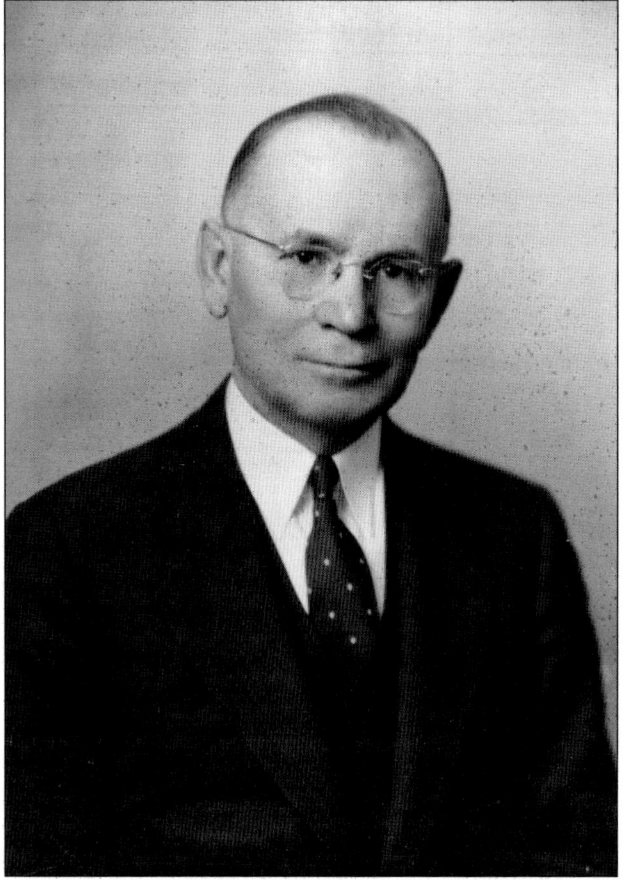

In the late 1920s, the park board adopted a unique approach to the construction of shelter houses. These structures were a combination of shelter house, comfort station, and little theater or bandstand and were featured in *Playground* magazine. They were credited with stimulating an increase in theatrical activity in the neighborhoods in which they were located. This example at Capps Park was constructed in 1929. (FWBG.)

Marvin D. Evans, a printer by trade, served as the president of the recreation board when that body was created in 1922. He remained in that capacity for 10 years. During his tenure, demand for recreational services increased, as did the city's population. Evans also served on the city council from 1938 to 1944. (FWSTC/SCUTA.)

Three

Depression, War, and Creativity 1930 to 1945

The decade of the 1930s started off with an unusual occurrence in Fort Worth. January 1930 was so cold that Lake Worth froze over for the first and, so far, only time in its existence. People drove their cars out on the ice, and the lake's surface became one big skating rink. This rare occurrence serves as a metaphor for life in Fort Worth during the Great Depression. Although all was not fun and games, residents and city government alike found creative ways to meet new challenges during a difficult time.

Like other major cities across the country, Fort Worth's population grew during the 1930s as people moved from rural to urban areas seeking employment. Between 1930 and 1940, the city's population grew from 154,847 to 177,662. For some, life continued much as it had before the stock market crash of 1929. But many others lost their jobs and could not find new ones. By 1932, some 20,000 people were asking for some type of public assistance. For them, work-relief jobs provided through the federal government gave them employment and made it easier for them to meet their families' basic needs. Fort Worth's parks and recreation facilities also were among the beneficiaries of these programs.

The Fort Worth Botanic Garden was the first park property to be improved using federal funds. Men employed through the Reconstruction Finance Corporation began construction on its Municipal Rose Garden in February 1933 during the final months of Herbert Hoover's administration. Franklin Delano Roosevelt's New Deal programs, such as the Civil Works Administration (CWA), Civilian Conservation Corps (CCC), and Works Progress Administration (WPA), allowed for the implementation of park plans created a few years earlier but not initiated because of the lack of funds.

As the country entered World War II, work-relief programs became unnecessary as citizens found employment by entering military service or working in defense-related industries. Few improvements were made to park and recreation facilities because of the war efforts. Yet residents flocked to parks to participate in patriotic programs or to seek solace from war worries.

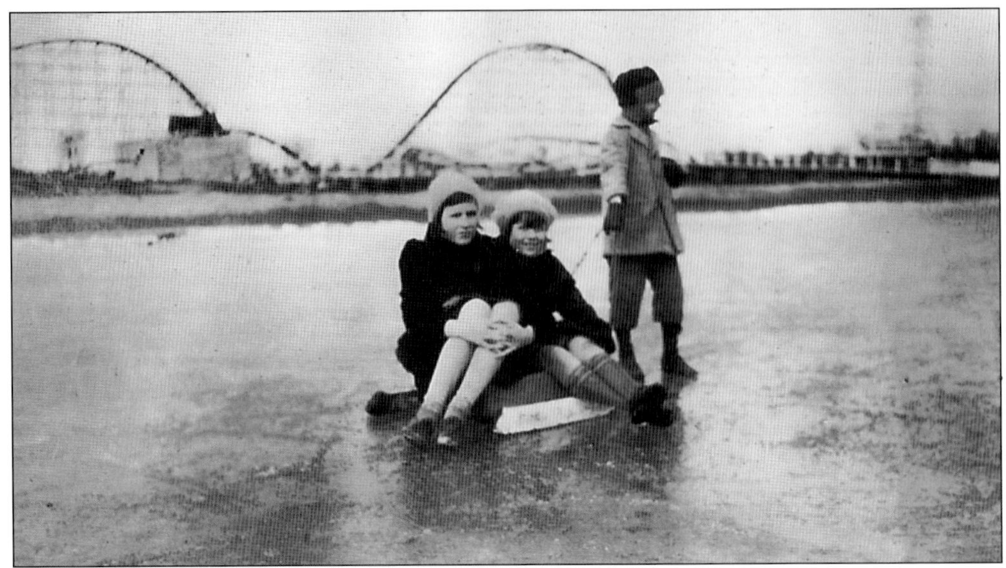

January 1930 was cold enough to solidly freeze Lake Worth. The Magoffin children—from left to right, Bernice, Elizabeth, and Robert—made the most of an unusual situation. The parks and recreation departments did the same during the Great Depression by using work-relief funds to beautify parks and playgrounds for the benefit of residents while providing jobs for the unemployed. (Lisa Helbing and Dorothy Magoffin.)

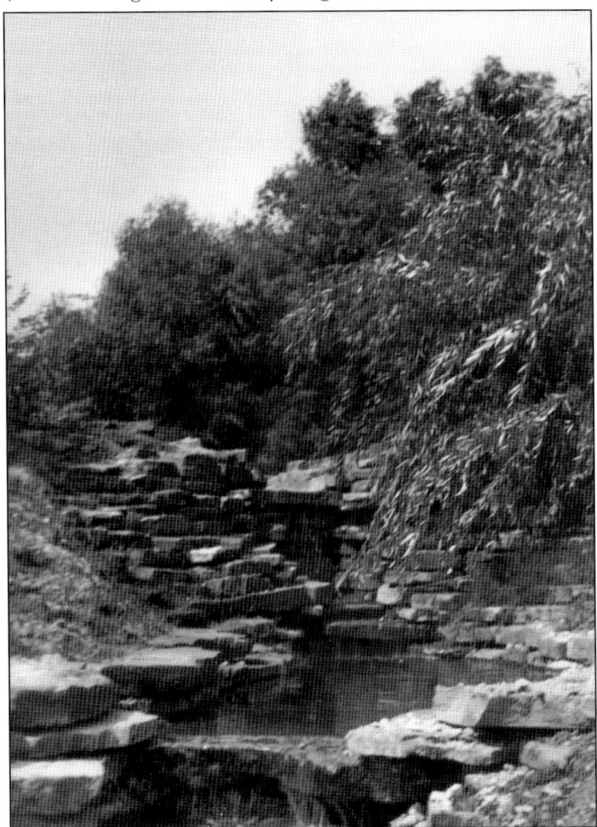

Rock Springs Park was acquired in 1912 upon the advice of George E. Kessler. Known for its forest-like qualities and the natural springs for which it was named, it remained largely unimproved until 1929, when work began on the construction of naturalized waterfalls, trails, lagoons, and a stone overlook under the direction of city forester Raymond C. Morrison. The projects were completed in about 1931 prior to the use of work-relief funds. (FWBG.)

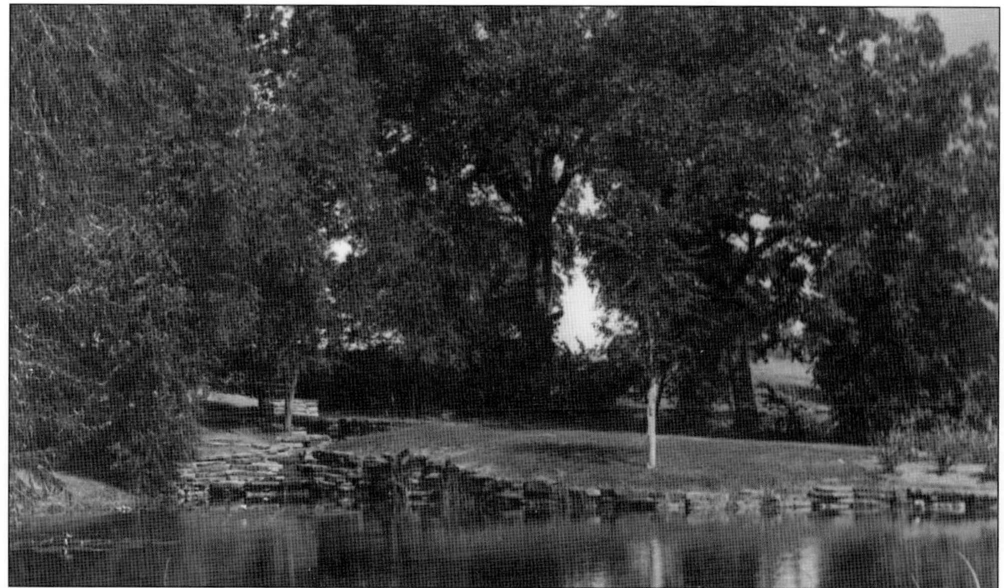

When one of the lagoons at Rock Springs Park would not hold water, Queen Tut, the elephant, was walked over from nearby Forest Park Zoo and allowed to wallow on the ground, compacting the earth. That did the trick and proved to be another example of creative minds solving a problem. The work in the Rock Springs area was the first completed component of the future Fort Worth Botanic Garden. (FWBG.)

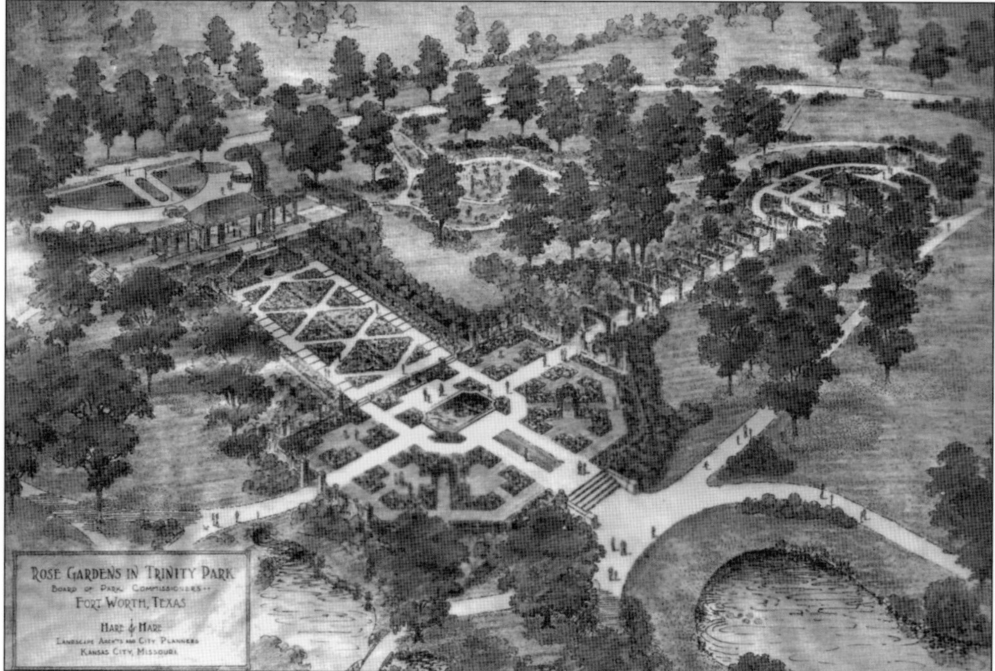

The Tarrant County Rose Society began advocating for the construction of a municipal rose garden in 1926. Rock Springs Park was chosen for the garden's location. In S. Herbert Hare's initial concepts, the garden was to have roses, perennials, and annuals, and its architectural features were to be constructed of brick. The final plan called for roses and stone features. (FWBG.)

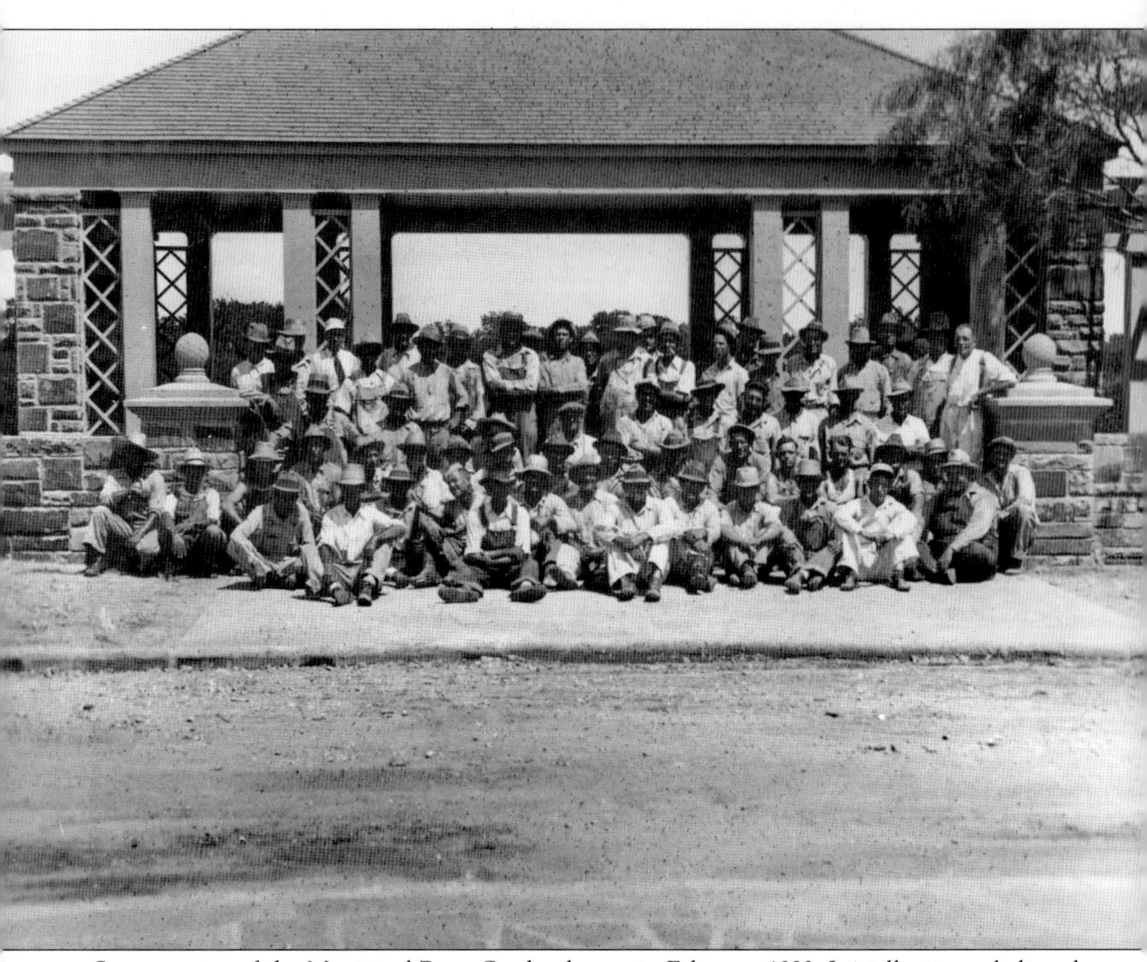

Construction of the Municipal Rose Garden began in February 1933. Initially, it was believed that it would take decades to complete thanks to the ambitious nature of its design. But when the chairman of the Reconstruction Finance Corporation's (RFC) Relief Committee in Tarrant County offered the use of RFC labor for the construction of the garden, the park board quickly agreed. With the exception of planting the roses, the garden was completed in nine months. The men who built the garden were paid $2 a day. They worked in shifts of 40 to 50 men two days a week. Many of them took such an interest in the garden's progress that they worked some days without compensation. In tribute to their selfless actions, the garden's dedication plaque acknowledges the "artisans and laborers who wrought the beauties of this garden and gave of their best to a degree far exceeding their monetary reward." Shown here are just a few of the hundreds of men who constructed the garden. (FWBG.)

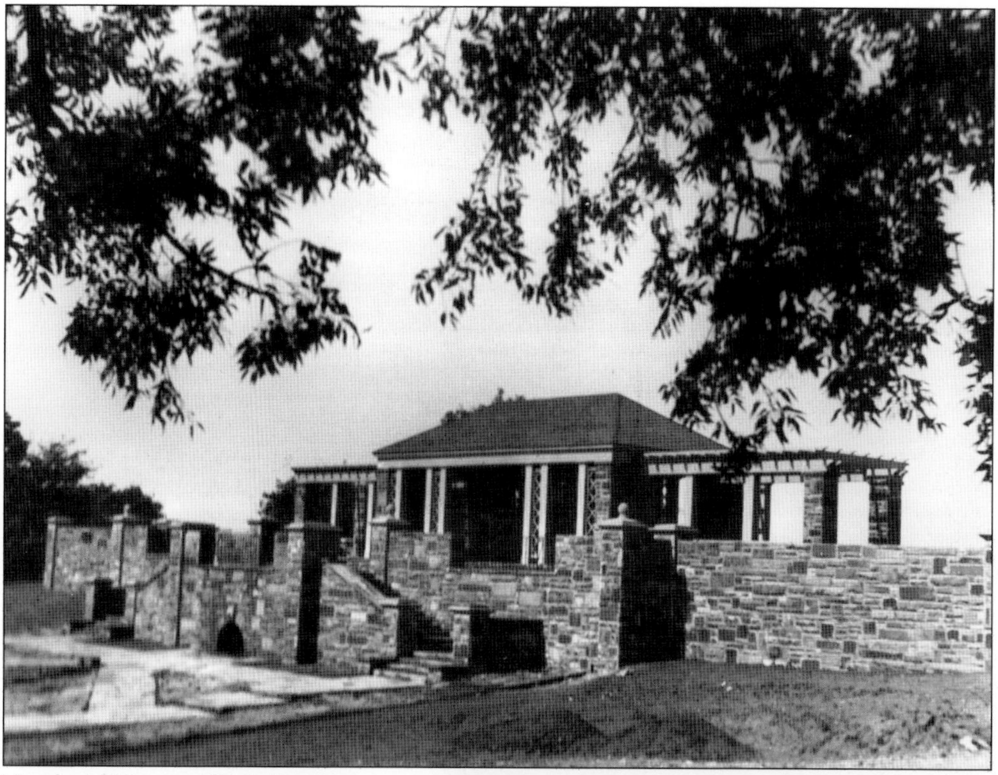

Nearly 4,000 tons of Palo Pinto sandstone were hauled to the site from Millsap, Texas. Work on the garden was labor intensive. A small number of skilled stonemasons trained unskilled laborers to artfully cut the stone by hand. This photograph is of the overlook shelter, terrace, and upper rose garden shortly after it was completed but before it was planted with roses. (FWBG.)

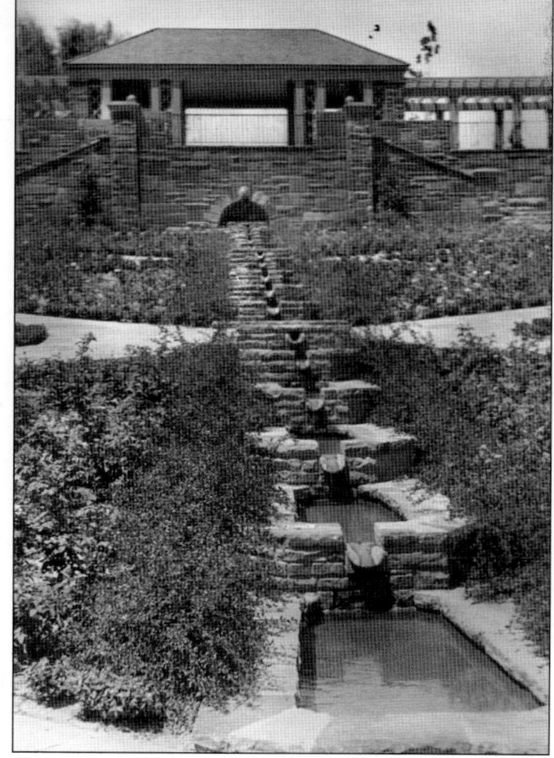

Hare's design for the rose ramp and water cascade in the upper rose garden was inspired by Villa Lante, a 16th-century Italian garden. Although the garden was dedicated in October 1933, the roses were not planted until April 1934. Most of the roses were donated or purchased with donated funds. The men who built the gardcn gavc $70 for the roses planted on the rose ramp. (FWBG.)

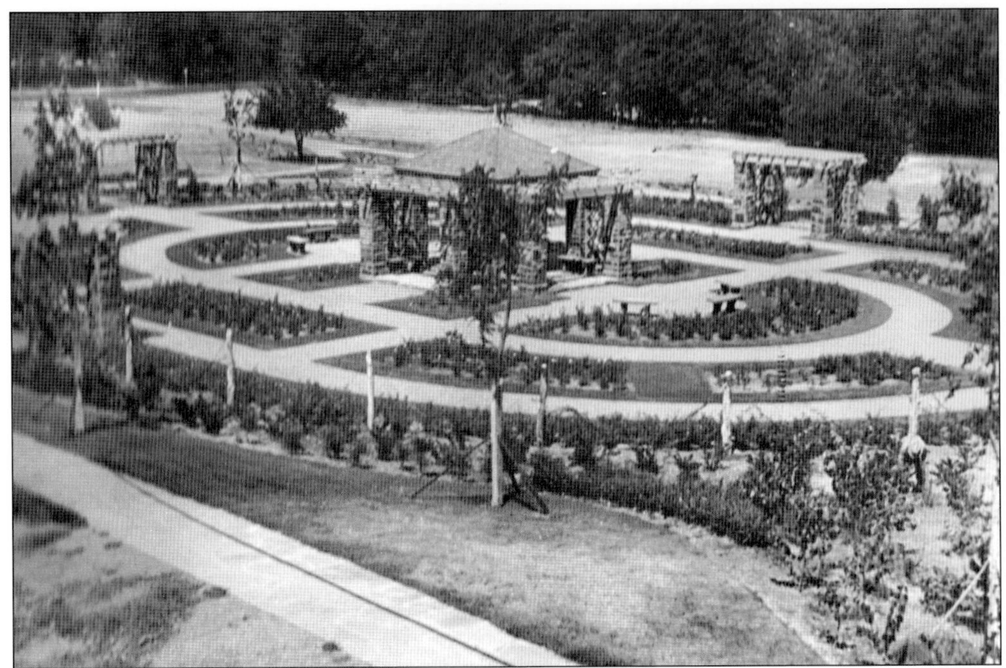

The oval rose garden is connected to the main rose garden by a colonnade of nine stone and wood trellises. The colonnade became a popular place for people to stroll between the gardens and was known as "Peacock Alley." Four portals provide entrances to the oval rose garden, and at its center is a small stone gazebo. (FWBG.)

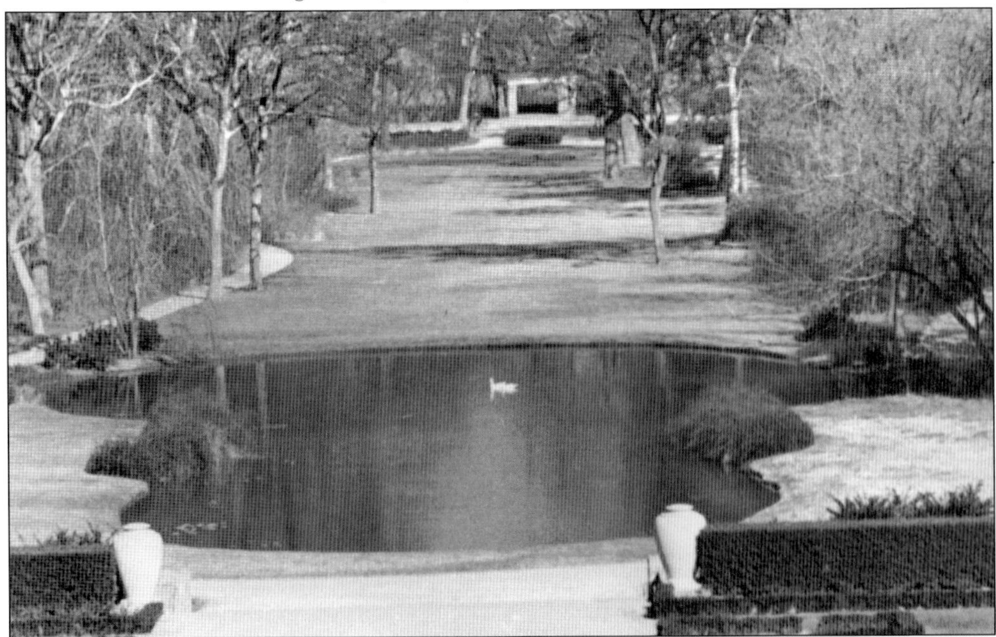

An important visual component for Hare's design was the vista that terminated at a small stone shelter on the bank above the Clear Fork of the Trinity River, approximately 800 feet east of the reflecting pond. This view, captured by amateur photographer Lewis Fox, can no longer be replicated because University Drive now severs the shelter from the rest of the garden. (FWL.)

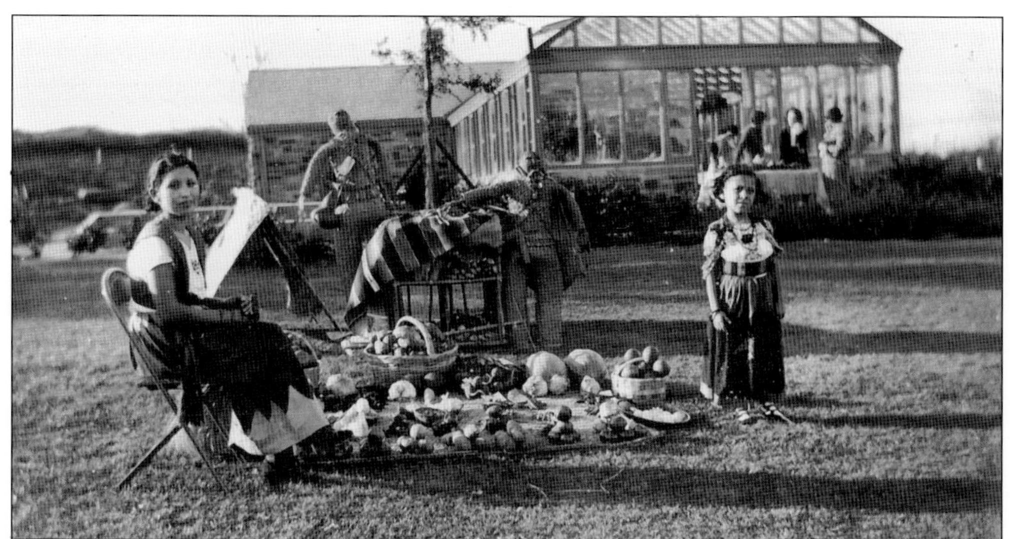

Through the CWA, funds were provided for the construction of the Horticulture Building for Rock Springs Park. The park board voted to allow the Fort Worth Garden Club to maintain a garden center in the building with an office and library. This photograph of the building is from the center's 1937–1938 Annual Report and was captioned "Mexican Street Scene in Spring Flower Carnival." (Fort Worth Garden Club.)

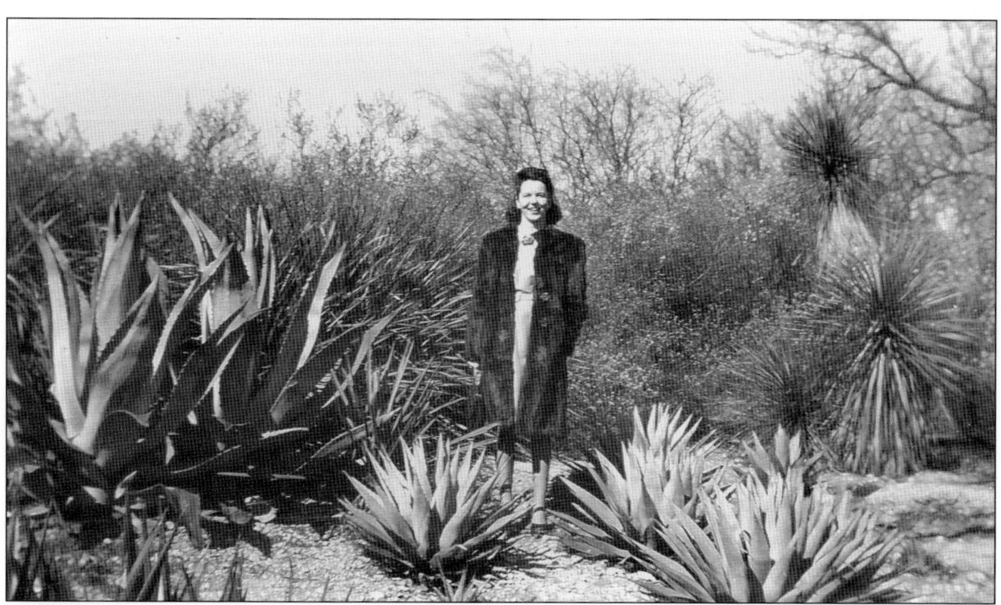

On December 14, 1934, the park board voted to change the name of Rock Springs Park to Fort Worth Botanic Garden. This was an appropriate name for an environment that included a wide variety of plants, including this cactus garden, constructed in 1935. Here Peggy Sue Wiese poses in that garden in February 1946. (Peggy Strange.)

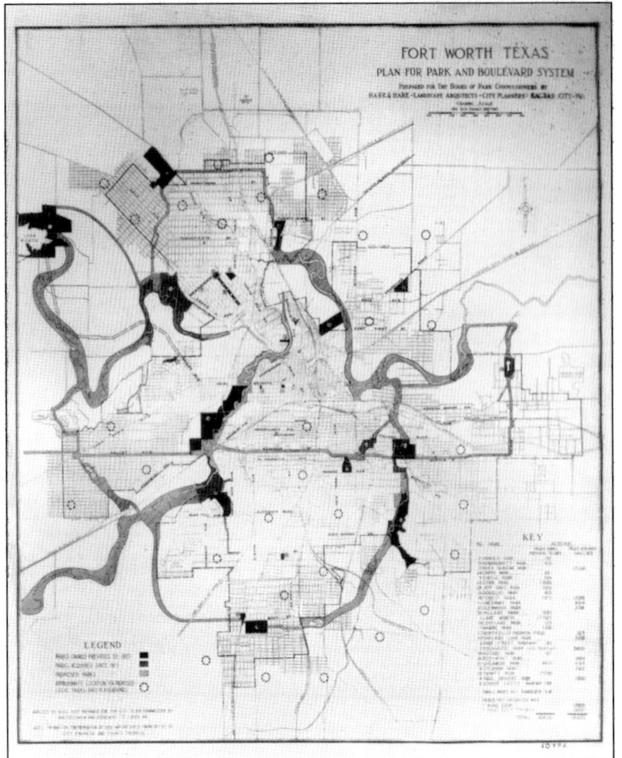

Hare and Hare completed a master plan for the city's park and boulevard system in 1930. It built upon Kessler's idea of linking parks with scenic drives and greenways along the rivers. This map shows the location of existing parks as well as proposed parks and boulevards. Today improvements such as the trails along the river allow users to experience much of the city as Kessler and Hare intended. (FWBG.)

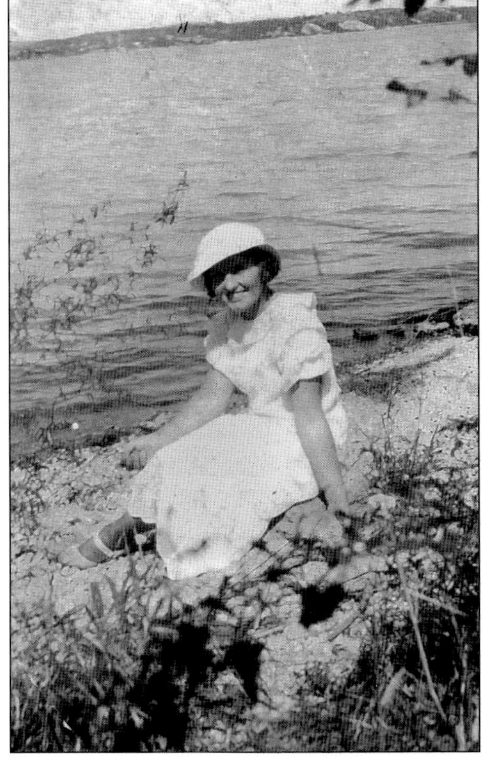

In April 1934, Albert and Marguerite Triplett Croix traveled to Fort Worth from a small community near Houston to celebrate their honeymoon. While staying with friends, the newlyweds visited the Municipal Rose Garden and Lake Worth, as seen in this photograph of Marguerite on the lake's shore. During the Depression, Fort Worth's parks provided residents and visitors an economical way to celebrate special occasions. (Mary Ludwick.)

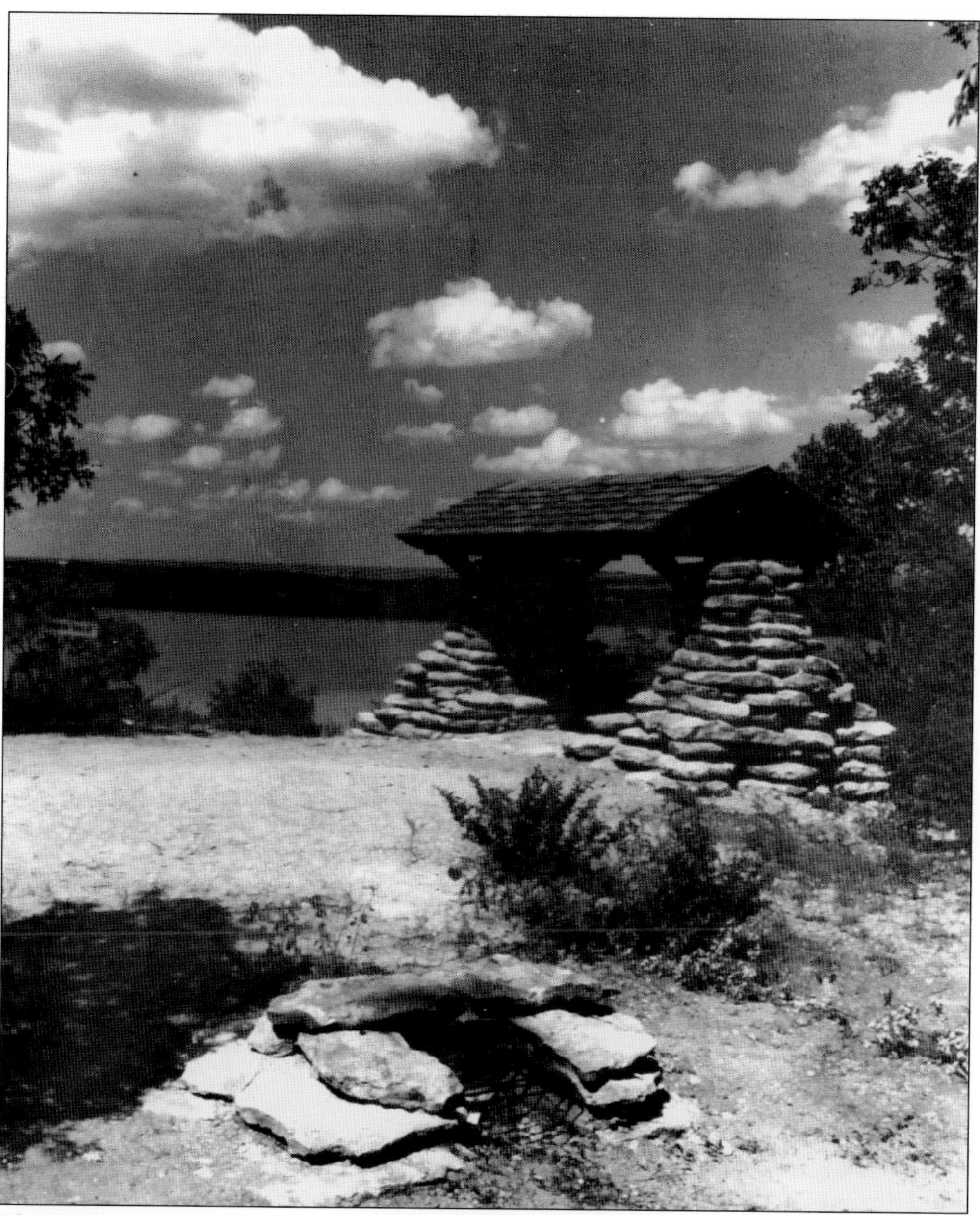

The Civilian Conservation Corps (CCC) became one of the most popular of FDR's "alphabet agencies." Created just days after his inauguration, the program was specifically designed to provide employment for young men between the ages of 18 and 25. While grouped in camps that were run in military-type fashion, the "boys" worked on conservation-related projects for a variety of federal agencies. Company 1816 began work at Lake Worth in May 1934 under the supervision of the National Park Service. There they built recreational structures such as shelters, picnic tables, and trails, and toiled at landscaping, fighting forest fires, and improving the lake's banks. The camp's tenure at Lake Worth ended on December 31, 1937, after putting in 99,000 man-days of work. Pictured here are the Lone Point shelter and a fire pit, both of which were likely constructed in 1935. This location is now within the boundaries of the Fort Worth Nature Center and Refuge. (FWBG.)

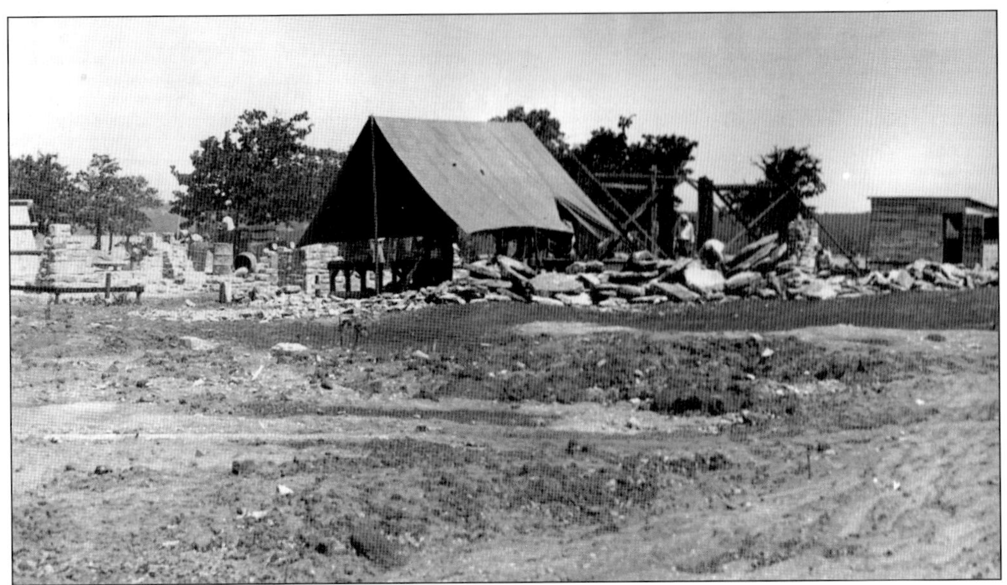

The Mosque Point Shelter was also built by the CCC. Note the piles of large rocks yet to be cut into blocks for use in the construction of the shelter. The tent was likely used to protect the stonecutters from the intense Texas sun. The location of all of the CCC-built shelters provided picturesque views of Lake Worth. (FWBG.)

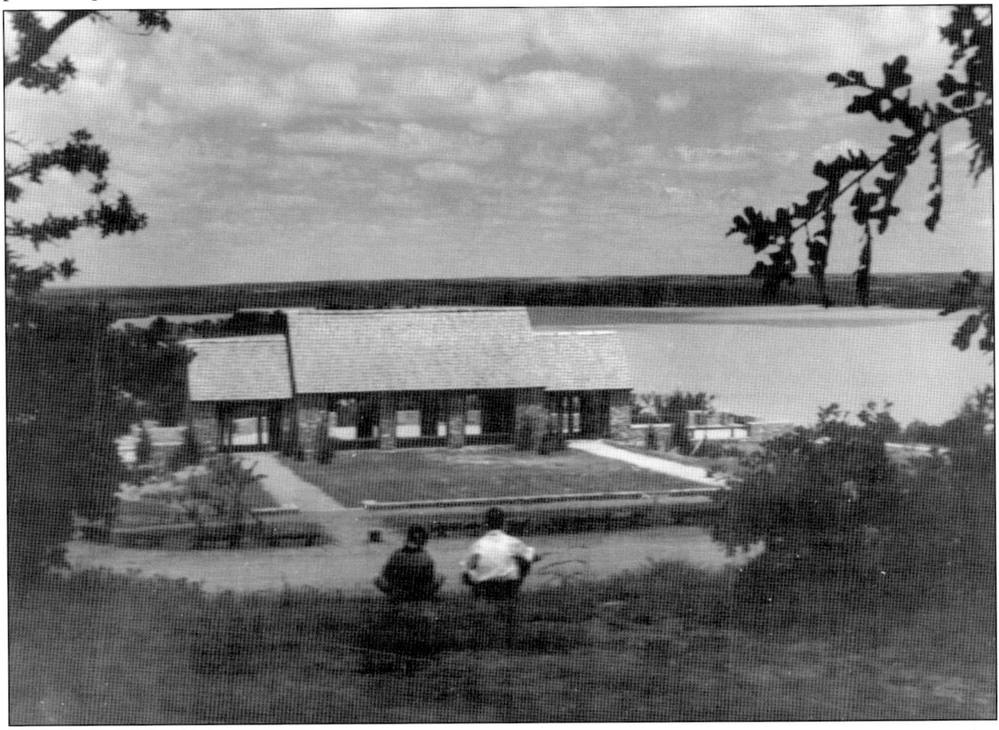

This view shows the completed shelter at Mosque Point. It is located on the former site of the Moslah Temple's mosque, which was constructed around 1918 and destroyed by fire in 1927. Other CCC structures on this site included a comfort station (since demolished) and stone stairs leading to the lake's shore. (FWBG.)

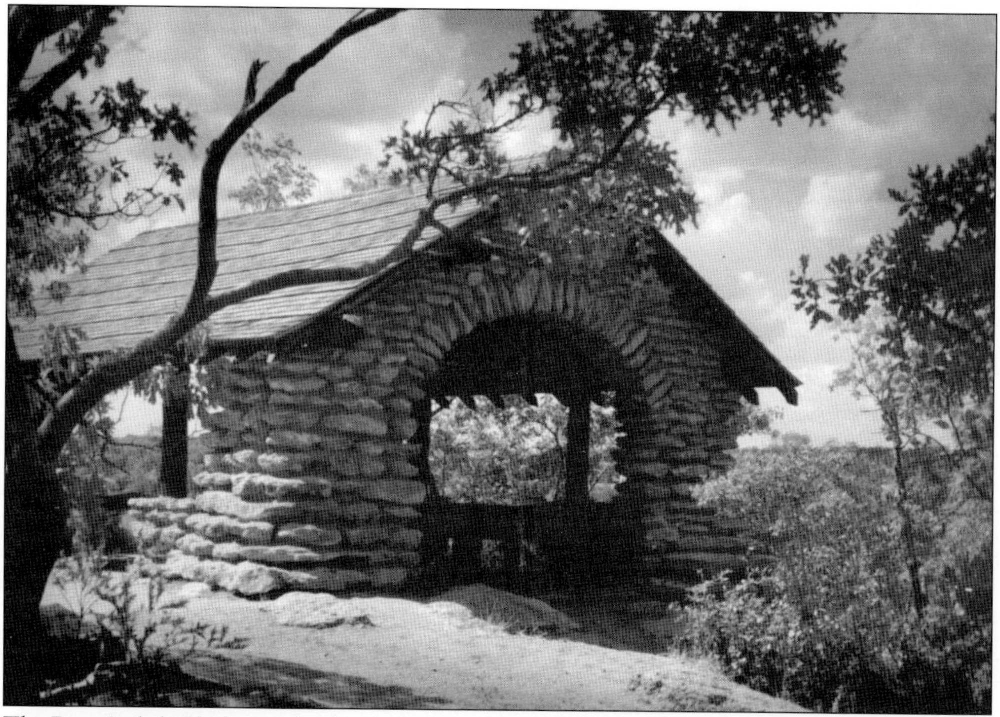

The Rest-Awhile Shelter and other structures at Lake Worth were featured in the book *Park and Recreation Structures* by Albert H. Good. Published by the U.S. Department of the Interior in 1938, the book highlighted the various types of facilities built by the CCC across the country. Remnants of this shelter are now within the boundaries of the Fort Worth Nature Center and Refuge. (FWBG.)

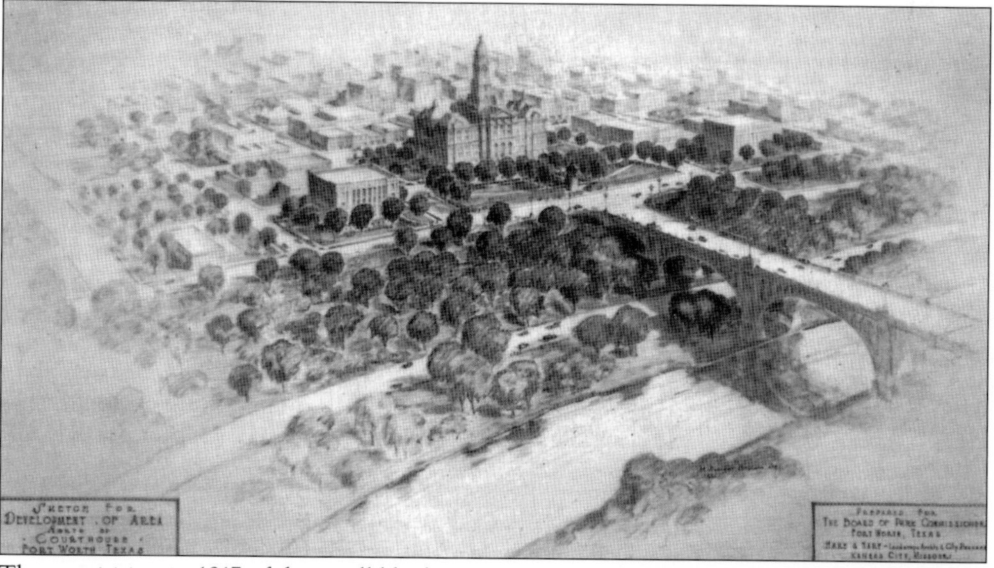

The acquisition in 1917 of the small block immediately north of the courthouse allowed for the creation of Paddock Park. But throughout the 1920s and 1930s, city officials were still advocating for the creation of a park-like setting on the bluff above the Trinity River. Hare and Hare's plan from 1935 shared similarities with Kessler's plan from 1909. (FWBG.)

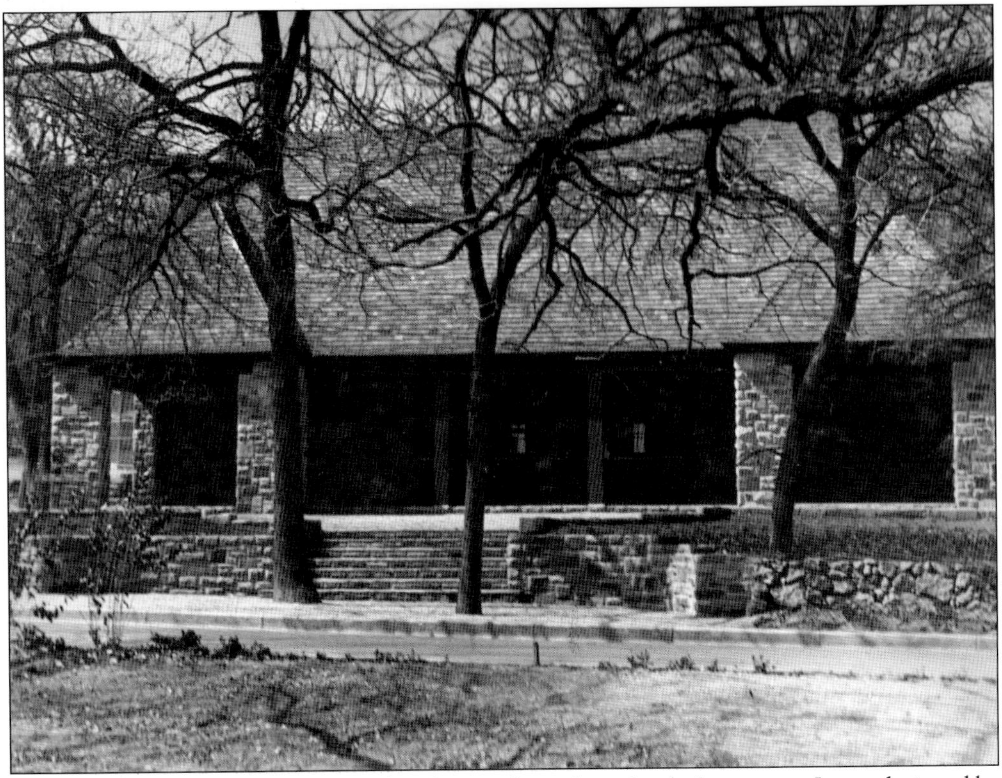

The Forest Park refectory was erected at the zoo through work-relief programs. It was designed by Hare and Hare and was constructed in 1934 with CWA funds. The irregular-coursed sandstone structure served as a pavilion but also contained offices for the zookeeper. It has since been modified but is still in use at the Fort Worth Zoo. (FWBG.)

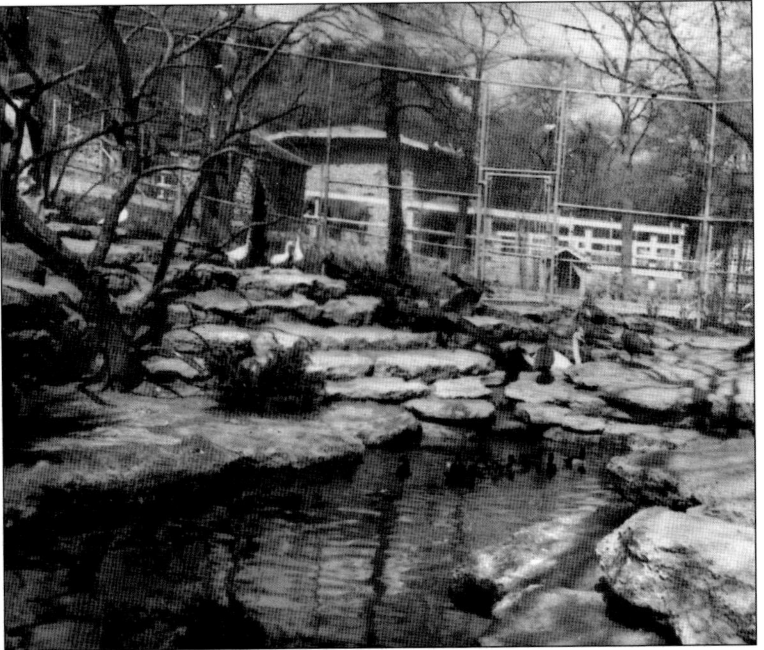

Work-relief funds were used to build new quarters for animals at the Forest Park Zoo. This enclosure for water fowl and other birds included a waterfall of naturalized stonework and a small pond. Such improvements not only beautified the zoo and created jobs, but also provided more humane habitats for the creatures under the zoo's care. (FWBG.)

Schoolchildren across Fort Worth raised the funds necessary to purchase Patsy, the chimpanzee, in 1931. She came to the zoo when she was three years old. There she put on a daily show performing tricks such as riding a tricycle and walking a tightrope. Her favorite treats were a plate of bananas and a popular soft drink. (Larry Schuessler.)

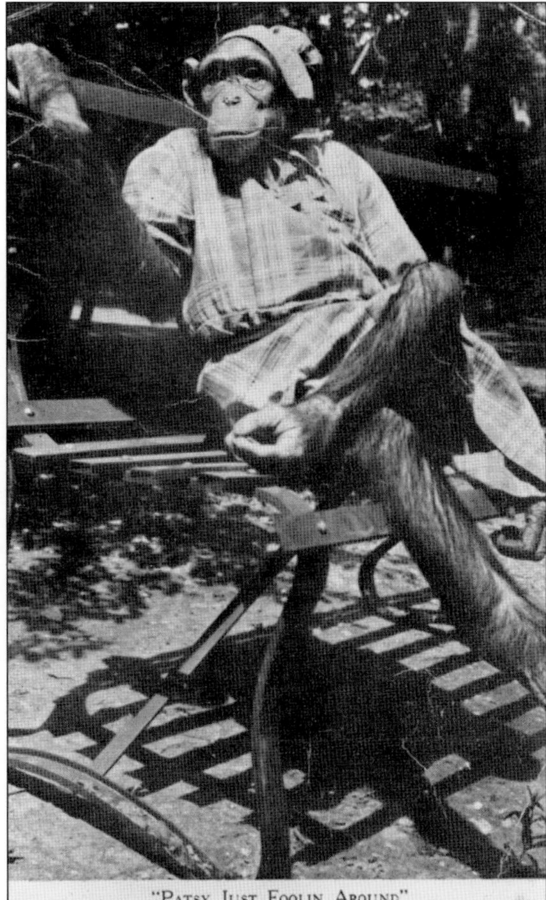
"PATSY JUST FOOLIN AROUND"

A renewed interest in archery emerged among both men and women in Fort Worth during the Great Depression. An archery range was located on the north side of Forest Park for many years. Here members of the Fort Worth Archery Club take aim at distant targets. (FWBG.)

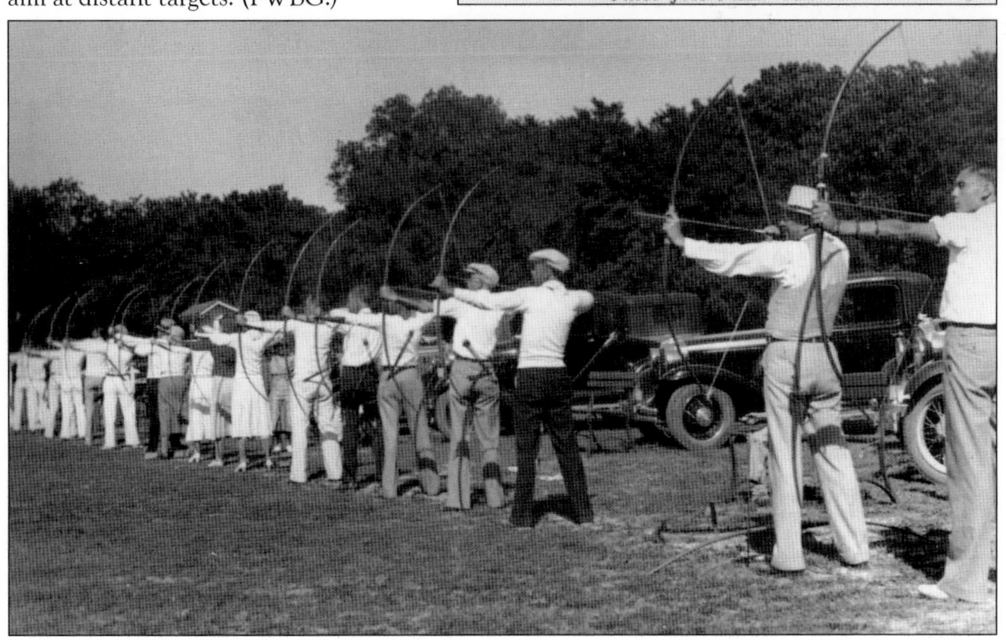

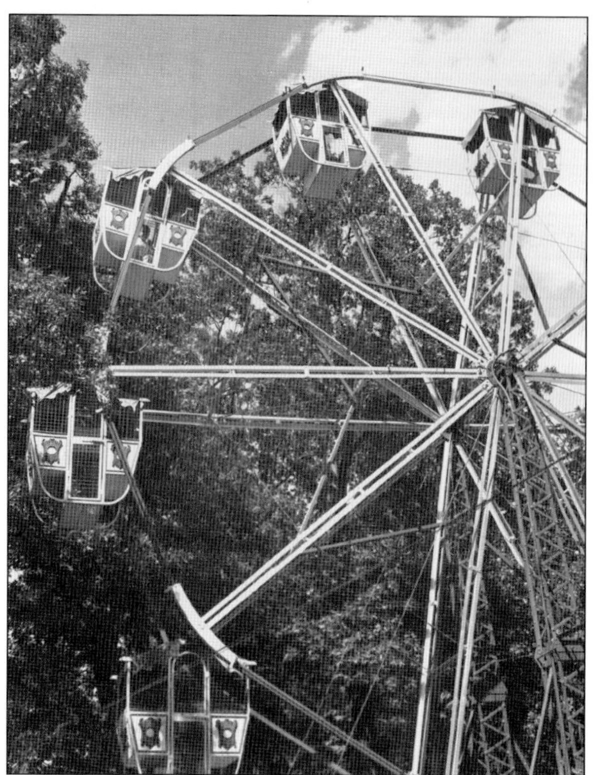

In 1924, William H. "Bill" Hames entered into a contract to furnish amusement rides in Forest Park. This was the beginning of a long association with Forest Park and the zoo. Rides at Forest Park included a miniature train, a merry-go-round, and a Ferris wheel, pictured here in 1937. (FWSTC/SCUTA.)

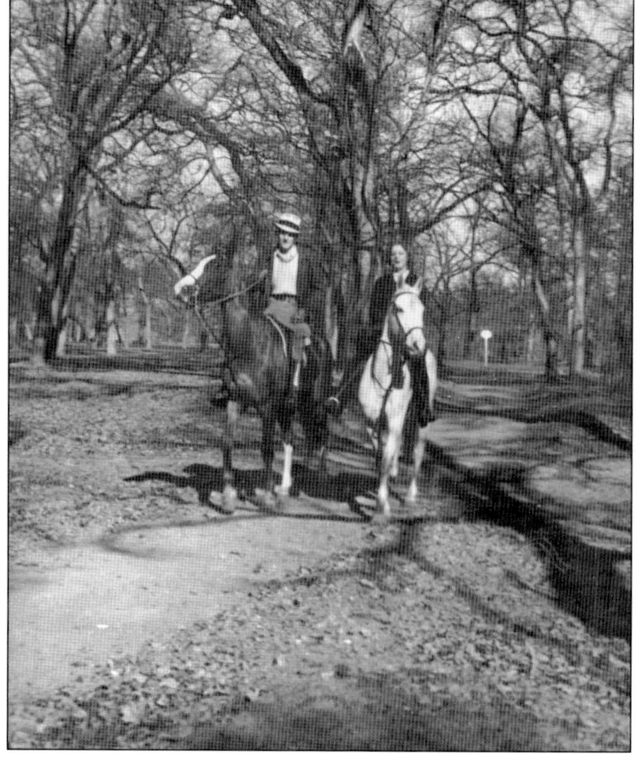

Horseback riding through city parks was a popular pastime. Several parks had stable concessions in them or nearby. WPA labor was used to construct bridle paths in some parks. This image of a couple riding on a bridle path in Trinity Park frequently was used in the promotion of the city's park system. (FWBG.)

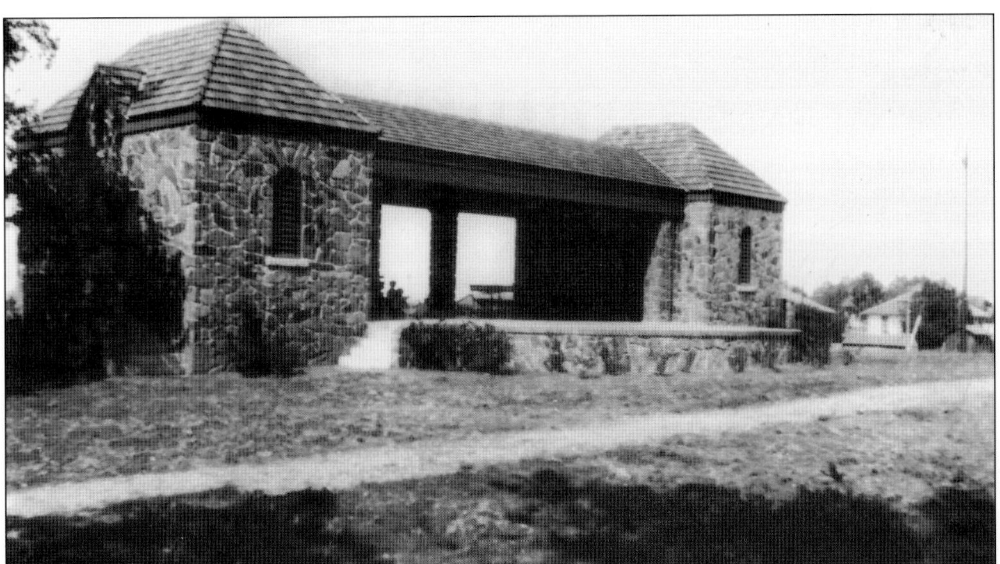

Land for Hillside Park was purchased in 1911, with additional acreage acquired in 1923 and 1927. Located on one of the highest points in southeast Fort Worth, the park provides an exceptional view of the downtown skyline. This shelter, no longer extant, was constructed of native stone and was sited so that the skyline provided the backdrop for its stage. (FWBG.)

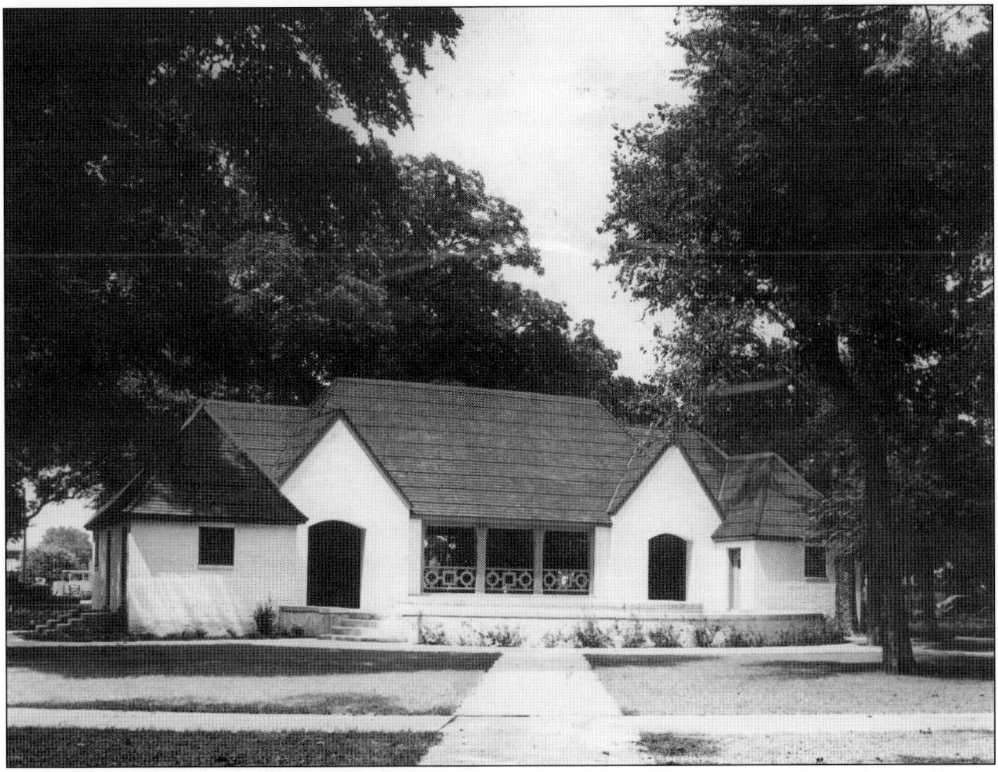

Travelers on West Seventh Street are familiar with this shelter in Trinity Park, although they might not recognize it here in its original white coat of paint. It was another design of Hare and Hare constructed by the WPA. It has long been used for concerts and theatrical performances. (FWSTC/SCUTA.)

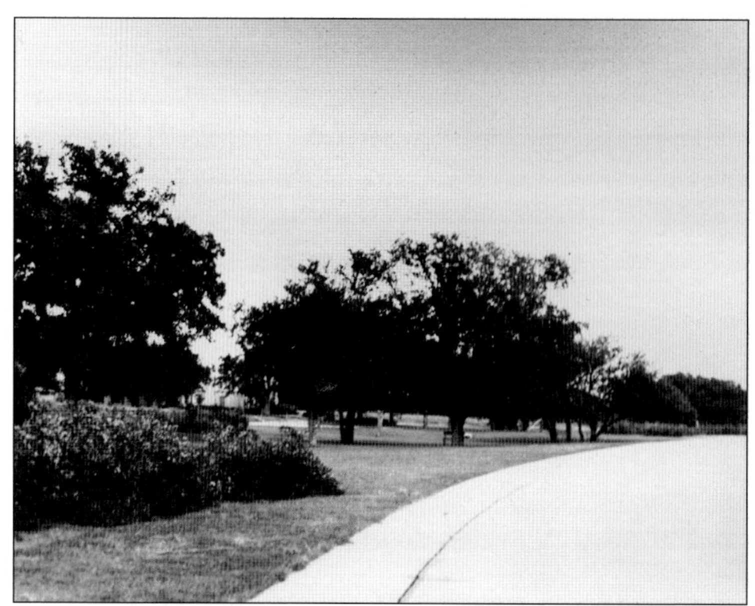

In January 1929, the William E. Harmon Foundation of New York gave $2,000 to the Monticello Land Company for the development of a park in the Monticello subdivision in west Fort Worth. The company gave the funds to the recreation department for the construction of tennis courts and a playground. Known as Monticello Harmon Field, this is how it looked in the mid-1930s. (FWBG.)

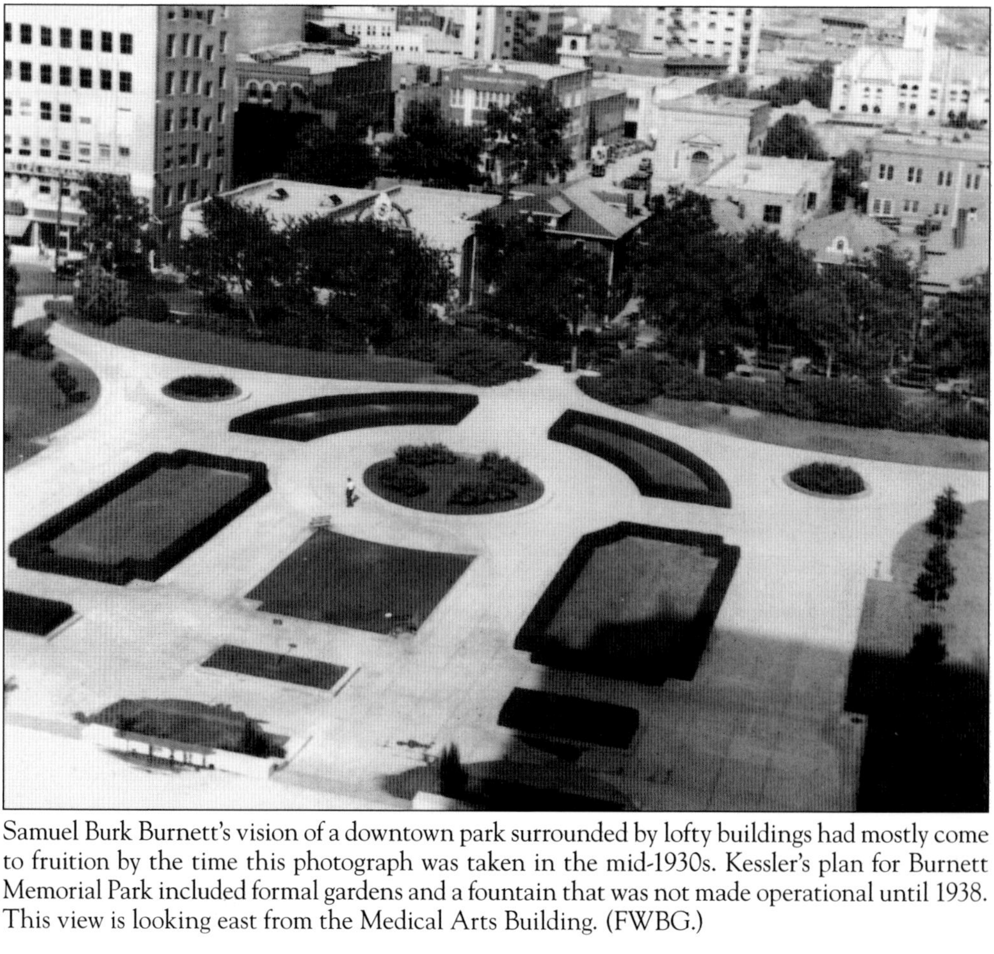

Samuel Burk Burnett's vision of a downtown park surrounded by lofty buildings had mostly come to fruition by the time this photograph was taken in the mid-1930s. Kessler's plan for Burnett Memorial Park included formal gardens and a fountain that was not made operational until 1938. This view is looking east from the Medical Arts Building. (FWBG.)

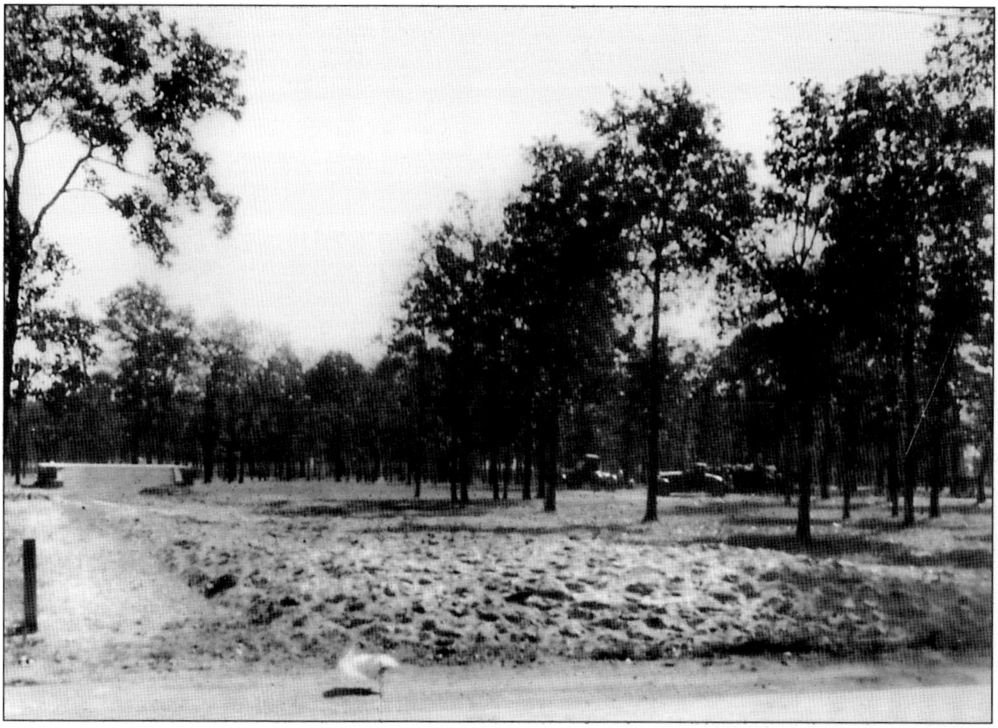

Sylvania Park, a popular neighborhood park located in the Riverside area of Fort Worth, was one of the many parks beautified under the WPA program. The above photograph depicts a shelter under construction and the entrance prior to being landscaped. The photograph below shows nearly the same view after the formal walks at the entrance and the shelter were completed. The shelter's platform could be used for band concerts or other performances. The park's 29.22 acres also contained picnic areas, tennis courts, baseball diamonds, and a small children's play area. It also received a pool and bathhouse built by the WPA. (Both, FWBG.)

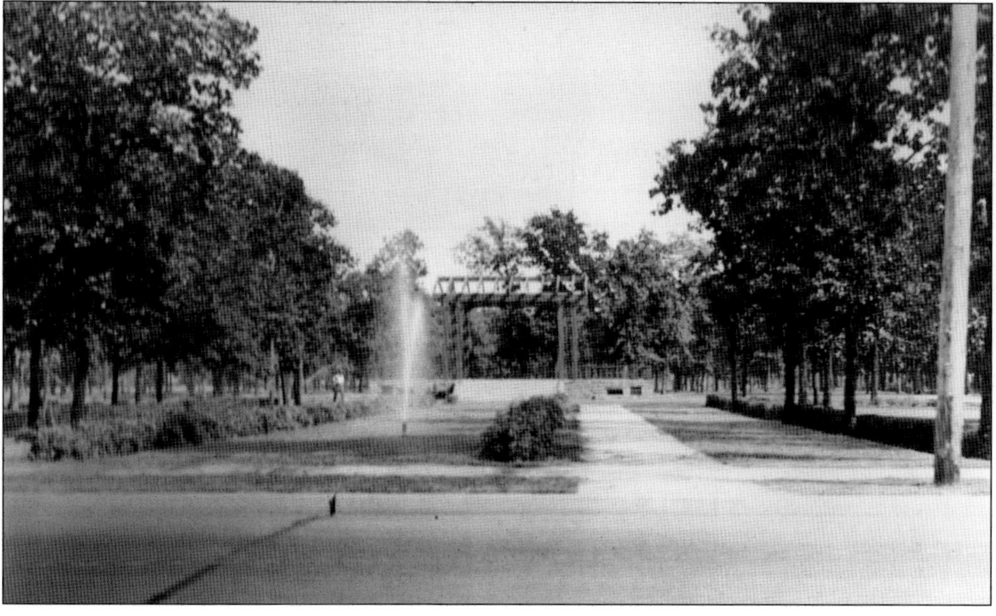

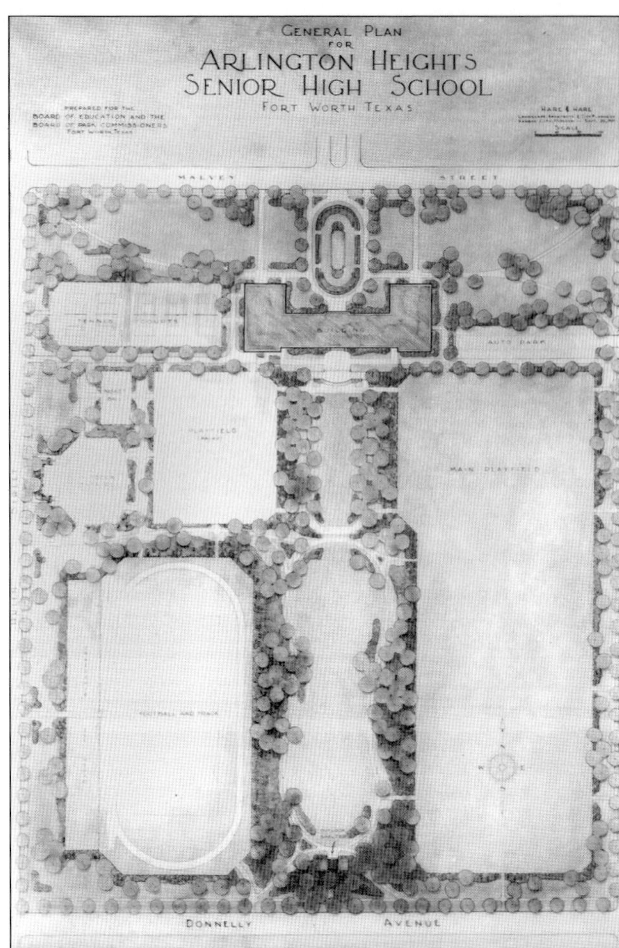

Arlington Heights High School was constructed in 1936–1937 with funds from the Public Works Administration (PWA). Its grounds were landscaped using WPA labor through a joint project of the park board and the school district. Hare and Hare's design included a park-like treatment with a formal entrance, a vista lined by informal paths, a small shelter amid clusters of trees, playfields, an amphitheater, and a football field and track. (FWBG.)

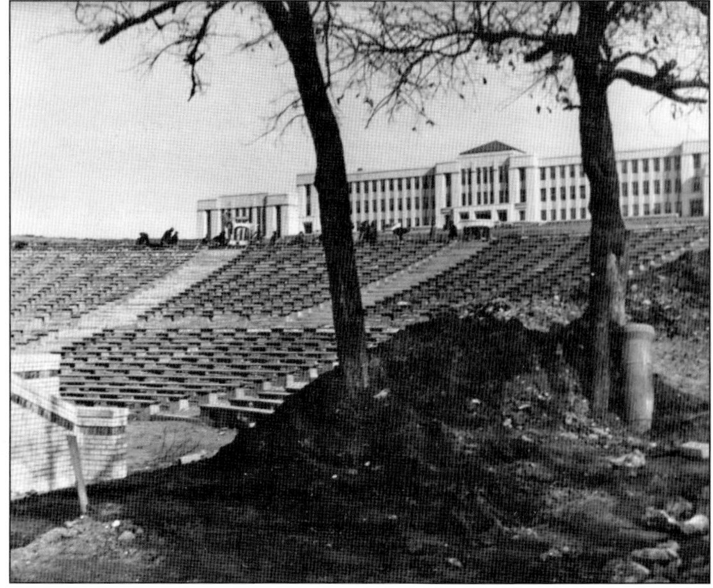

North Side Senior High School was also constructed in 1936–1937 through the PWA, and its grounds were landscaped by the WPA. Among the WPA work was this amphitheater. In all, 54 schools were landscaped. Besides the laborers, 60 engineers, 40 draftsmen, 20 estimators, a sculptress, and several architects and landscape architects found employment through this program, which became a model for other cities. (FWBG.)

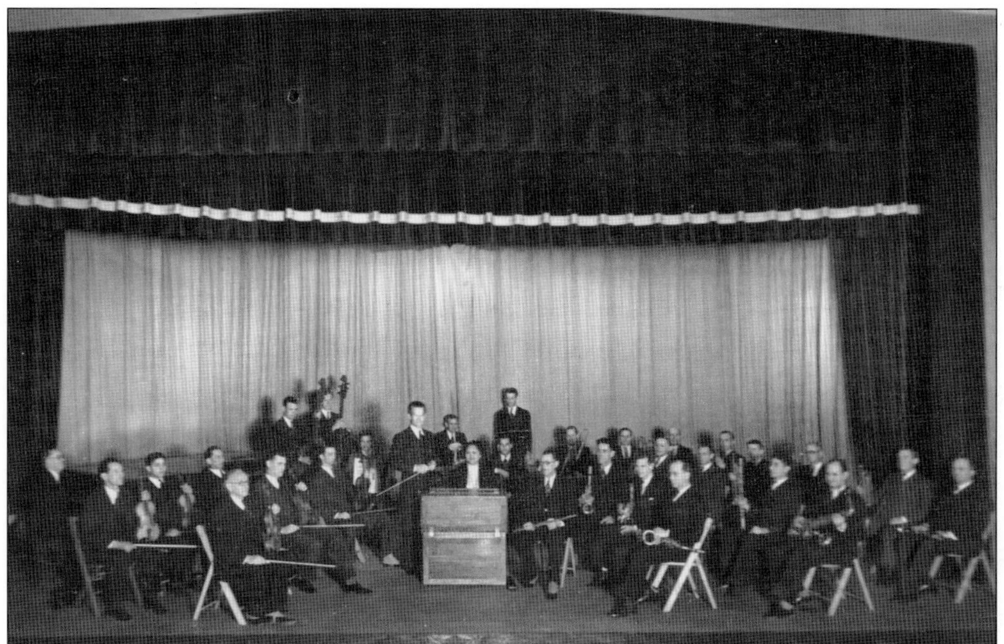

Fort Worth was one of four cities in Texas that participated in the WPA's Federal Music Project. The recreation department was the sponsor of the program in Fort Worth. Between March 1936 and March 1938, this branch gave 878 concerts. The musicians also conducted free music classes on Saturday mornings. (W. D. Smith photograph, D. Lynn Smith.)

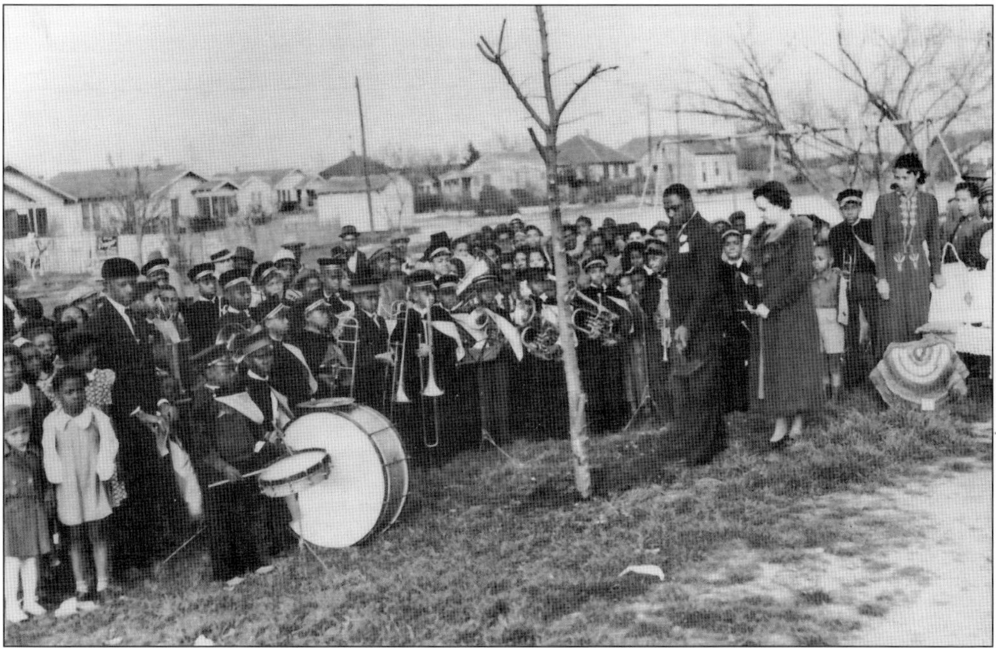

The Colored WPA Recreation Playground Orchestra was composed of students who took lessons from the members of the Fort Worth Federal Music Project. Here the orchestra is pictured at a tree-planting ceremony in Dixie Park. Located at Fabons and East Rosedale Streets and acquired in 1926, Dixie Park was one of the parks established for African American residents in the era of segregation. (FWBG.)

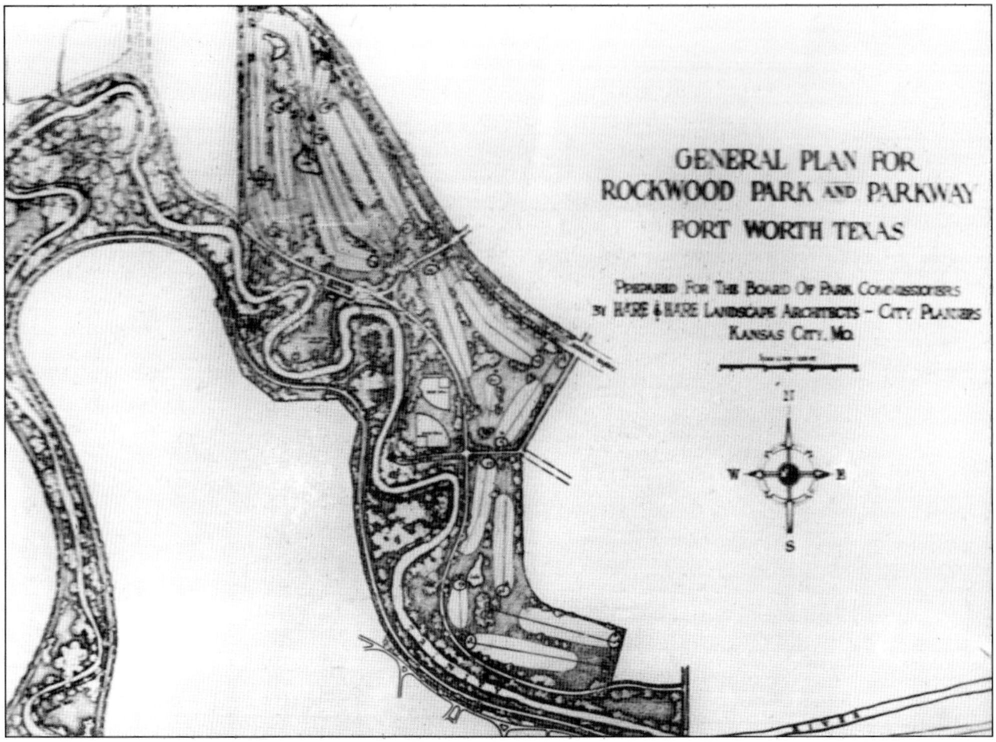

Prior to its realignment, the West Fork of the Trinity River snaked along Rockwood Park, as shown in this plan prepared by Hare and Hare. The park's golf course was the recreation department's first work program under the CWA. The first nine holes of the course were constructed by the CWA. Additional work was completed by the WPA. (FWBG.)

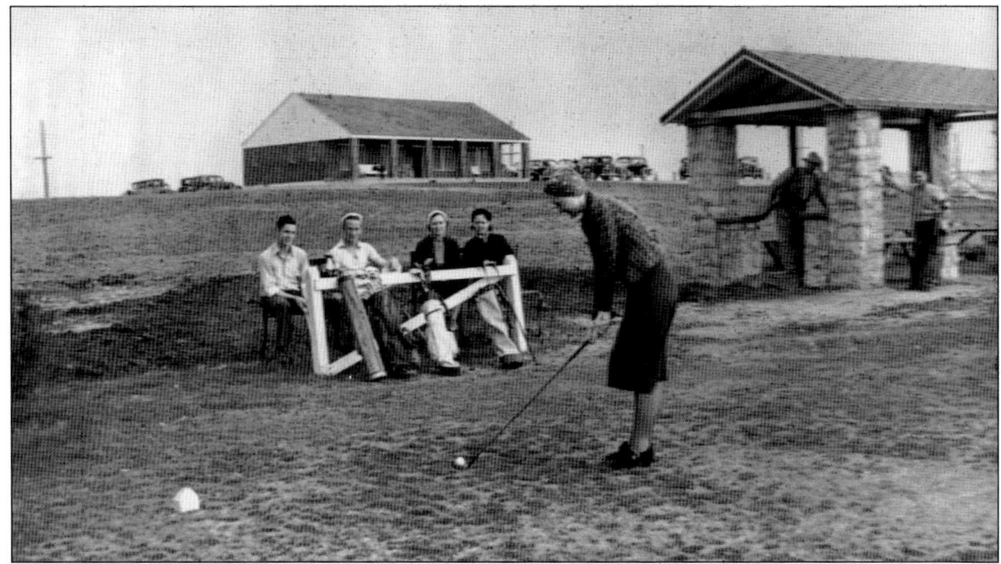

The 140-acre Z. Boaz Municipal Golf Course, located on Fort Worth's west side, received numerous improvements under the WPA. Work there included the construction of a clubhouse, a starter shelter, and a practice putting green. In this photograph, a golfing party observes one of its members as she is about to tee off. (FWBG.)

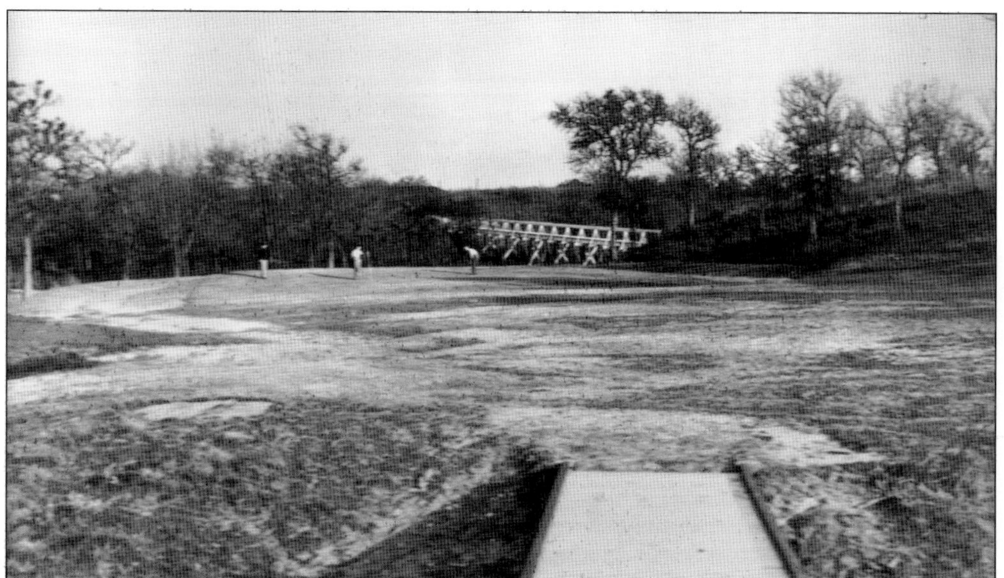

Meadowbrook Municipal Golf Course on the city's east side started out as a private club. The city purchased it in 1936–1937 for $30,500. At that time, it contained 118 acres, a large clubhouse, and a swimming pool. Through the WPA, the course received new footbridges and improvements to bunkers, tees, and fairways. (FWBG.)

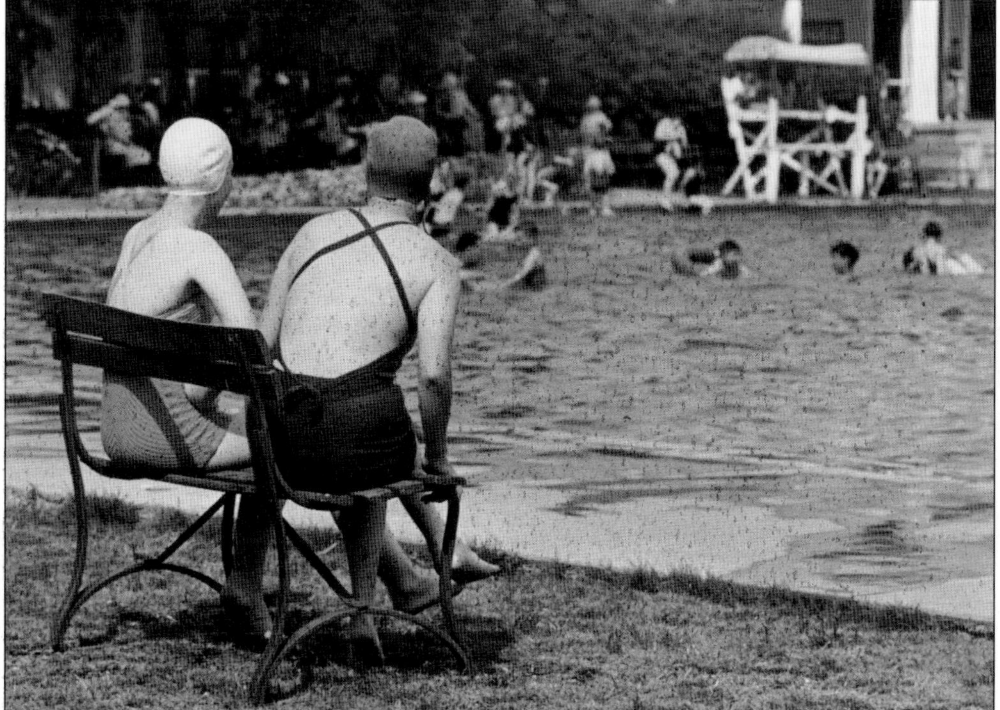

Approximately 20 years before this photograph was taken, a local newspaper commented about the shocking behavior some women displayed when they entered the Forest Park wading pool without their stockings. The stylish swimming attire worn by these two women at the Forest Park swimming pool in the mid-1930s does not appear to have shocked anyone. (FWL.)

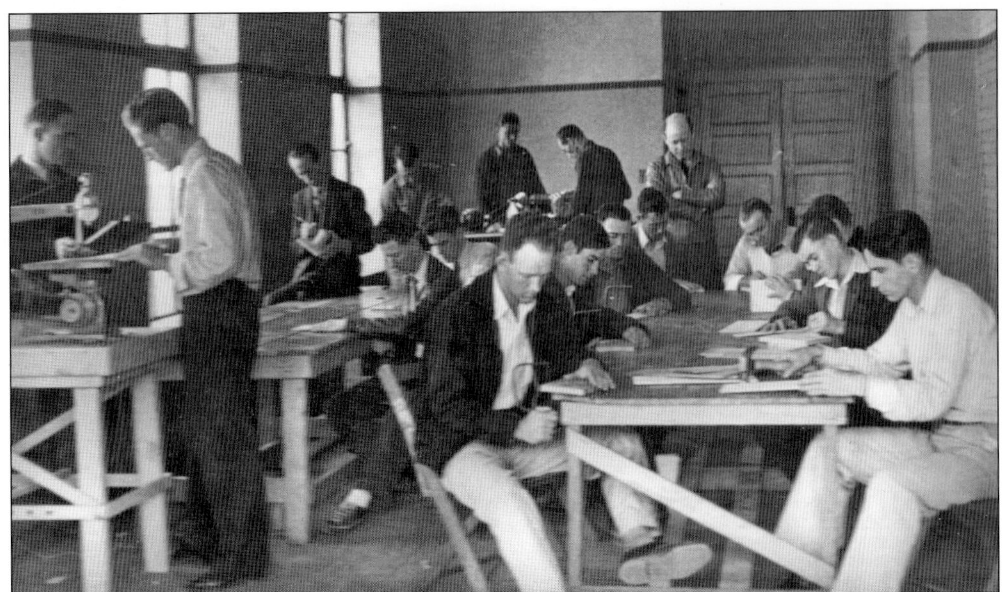

With the assistance of work-relief funds, the recreation department was able to increase its general programming by 80 percent and participation by 69 percent. Supervision increased from 17 to 60 playgrounds during the summer and from 8 to 21 playgrounds during the school year. All directors went through a training school sponsored by the department. In the photograph above, directors are shown receiving handcraft instructions. Numerous classes were also offered at the Recreation Building every day of the week. In the photograph below, young children in a dance class follow the instructions of their teacher, who was paid through the WPA. City officials noted that one of the prime benefits of the WPA recreation programs was the reduction in juvenile delinquency. (Both, FWBG.)

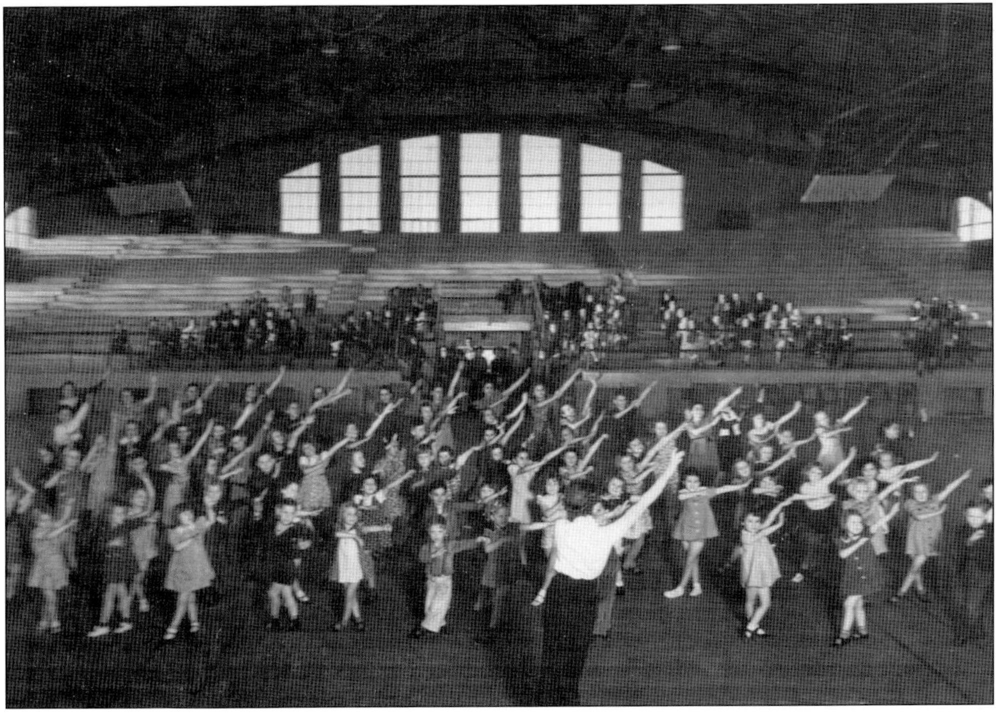

Rosa Mae Steverson (1896–1995) was hired through the WPA as recreation director for Dixie Park. She stayed with the recreation department for 28 years and retired in 1965. A talented ceramics and leatherwork instructor, she later commuted to Hillside, Lincoln, and Lake Como Parks as well as Harmon Field and Butler Place, working with all age groups. (Loyce Steverson Whitted.)

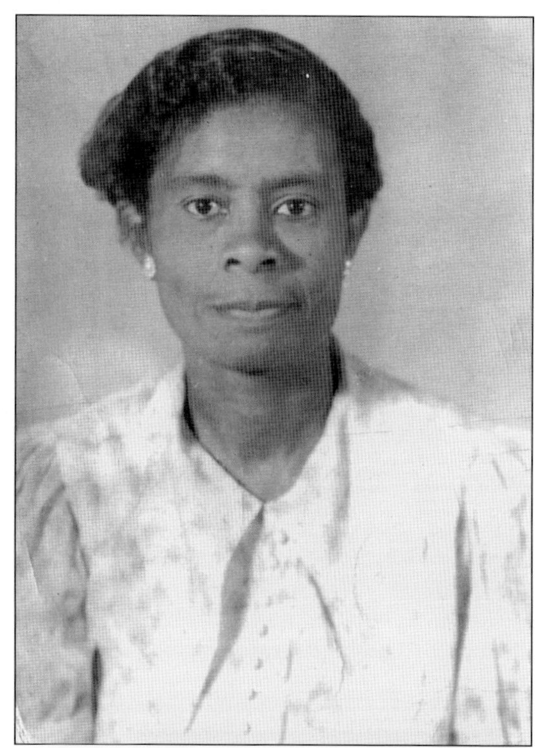

Alfred T. Palmer, a photographer for the Farm Security Administration–Office of War Information, captured this idyllic scene in the Fort Worth Botanic Garden. The image was used in a montage of photographs from across the country to illustrate the concepts expressed in President Roosevelt's "Four Freedoms" speech. This was one of the images used to represent the ideal of "Freedom from Fear." (Library of Congress, Washington, D.C.)

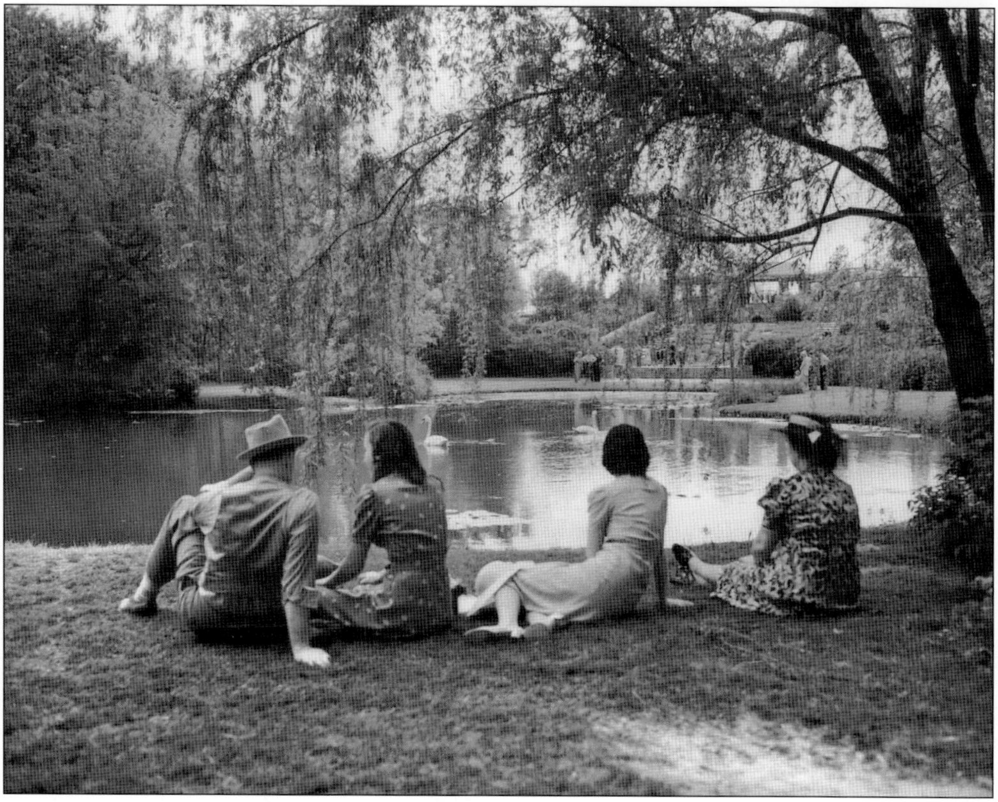

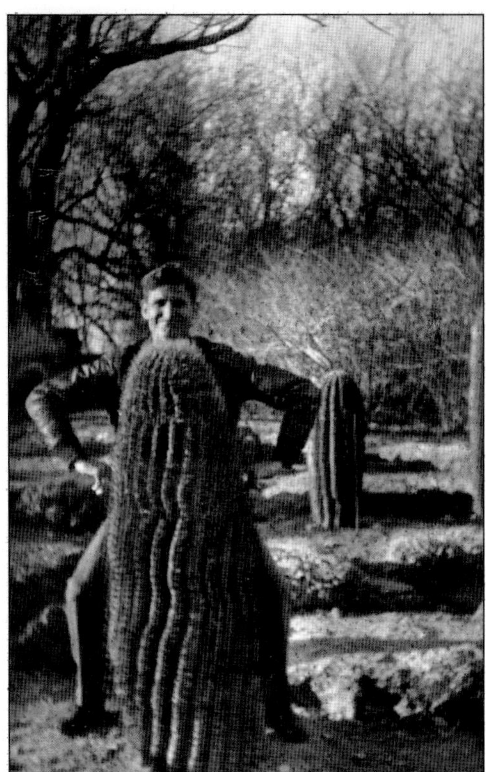

George G. Curl was an experienced aviator when he joined the U.S. Army Air Corps in 1943. Here he is shown wearing his flight jacket while clowning around in the Fort Worth Botanic Garden's cactus garden. Many military personnel on leave or stationed nearby found refuge at the city's parks and recreation spots during World War II. (Taddie Hamilton.)

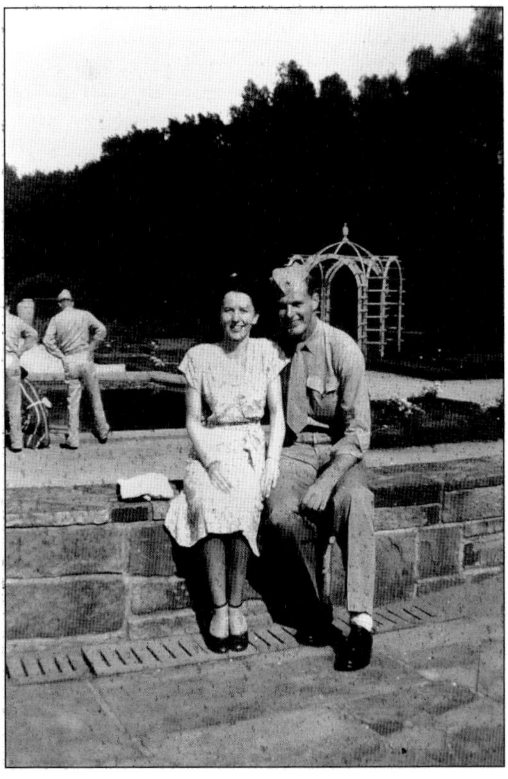

Frederick Rea Strange (right) served in the U.S. Marine Corps and was stationed at Eagle Mountain Lake north of the city during the waning months of World War II. He met Peggy Sue Wiese in May 1945. Before marrying in May 1946, their courtship included frequent trips to Fort Worth area parks. Here the couple enjoys a moment together at the Fort Worth Botanic Garden. (Peggy Strange.)

Four

Postwar Boom 1946 to 1963

After World War II, Fort Worth's population continued to grow as its economy benefited from industries attracted to North Texas, particularly those associated with aviation and aerospace industries. By 1950, it had 278,788 residents, an increase of 57 percent from 1940. By 1960, the population had increased nearly 25 percent to 347,368 residents.

As the city's boundaries expanded, so did the number of parks. New parks included Wedgewood, Springdale, Kellis, Bluebonnet Circle, Newby, Harrold, and Tandy Hills. The Forest Park Zoo grew with the construction of the Children's Zoo (1953), the Record Aquarium (1954), and the Herpetarium (1960). The Log Cabin Village also got its start during this period.

The recreation department experienced an increase in resources and responsibilities following the passage of a $500,000 bond issue in 1946. One of its first priorities was the construction of more recreation centers across the city. The first to be completed was the Northside Recreation Center; it opened in 1948. Two centers were constructed in 1954, one on the west side and one for African Americans east of downtown. These were followed by the Riverside Center at Sylvania Park in 1955 and the Sycamore Center at Sycamore Park in 1956. The department moved its headquarters to the Sycamore Center, and the South Side Center on Vickery Boulevard became the headquarters for the Athletic Division. Five swimming pools were constructed by 1960, four of which served largely African American neighborhoods.

As the civil rights movement gained momentum in the 1950s, Fort Worth's African American community became more vocal about equal access to park and recreation facilities. In 1951, African Americans were granted limited access to the zoo and amusement rides at Forest Park, the botanic garden, and the Broadview picnic area at Lake Worth. When the Harmon Center opened in 1954, so too did an adjacent golf course. The four swimming pools for African Americans were built in previously underserved neighborhoods. These facilities largely preserved the status quo. Progress was made in 1961 when the city's first African American was appointed to the park board.

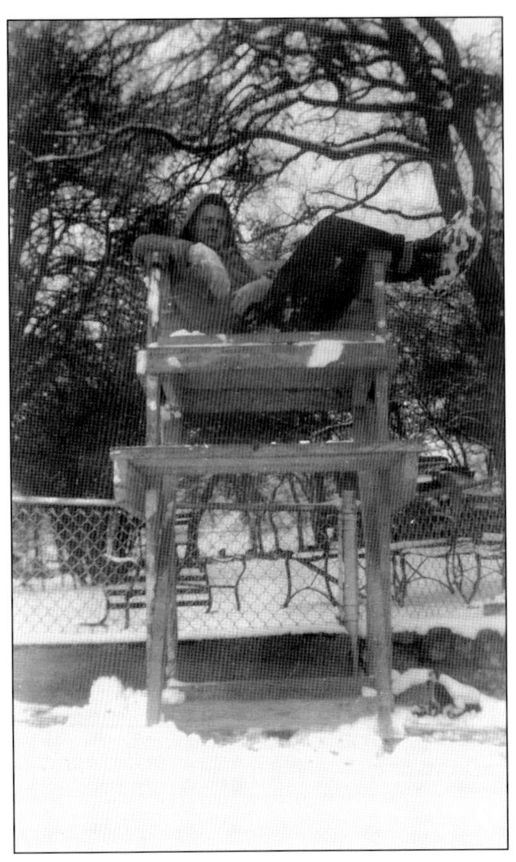

A summer job as a lifeguard has long been the dream of many young men and women. Hugh Bryant was fortunate to have worked as a lifeguard at the Forest Park swimming pool part-time in the summer of 1946 and full-time in the summers of 1947 and 1948. His fondness for the place extended to the off-season as well. The photograph at left shows him lounging in the lifeguard's chair in January 1947. In the photograph below, he is standing on the diving board in the center of the pool. This view reveals the concavity of the pool's bottom, a design feature that made it difficult to keep inexperienced swimmers from literally getting in over their heads. (Both, Hugh Bryant.)

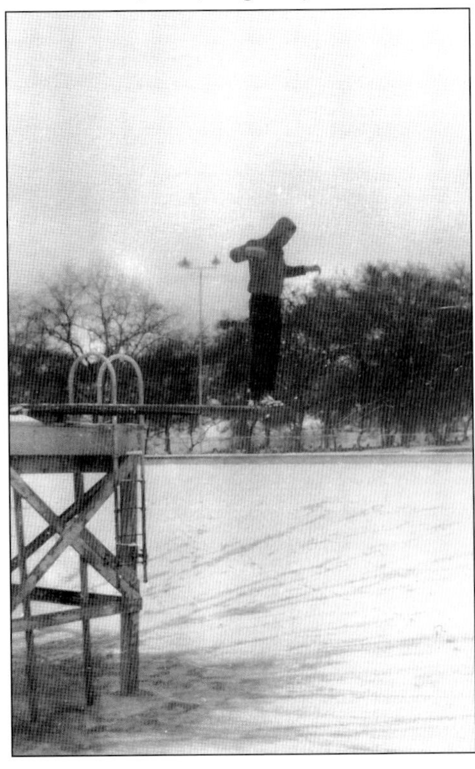

Hampton "Hamp" Cottar, along with 11 fellow sailors, founded the Lake Worth Sailing Club in 1935. The club established its headquarters near Sunset Park where it remains today. Here Hamp is pictured with his wife, Doty, as they enjoy a day on the lake in their Snipe sailboat. (Lake Worth Sailing Club.)

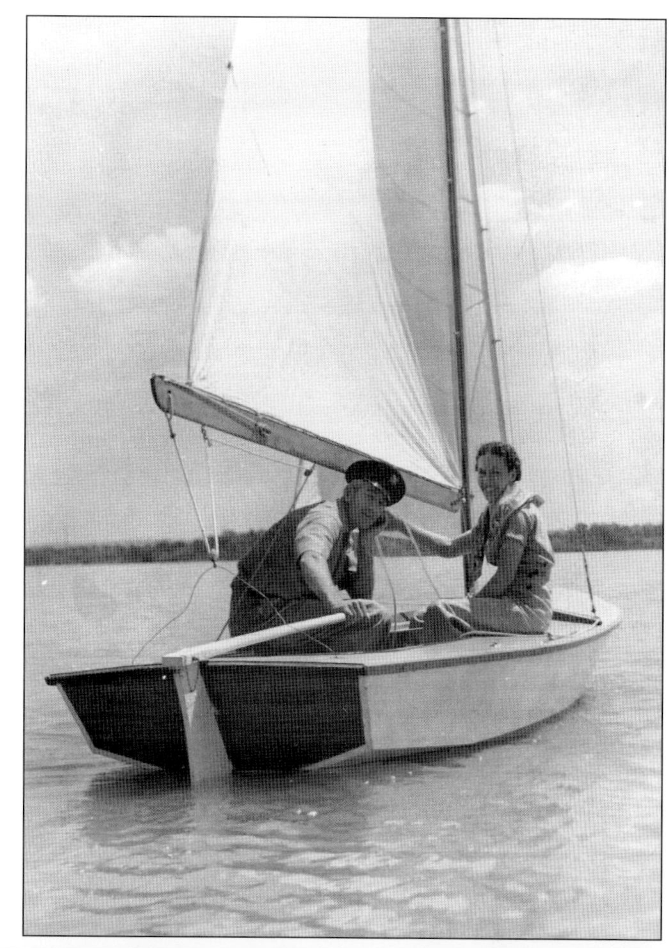

Under city forester D. D. Obert, the park department implemented a citywide tree-trimming program in 1939. The program was not always looked upon favorably by property owners, but the *Fort Worth Star-Telegram* praised the work done in the 2200 block of Huntington Lane, as shown in this photograph below from May 1947. Today tree-trimming services are also performed by the Fort Worth Parks and Community Services Department. (FWSTC/SCUTA.)

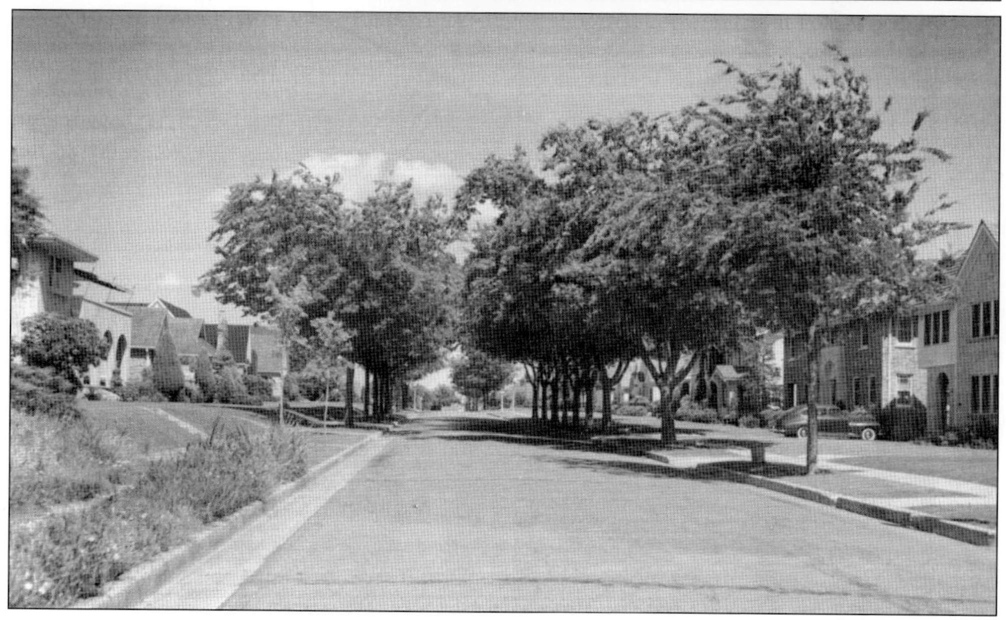

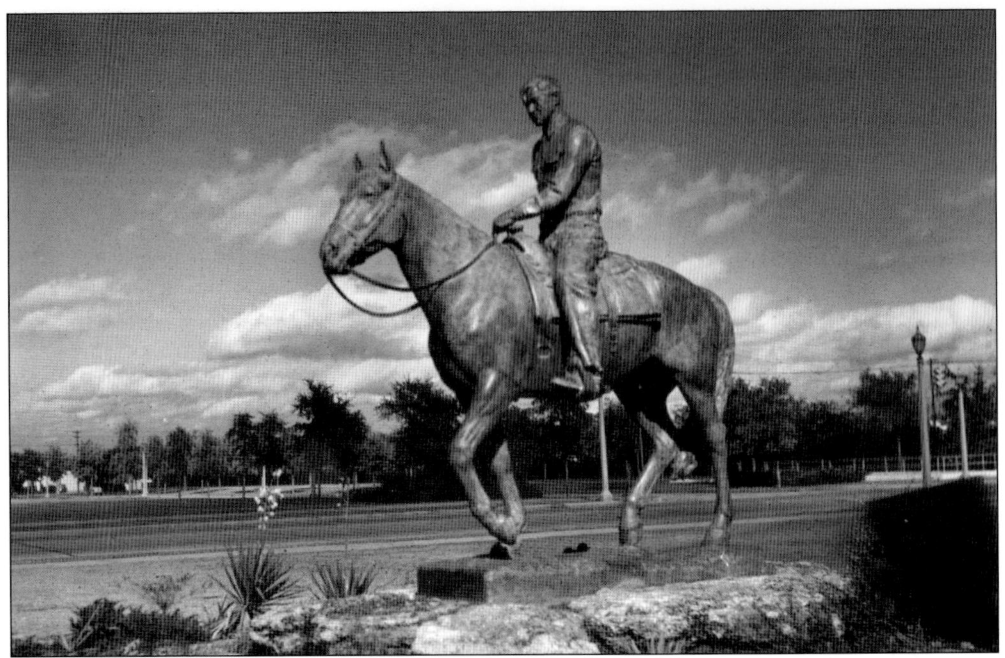

Amon G. Carter Sr. commissioned Electra Waggoner Biggs to craft this sculpture of his friend cowboy humorist Will Rogers on his horse, Soapsuds. Titled *Will Rogers Riding into the Sunset*, the sculpture was completed in 1941–1942. Placed at the Will Rogers Memorial Complex on grounds maintained by the park department, the sculpture was dedicated by Gen. Dwight D. Eisenhower on November 4, 1947. (FWL.)

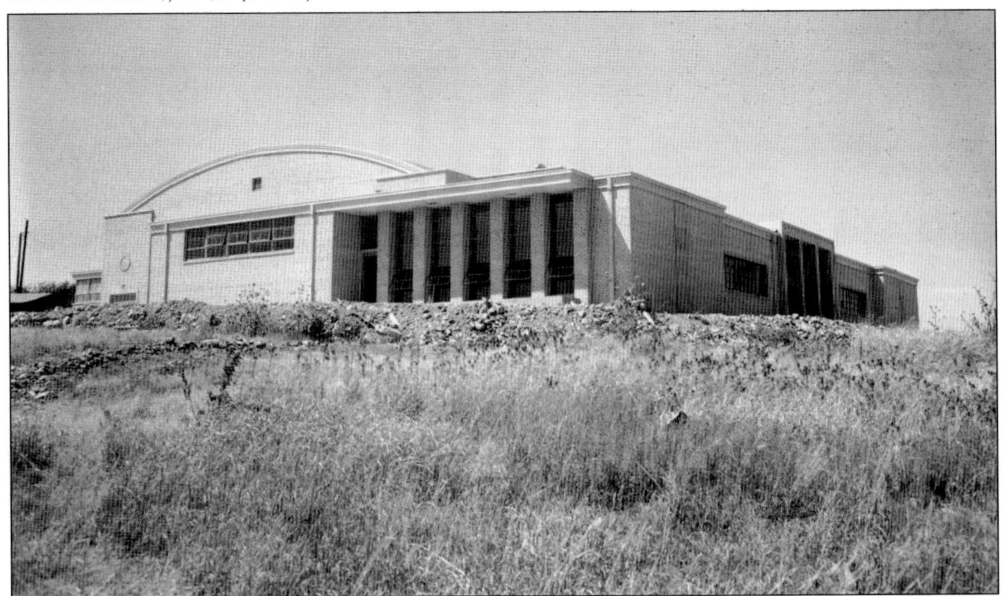

The Northside Recreation Center was the first center constructed after the passage of a recreation department bond issue in 1946. Designed by Wilson and Patterson, architects, and built by the Paschall-Sanders Construction Company, the building contained a gymnasium, a stage, and club rooms. This photograph of the building was taken in September 1948 as it neared completion. (FWSTC/SCUTA.)

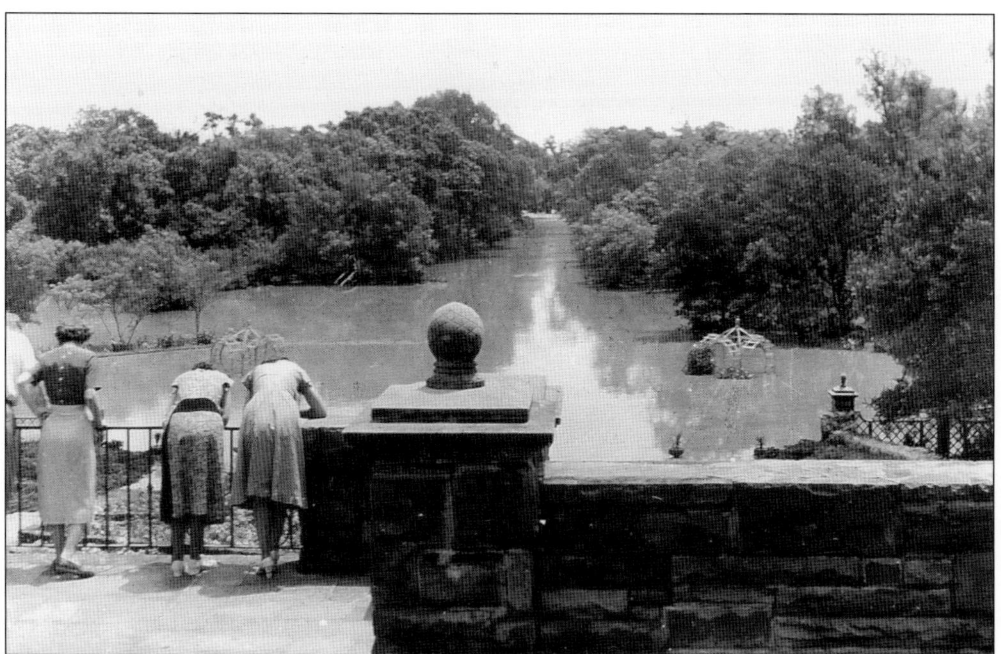

In 1949, the Fort Worth Botanic Garden was flooded twice, placing portions of the garden under 12 to 18 feet of water. Surprisingly, most of the plants survived, and the lawn actually thrived as a result of the deposit of topsoil. This view of the May flood was taken from the terrace overlooking the rose garden. (Larry Schuessler.)

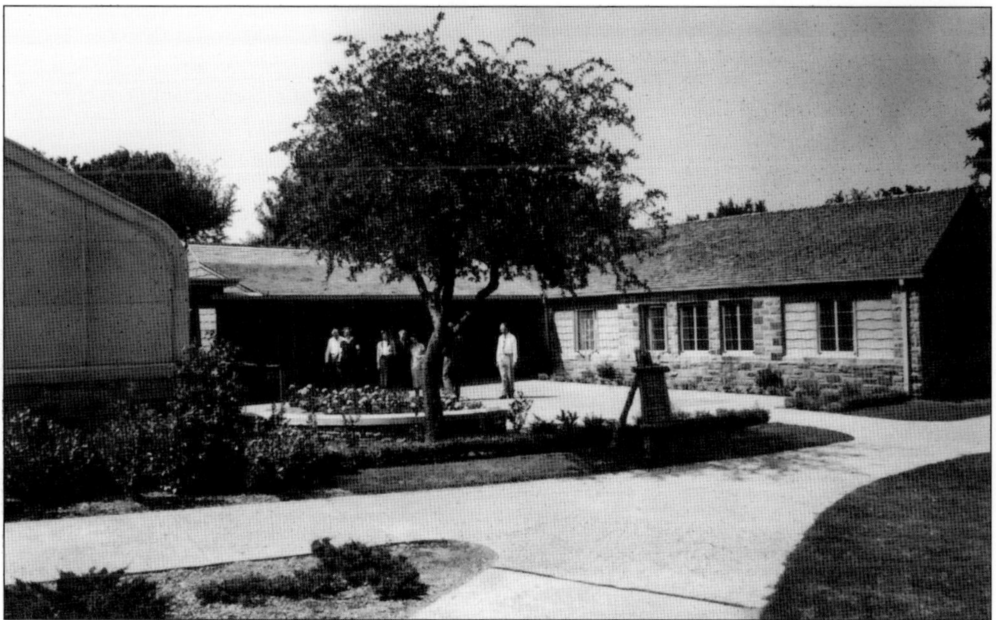

The garden center building at the Fort Worth Botanic Garden was enlarged in 1950 to accommodate new uses. The old greenhouse (right) was converted to an assembly room, and a new greenhouse was constructed to the west. The new greenhouse was designed specifically for conservatory plantations, which mostly consisted of rare tropical plants. Today it houses the garden's begonia collection. (FWBG.)

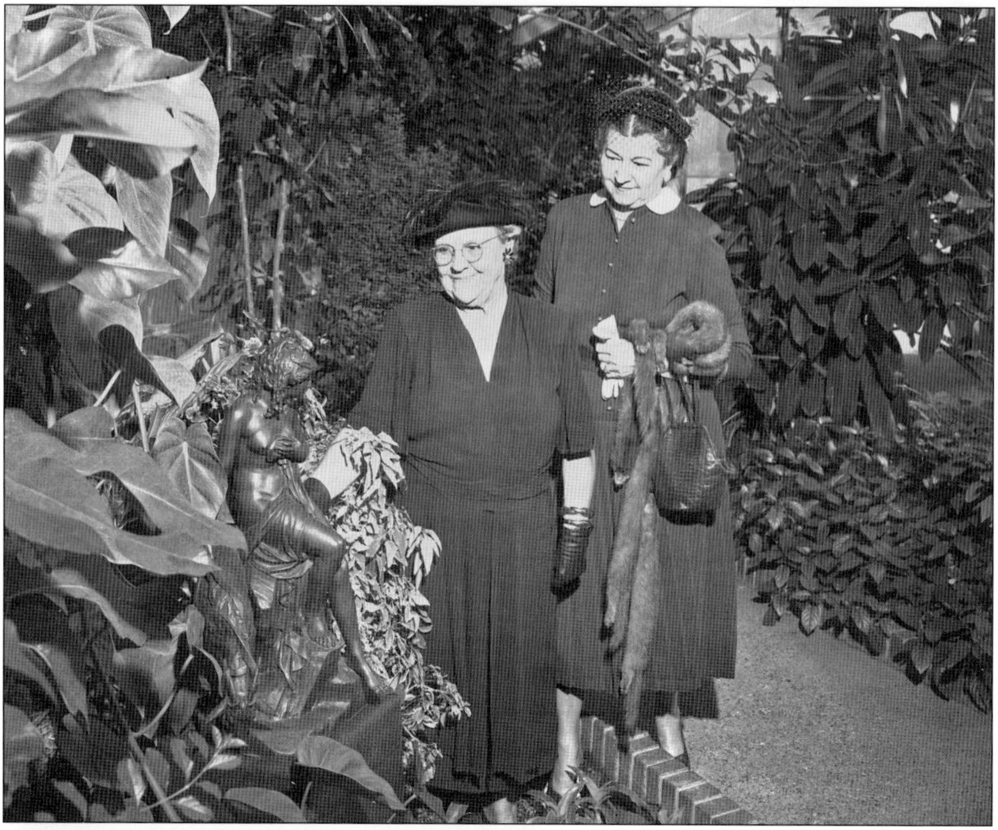

The North Fort Worth Garden Club presented the garden center at the botanic garden with this bronze sculpture in honor of Mary Daggett Lake (1881–1955) in 1952. Lake served as the center's director and a member of the park board for many years, and was a noted botanist and author. Admiring the sculpture are Lake (left) and the club's president, Edna Shine. (FWSTC/SCUTA.)

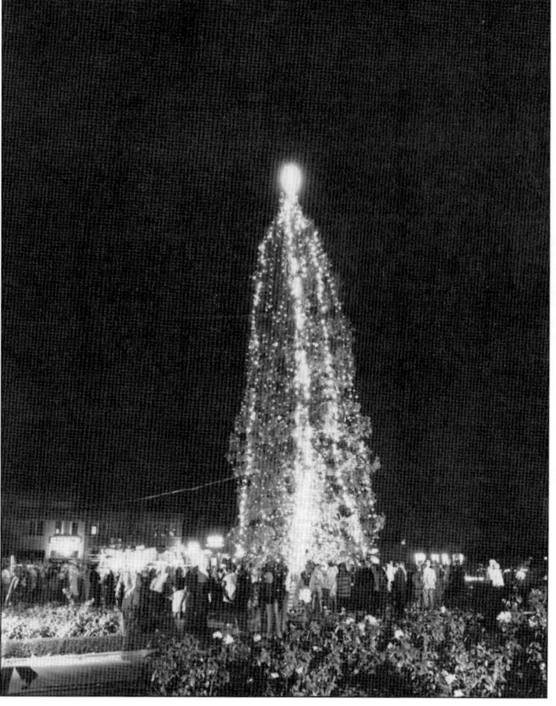

Beginning in the 1930s and continuing for many years, downtown's Burnett Park served as the location for the annual community Christmas tree. Over the years, the tree was sponsored by entities such as the Junior Chamber of Commerce, the *Fort Worth Star-Telegram*, and the recreation department. This nighttime view was captured in 1956. (FWSTC/SCUTA.)

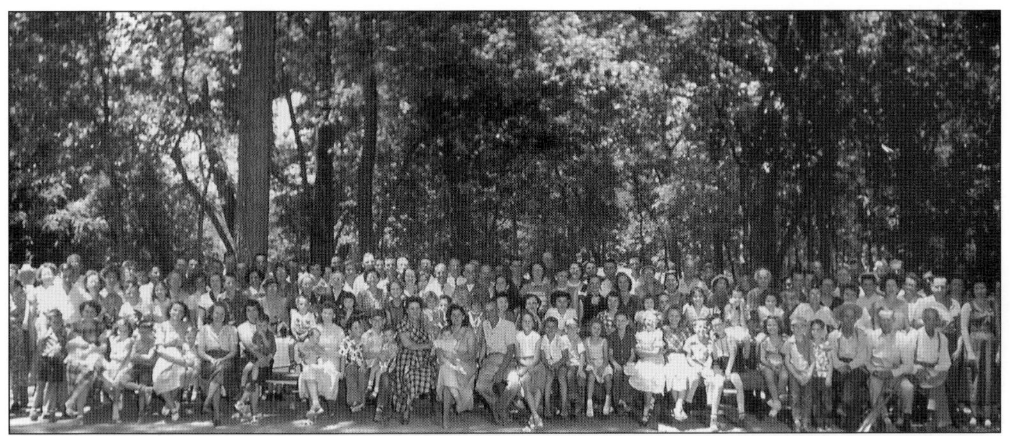

For generations, families have been enjoying reunions beneath the trees in Forest Park. The Faries-Stoker families, pictured in the above photograph from June 11, 1952, always held their reunion on the Sunday prior to Father's Day. The photograph below is of the c. 1951 Crew, Ellis, and Brumley family reunion. It depicts the accoutrements required for a successful reunion: picnic tables covered with tablecloths, loaves of bread, jars of canned goods, crocks, plates, glasses, large pots and pans filled with food, cardboard boxes and bushel baskets to carry things, and people of all ages. (Above, Bobby Faries; below, William Crew.)

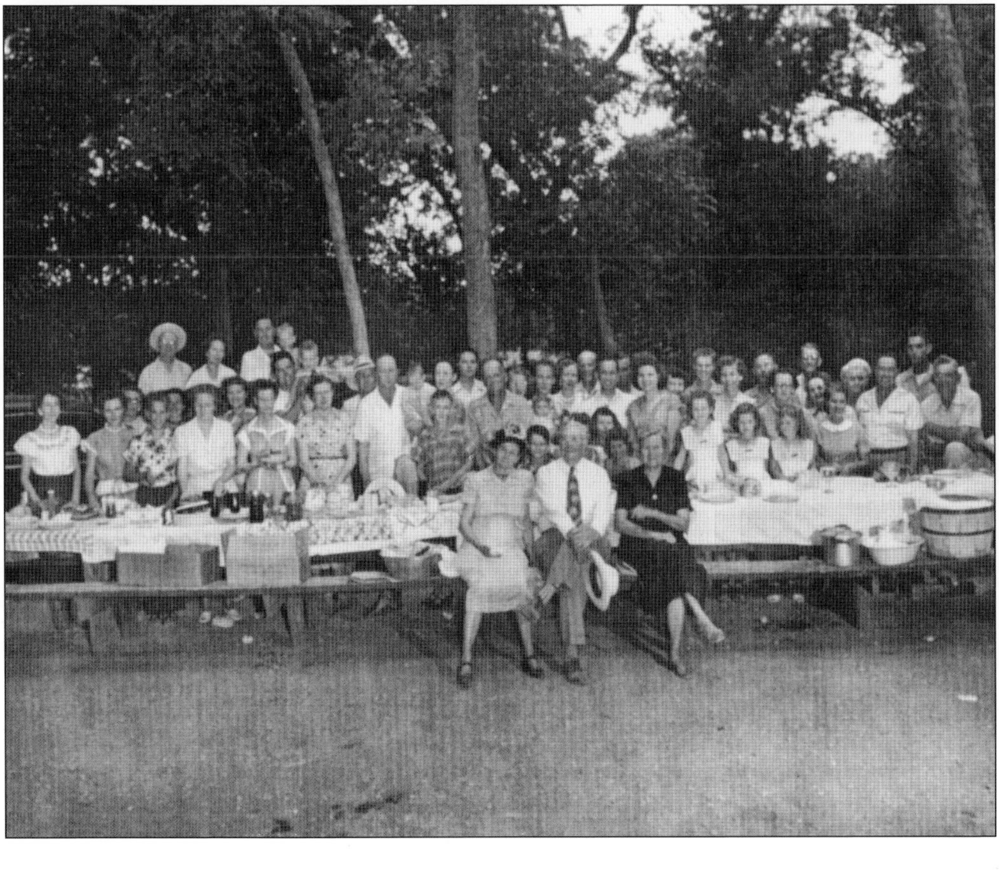

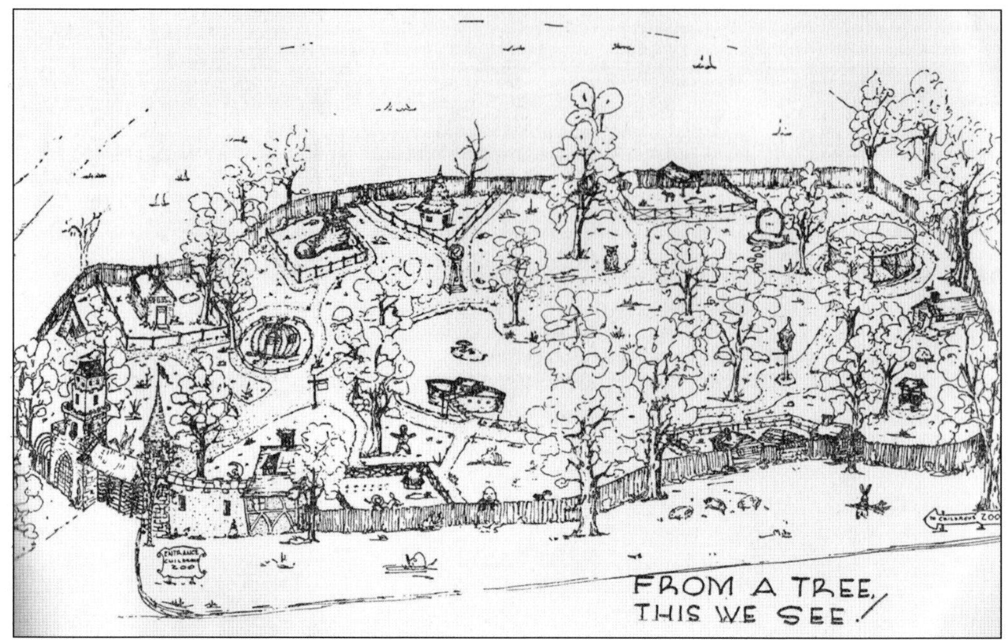

The Children's Zoo at Forest Park officially opened to the public in June 1953. Included within its confines were the homes of Peter Peter Pumpkin Eater, the Old Woman in the Shoe, and the Three Little Pigs. Architect Charles T. Freelove designed the attraction and created a booklet suitable for coloring as a memento. (Dalton Hoffman.)

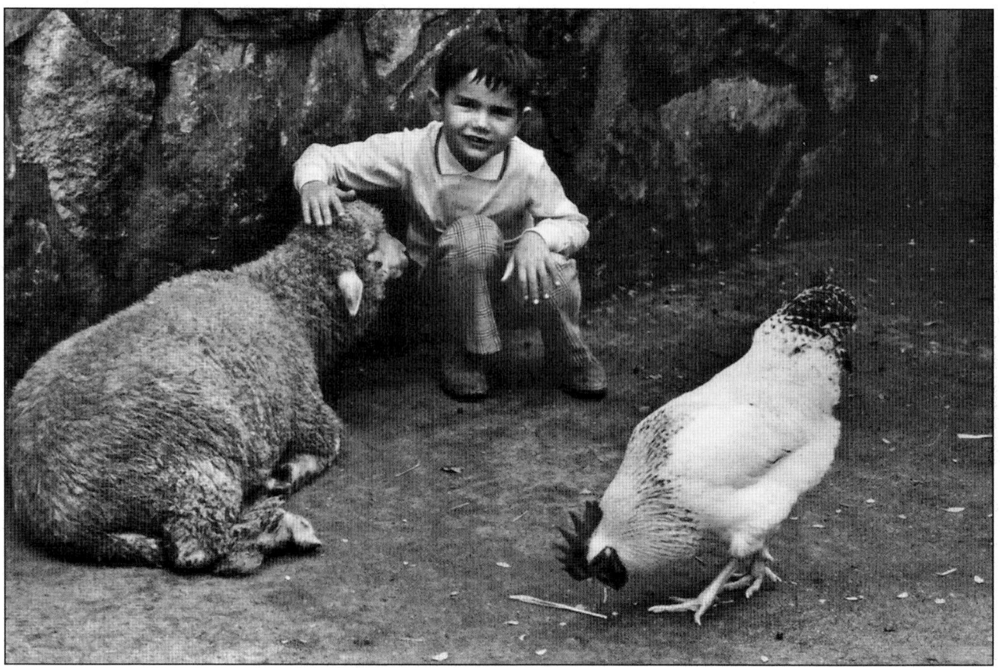

During the first year that the Children's Zoo was open, it received more than 200,000 visitors. An assortment of child-friendly animals such as sheep, baby goats, deer, de-scented skunks, puppies, ducks, and chickens added to its appeal. As shown here, young visitors eagerly interacted with the animals. (Fort Worth Zoo.)

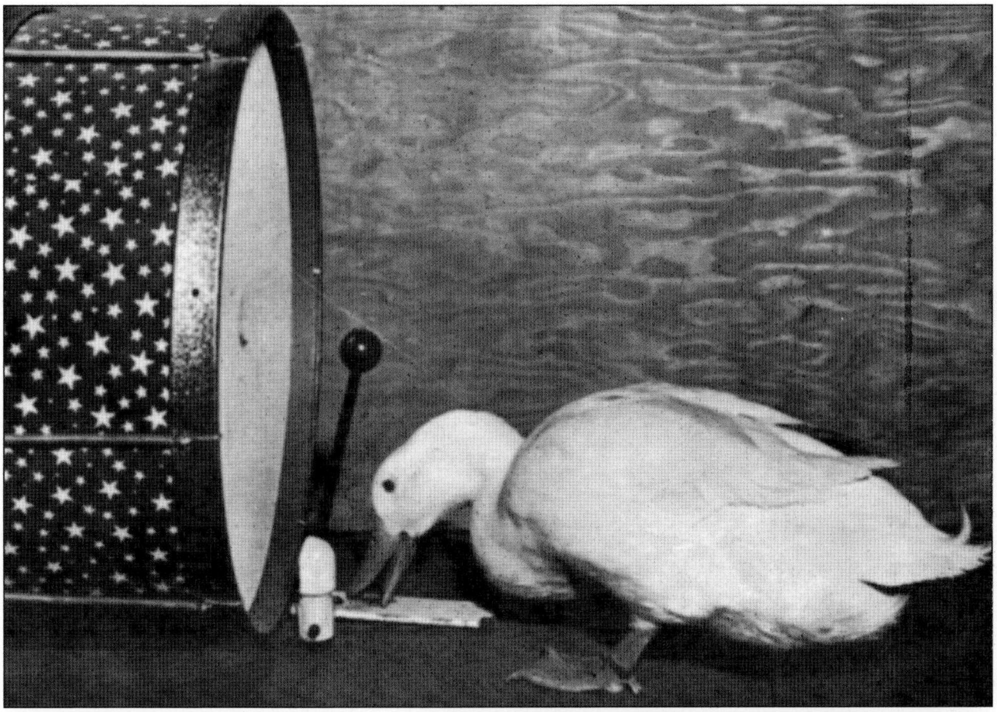

Some animals at the Children's Zoo performed tricks. When a nickel was dropped in a slot, Desmond the Drumming Duck would beat a drum 15 times to receive his reward—food. Other trained animals included a tightrope-walking chicken and a rabbit that kissed a plastic sweetheart until it blushed. (Larry Shuessler.)

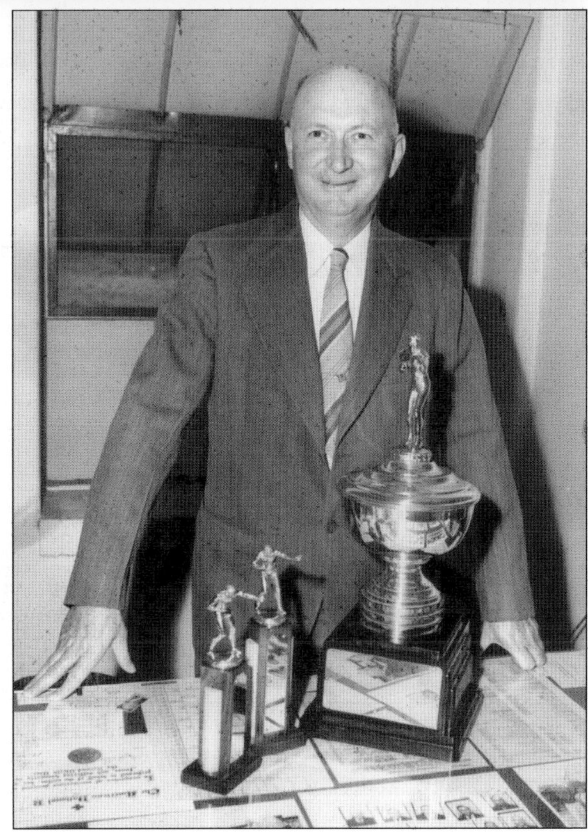

R. D. Evans was the recreation department's longest serving superintendent. He served as the athletic director from 1922 to 1924 and then as superintendent until his death in October 1953. Evans's accomplishments included organizing the Texas Amateur Athletic Federation and the annual Southwestern Recreation Track and Field Meet. When the new west-side recreation center was dedicated in March 1954, it was fittingly named the R. D. Evans Recreation Building. (FWSTC/SCUTA.)

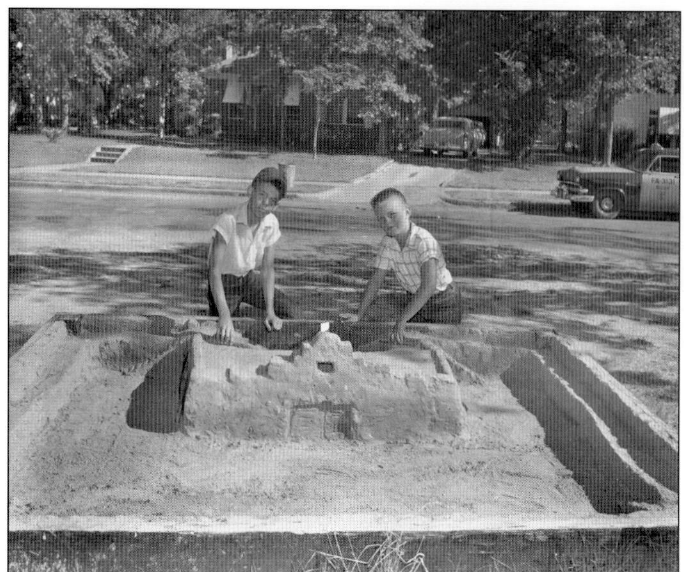

The recreation department sponsored a sand craft exhibition at neighborhood parks during July 1955. Freddy Drysdale (left) and Sparky Jones created their version of the famed Alamo at the Oakhurst Triangle in the Riverside area of Fort Worth. Judges went from park to park to choose the best creation. (FWSTC/SCUTA.)

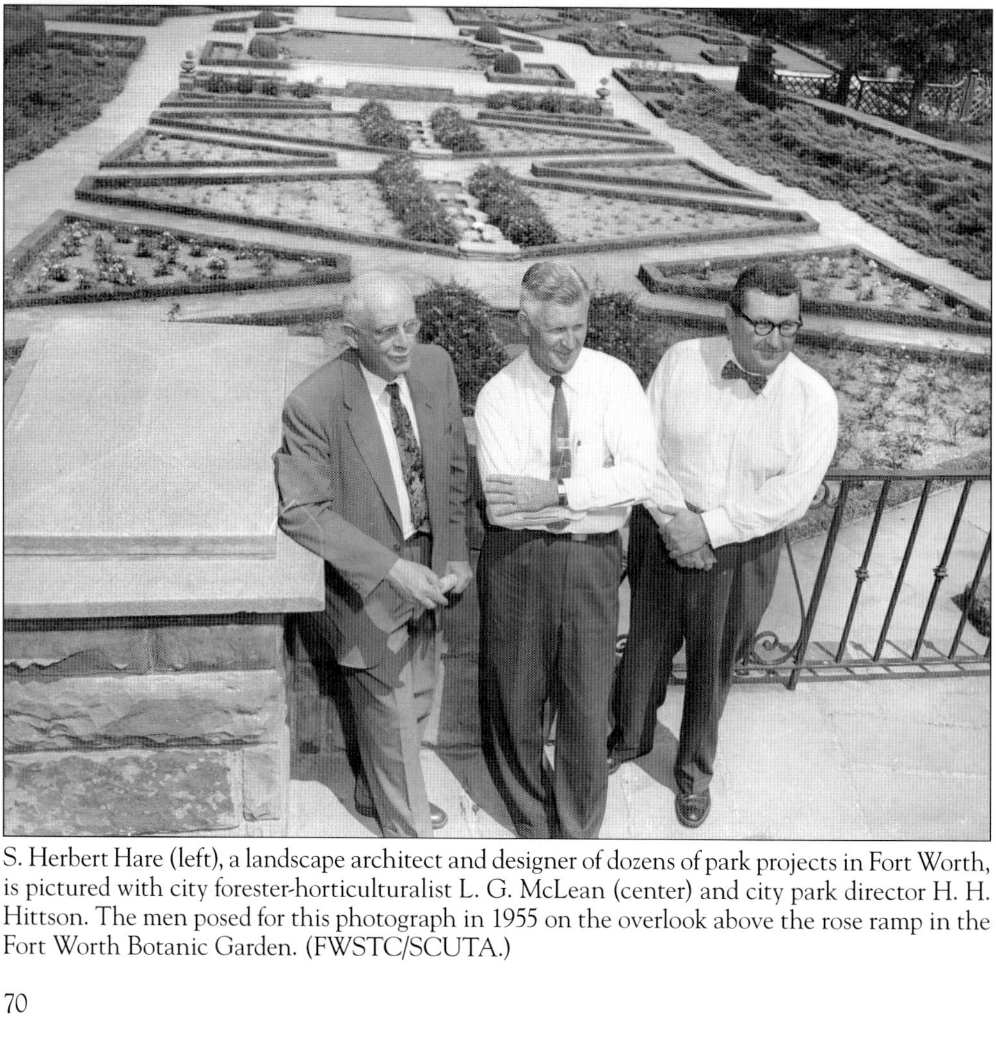

S. Herbert Hare (left), a landscape architect and designer of dozens of park projects in Fort Worth, is pictured with city forester-horticulturalist L. G. McLean (center) and city park director H. H. Hittson. The men posed for this photograph in 1955 on the overlook above the rose ramp in the Fort Worth Botanic Garden. (FWSTC/SCUTA.)

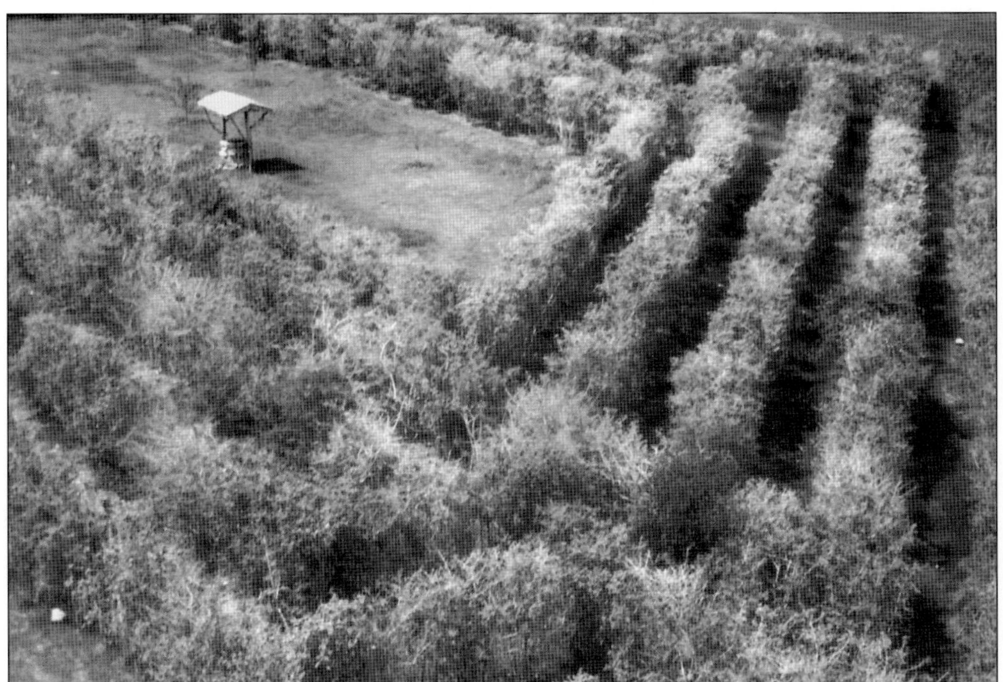

Inspired by the maze at the Hampton Court Gardens in England, park officials approved the construction of a similar feature at the Fort Worth Botanic Garden in 1956. Located on a quarter-acre site near the south end of the garden, the maze was composed of 6-foot-tall yaupon holly plants. Unfortunately, the maze never caught on with the public and was eventually removed. (FWBG.)

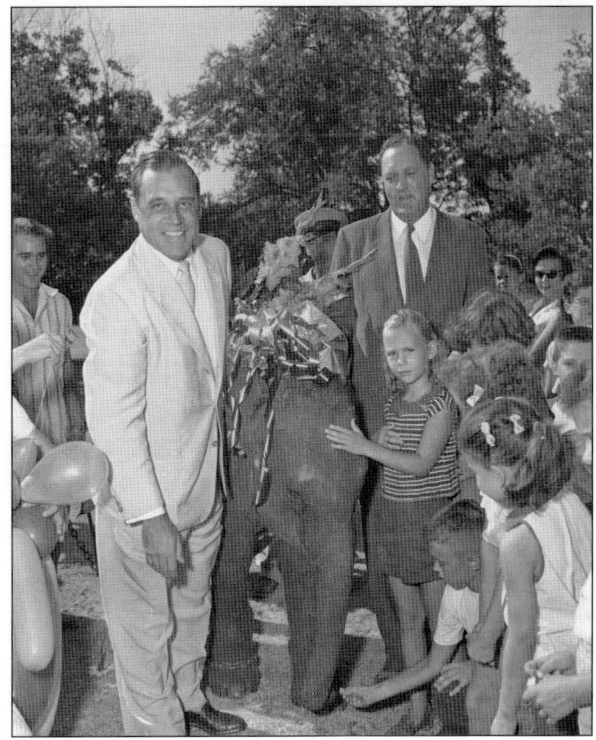

During the presidential election year of 1956, a group of Tarrant County Republicans purchased a young female elephant, later named Mamie, for the Children's Zoo. A sign on the vehicle bringing her from Vero Beach, Florida, to Fort Worth stated she was coming with "a Trunk Full of Votes for Ike." Pictured on either side of the elephant are Gordon Harriman (left) and O. Gene Murray. (FWSTC/SCUTA.)

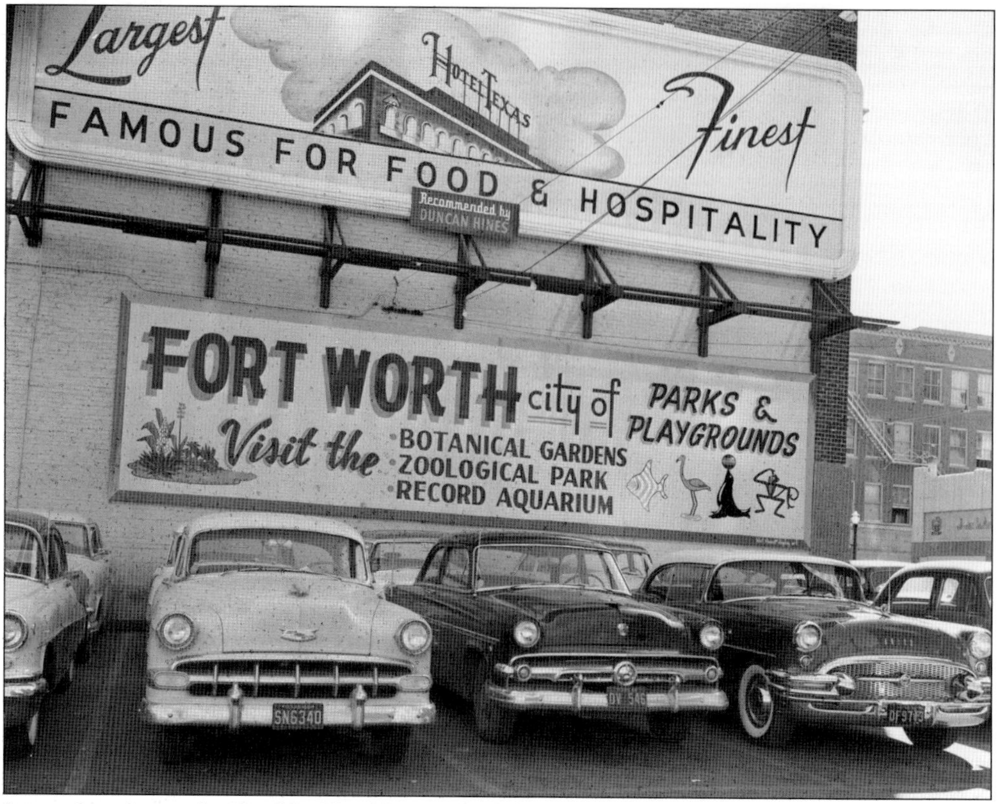

Located on the north side of the Hotel Texas, this billboard encouraged visitors and residents alike to patronize the city's parks and playgrounds, and listed three of its most popular attractions. When this photograph was taken in November 1956, the James L. Record Aquarium, located at the zoo, had been open for two years and was fast approaching its one-millionth visitor. (FWSTC/SCUTA.)

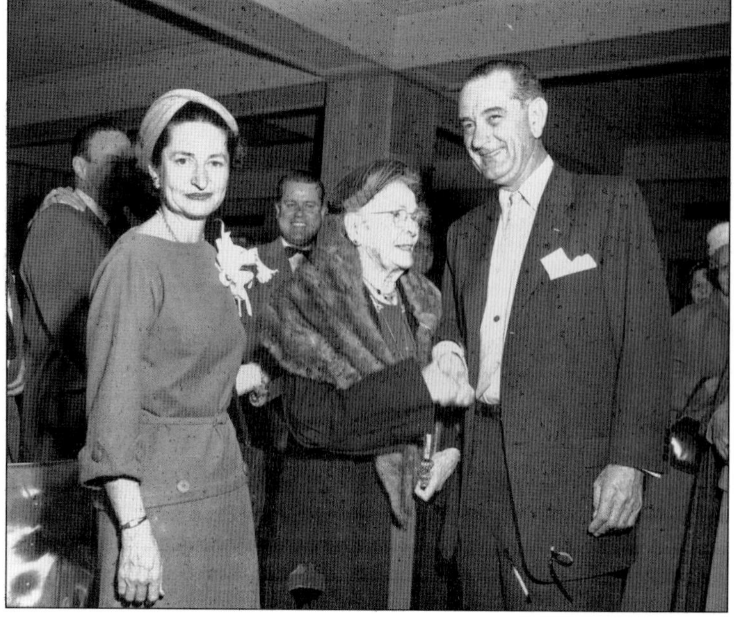

Margaret McLean (center) was appointed to the park board in 1921 after women received the right to vote. She served for 18 years, many of those as the board's secretary. Her radio addresses of the late 1930s informed listeners of park improvements made during that time. This photograph of her with Lady Bird and Sen. Lyndon Baines Johnson was taken in 1957. (FWSTC/SCUTA.)

On June 12, 1959, the Forest Park Miniature Railroad was placed into service connecting Forest Park with Trinity Park. Operated by Bill Hames and other family members, the 5-mile round-trip took 30 minutes to complete. Two types of trains were available, a miniature version of a streamlined *Texas Eagle* and a miniature version of an 1865 steam locomotive. In the photograph at right, a young boy identified only as Mark stands by the train in 1960. The photograph below, also from the early 1960s, shows the train as it is about to cross the truss bridge that would carry it over the Clear Fork of the Trinity River. Although the right-of-way has changed over the years, the Forest Park Miniature Train remains a popular attraction. (Right, Larry Schuessler; below, photograph by Daniel Zurovetz; Ann Zurovetz.)

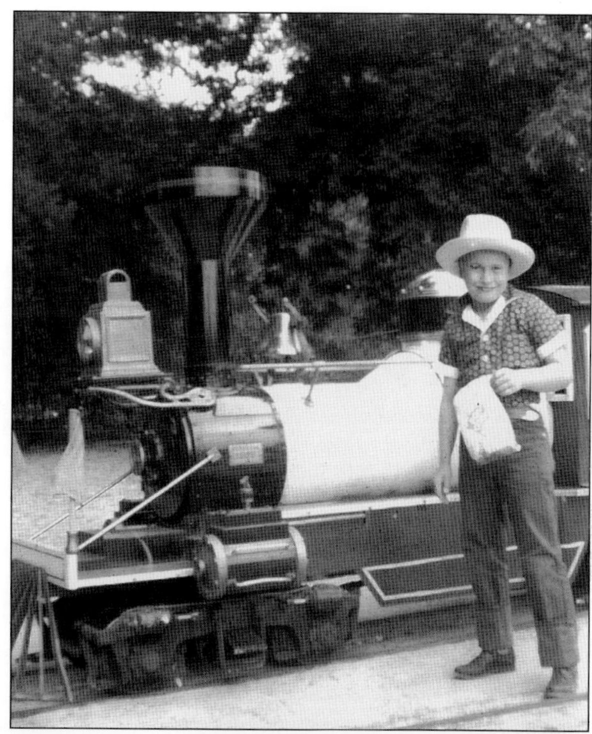

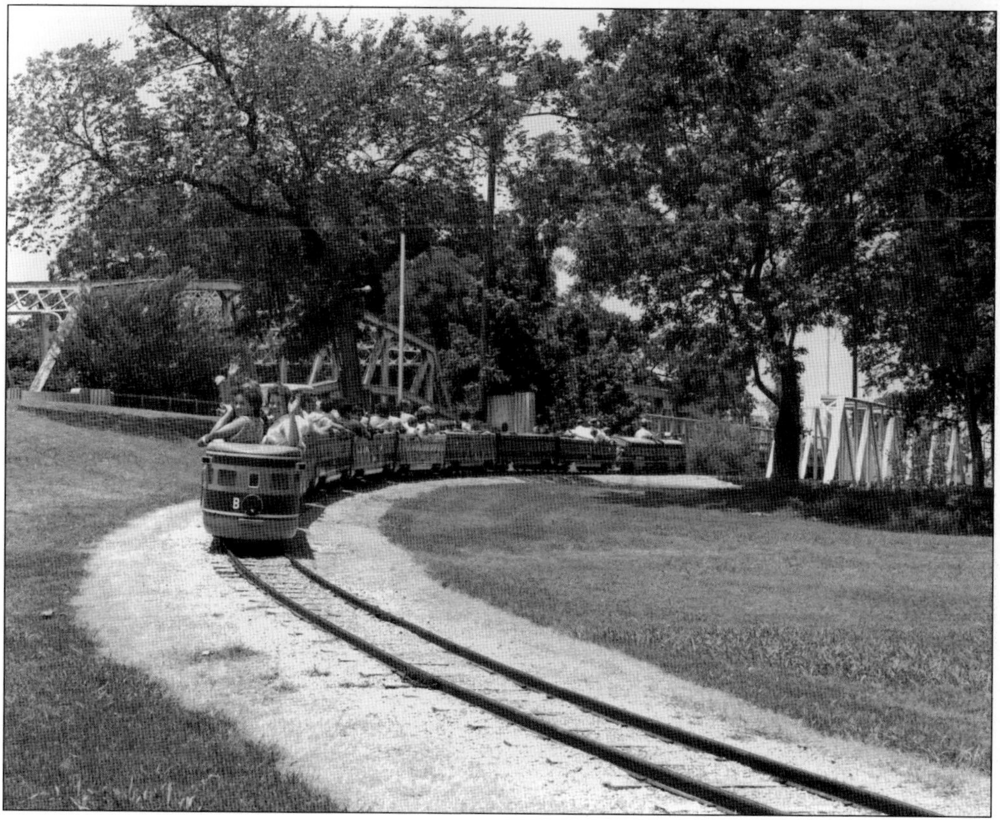

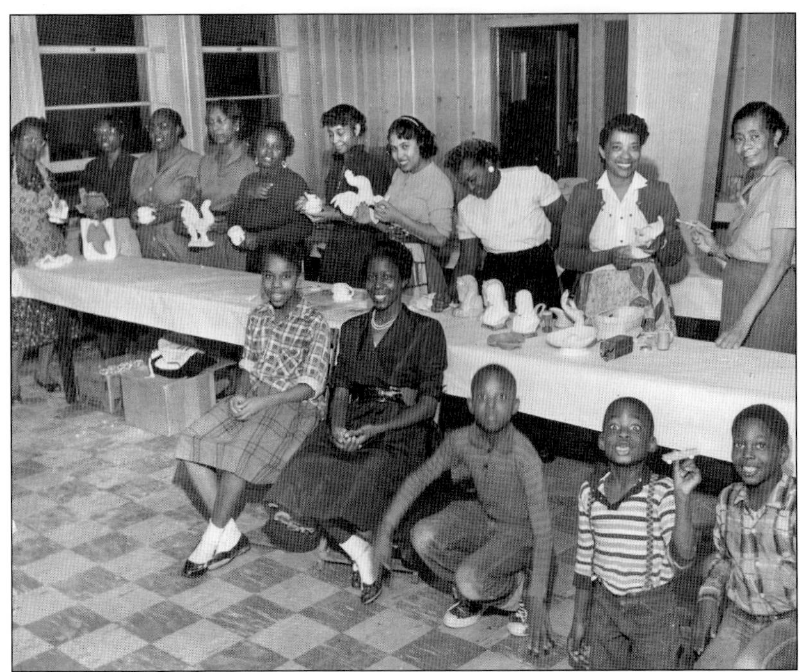

The Harmon Field Recreation Center and Golf Course were dedicated in June 1954. The land on which they were located was donated by the William E. Harmon Foundation of New York City in 1925. The African American community had long sought its own golf course because they were not permitted to play on the "white" public courses. Free instruction in many types of activities was offered at the recreation center. Among them were Rosa Mae Steverson's ceramics and leathercraft classes. Steverson is at the far right in the above photograph, taken in March 1957. Her grandson, Michael Whitted, is the little boy holding the toy car. The photograph below is of a hat-making class. (Above, photograph by John Turner; below, photograph by Lee Angle Photography; both, Loyce Whitted.)

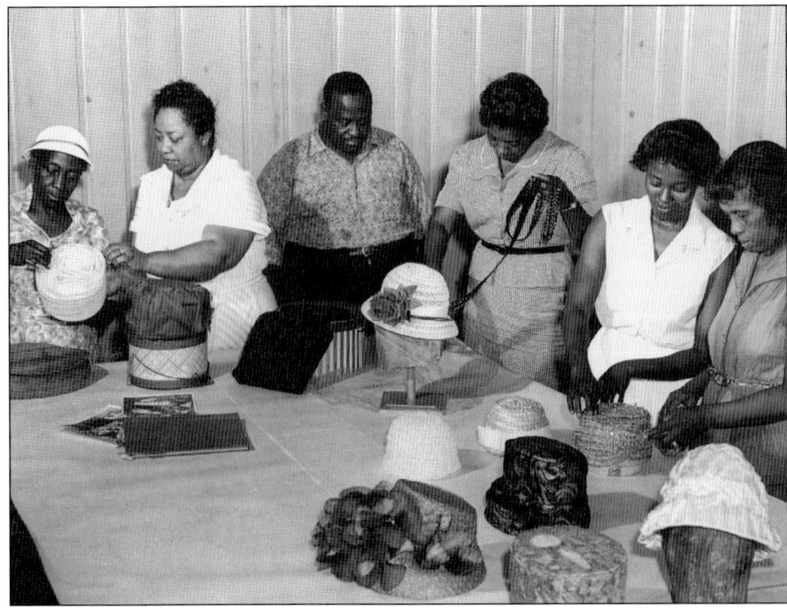

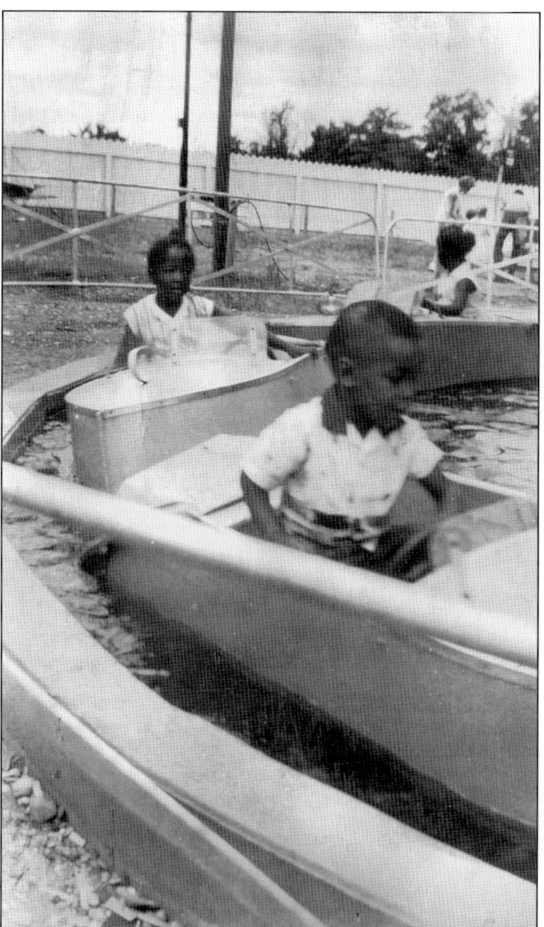

During the 1950s, property was acquired for African American parks in previously underserved areas. These included Bunche Park in far east Fort Worth and Lake Como Park in west Fort Worth. Dixie Park, one of the oldest black parks, continued to be a popular destination until the end of the decade. Its pool was closed in 1960, and the land was sold in 1962. These photographs from around 1959 show members of the Jefferson and Sanders families enjoying time together at the park. At right, Phillip Sanders (pictured at right, front) takes his turn on a miniature boat ride. Pictured at the park's wading pool below are, from left to right, Phillipa Jefferson, Tarvis Jefferson, Chorlette Sanders, and Phillip Sanders. (Both, Brenda Sanders-Wise.)

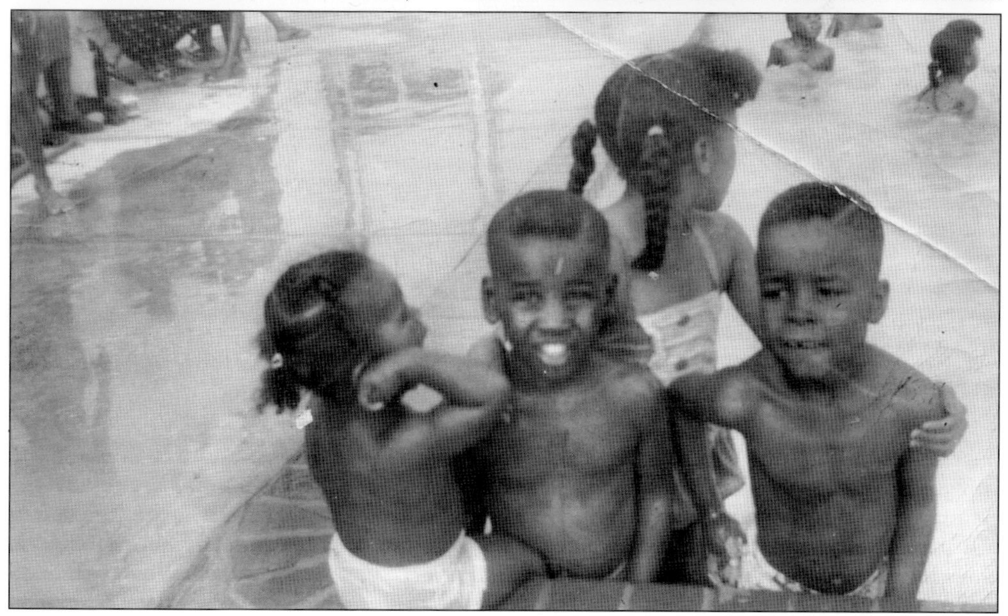

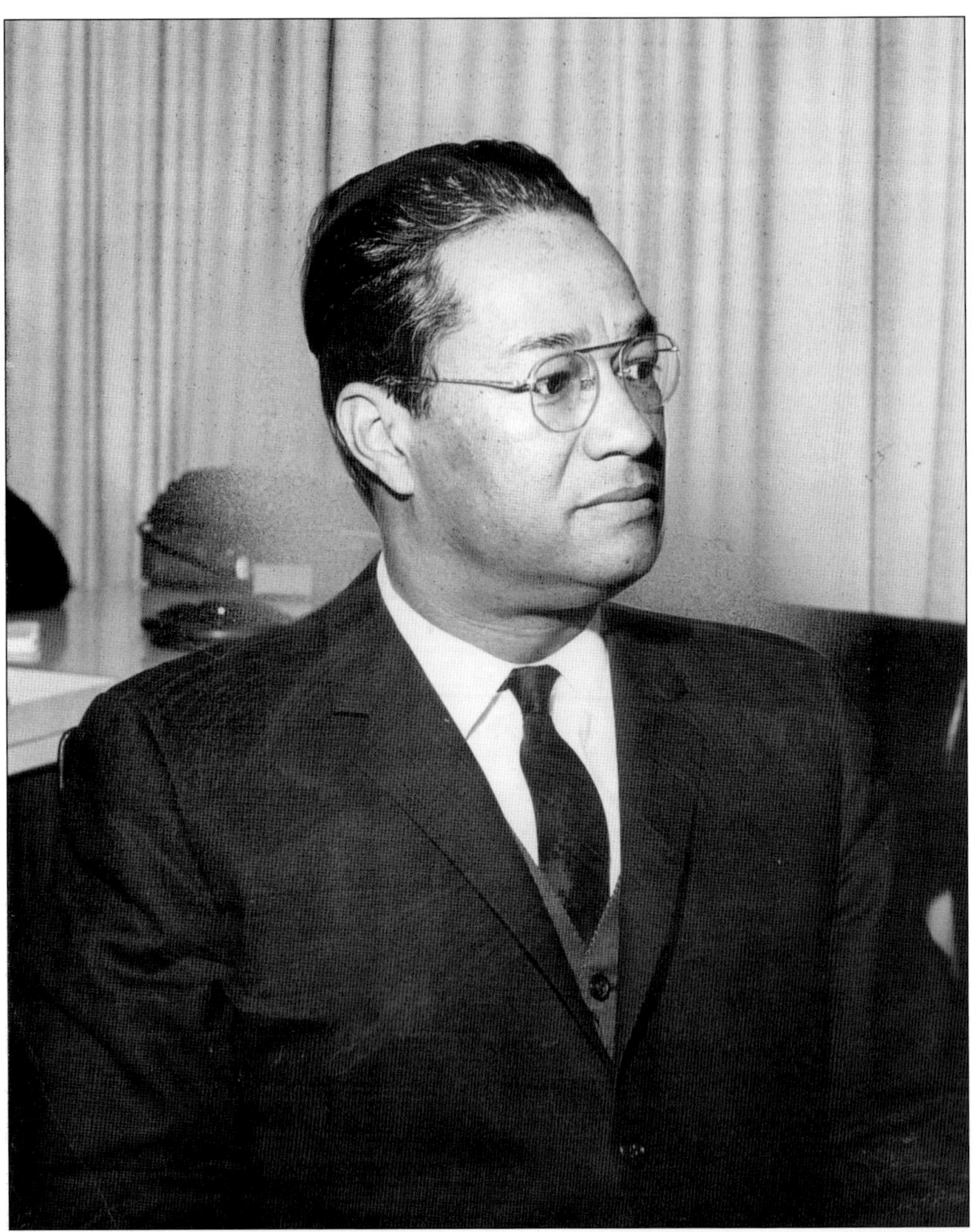

For the city's African American community, full access to parks and recreational amenities was not gained until the 1960s. After years of protesting the inequalities of the system, a hard-won victory was achieved in 1961 when Dr. Marion "Jack" Brooks (1920–2003) became the first African American appointed to the park board. When the park board was merged with the recreation board in 1964, Brooks was appointed to the new board and then served on it for another year. Brooks, a native of Fort Worth, received his medical degree from Howard University in 1951 and then returned to Fort Worth to practice. He established a clinic with his brother, Donald, and was instrumental in the integration of the city's hospitals for both patients and physicians. He also was a founder of Morningside United Methodist Church and devoted his life to civil rights and community activism. (FWSTC/SCUTA.)

From the Kessler Plan of 1909 to modern times, the beautification of many city streets has been under the purview of the park department. In April 1958, park department employees planted the 6300 block of Camp Bowie Boulevard with succulents. The drought-tolerant plants provided a "Western" theme to this section of the street. (FWSTC/SCUTA.)

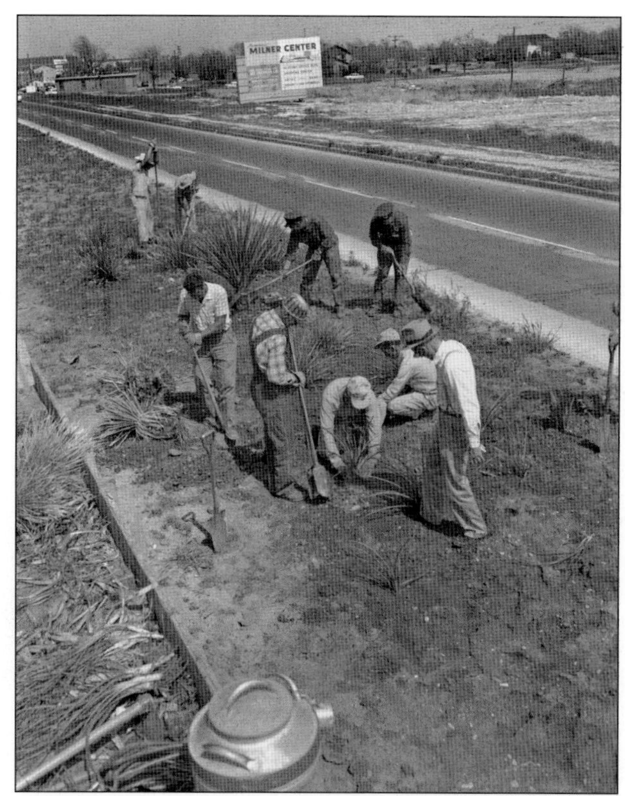

The Van Zandt Cottage, located in Trinity Park, was first restored in 1936 as part of Fort Worth's celebration of the Texas centennial. Once owned by Maj. K. M. Van Zandt, it is believed to be Fort Worth's oldest house on its original foundation. In 1960, the Daughters of the Confederacy undertook another rehabilitation of the structure and opened it to the public. (Photograph by Daniel Zurovetz; Ann Zurovetz.)

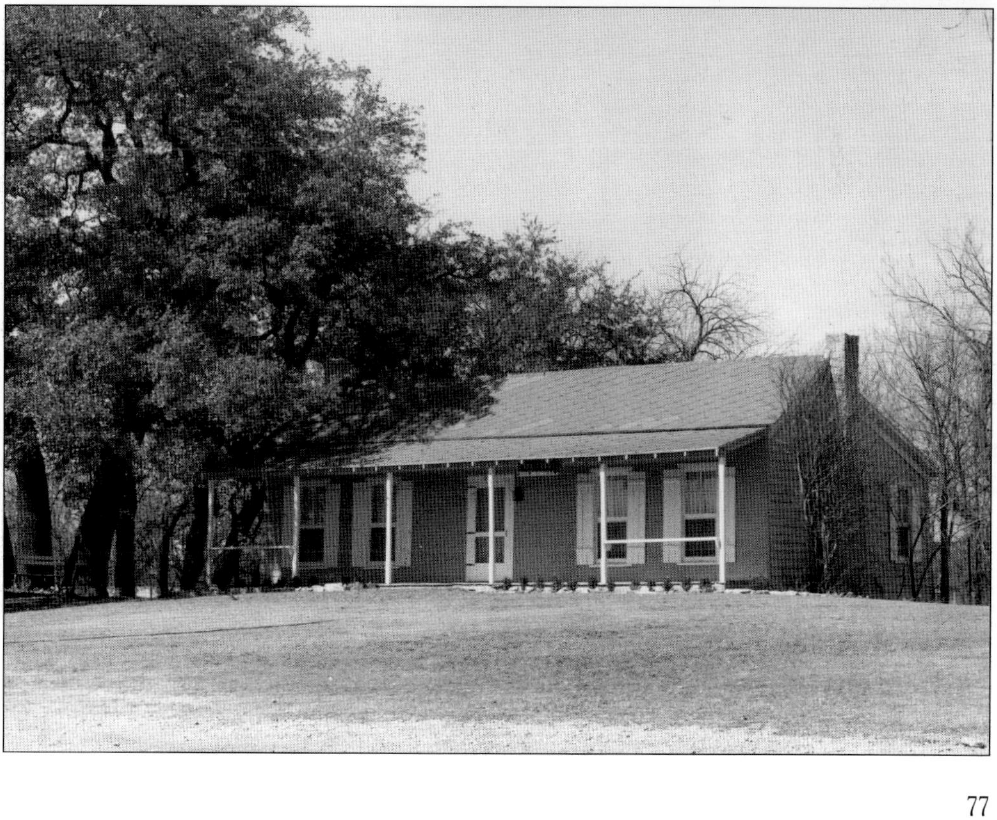

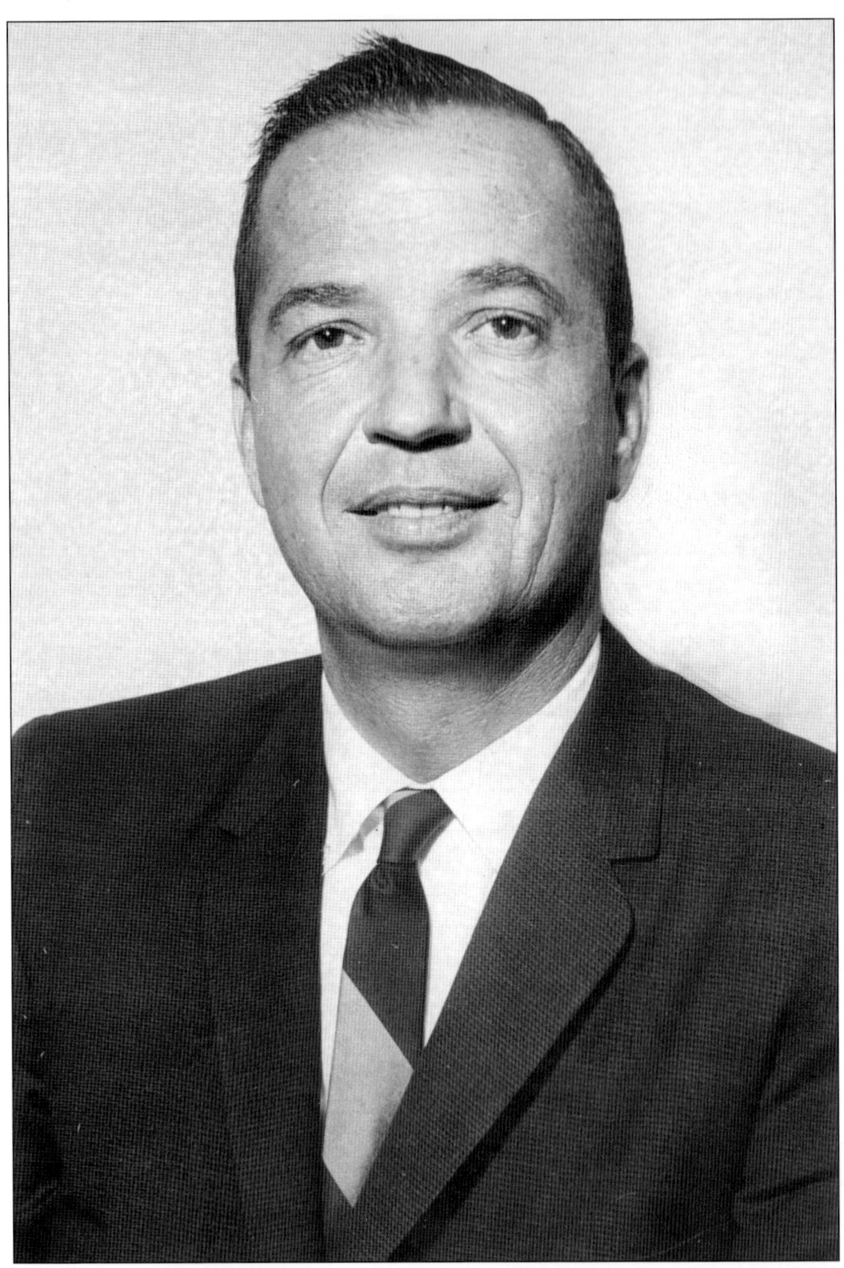

Charles B. Campbell (1922–2006), a landscape architect by training, was 39 years old when he accepted the position of director of Fort Worth parks in 1962. Previously, he had served as the parks and recreation director in Midland, Texas, and in landscaping and nursery firms prior to that position. After the merger of Fort Worth's park and recreation boards in 1964, Campbell was named director of the new park and recreation department. He served in that position until his retirement in 1987. Throughout his quarter-century of service, he was a strong advocate for the creation of green space, and during his tenure, city regulations were amended to require residential developers to set aside parkland in their subdivisions. During the years he served as director, the number of parks increased from 57 parks on 2,872 acres to 163 parks with 9,923 acres. (FWSTC/SCUTA.)

Five

Together Again
1964 to 1999

The park and recreation departments were merged in February 1964 following voter approval of an amendment to the city charter authorizing the move. The new department's board was appointed by the city council, with three members coming from the recreation board, three from the park board, and one newcomer. The new ordinance removed the authority of hiring and firing personnel from the board and gave it to the director of the Fort Worth Park and Recreation Department.

During the next 35 years, partnerships with individuals, nonprofits, private foundations, federal and state agencies, and other organizations brought creative programming to meet community needs and innovative designs to new and old parks. This was the era that saw the creation of the Japanese Garden, a new conservatory and garden center (now the Deborah Beggs Moncrief Garden Center), and the Fuller Garden, all within the Fort Worth Botanic Garden, as well as the Fort Worth Botanical Society as a nonprofit supporting the garden. Collaboration also brought about the creation of the Greer Island Nature Center and Wildlife Refuge (now the Fort Worth Nature Center and Refuge), Fort Worth Water Gardens, Heritage Park and its Plaza, and the redesign of Burnett Park. Mayfest helped revive interest in better stewardship of the Trinity River.

The Fort Worth Zoological Association took over management of the zoo in 1991. Since the 1930s, the association had been the zoo's principal benefactor. In 1994, the community services division was moved from the city's housing department to the park and recreation department. As a department with a multitude of services, its name was appropriately changed to the Forth Worth Parks and Community Services Department. Two years later, the department won the prestigious National Gold Medal Award from the Sports Foundation, Inc., for excellence in the field of park and recreation management.

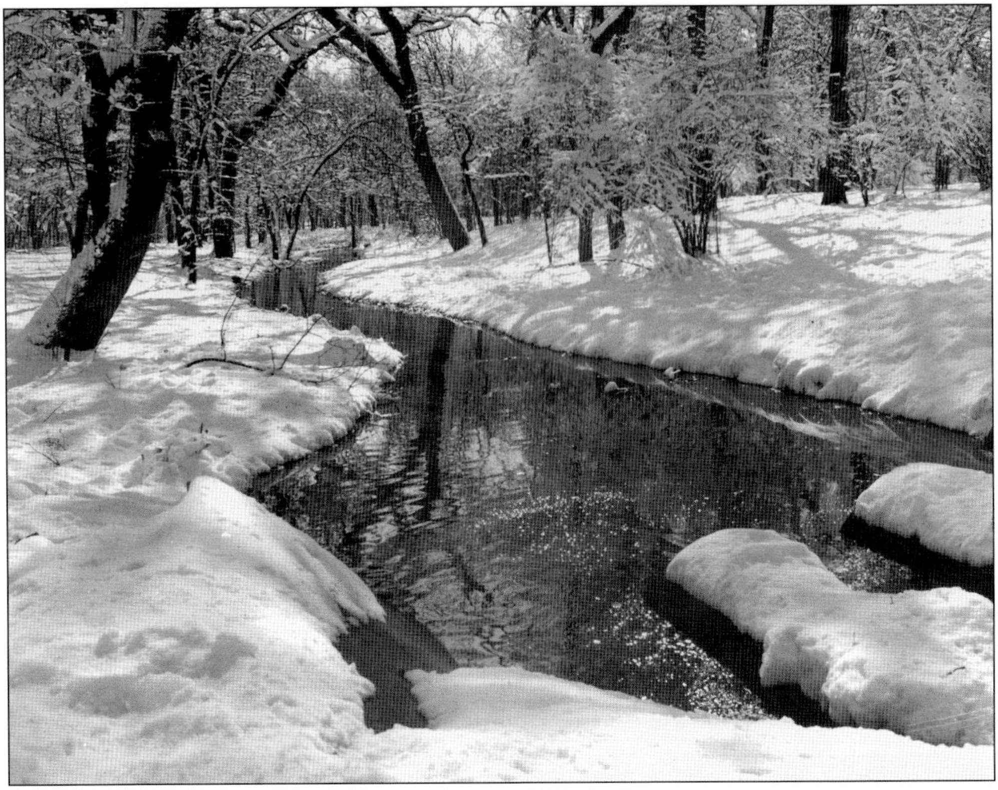

Record snowfall blanketed North Texas in January 1964. Such occurrences encourage many to try to capture the beauty before it is gone. Photographer Daniel Zurovetz recorded this fleeting but timeless view in Trinity Park as the sun shown through the bare trees casting graceful shadows on the snow below. (Ann Zurovetz.)

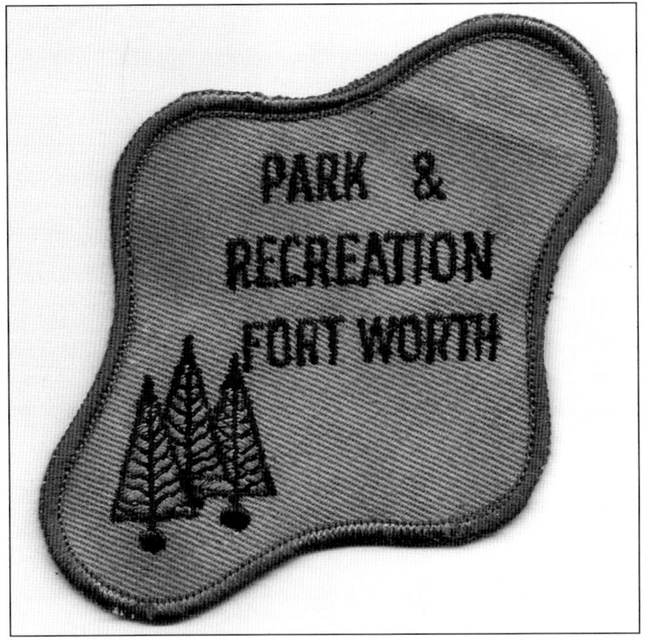

In 1964, the citizens of Fort Worth approved an amendment to the city's charter providing for the merger of the park and recreation departments under a single board. The members of the first board were Charles H. Haws, chairman; Dr. Bobby Brown, vice chairman; Patricia Purvis; Dr. Marion J. Brooks; Mrs. Jim McMullen; Mrs. Freddy Moore; and Harry L. Tennison. (Dalton Hoffman.)

Dr. Bobby Brown (right), former New York Yankee baseball player and president of the American League from 1984 to 1994, served on the recreation department board and then on the park board after the merger of the two departments. Here he is shown with Shirley Holmes of the Brown-Lupton Foundation in June 1964 as they sit by a plaque commemorating the foundation's donation of lights to the Rosemont Tennis Center. (FWSTC/SCUTA.)

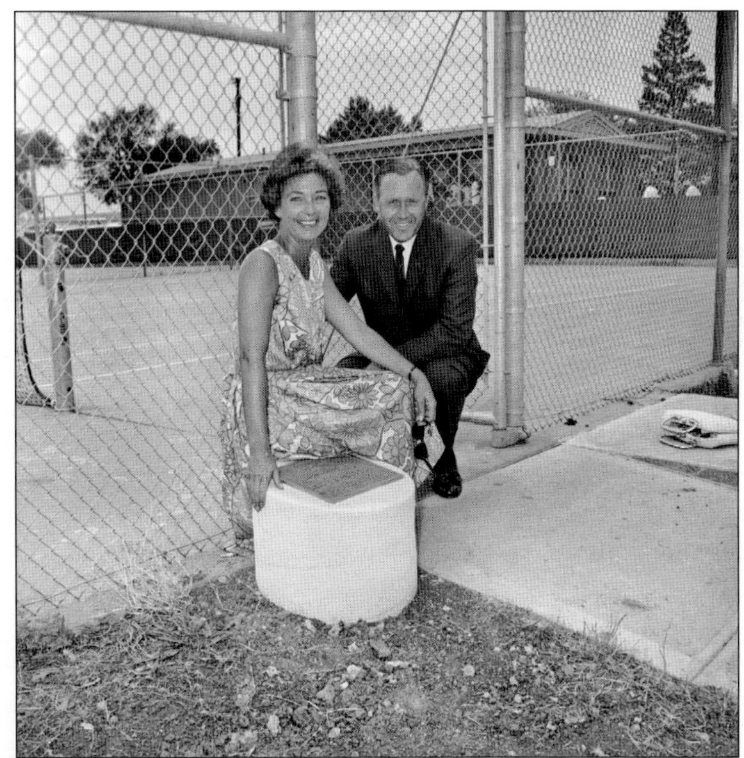

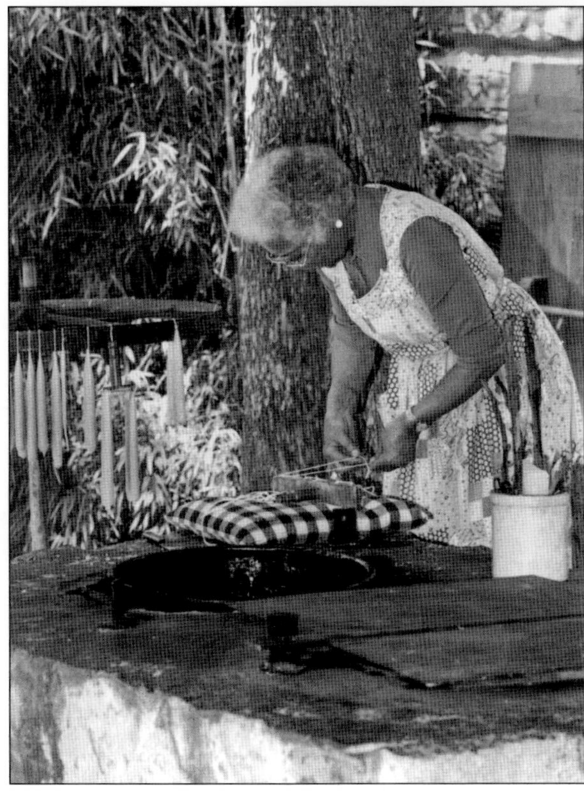

The Log Cabin Village, located in Forest Park, was established in the 1950s by organizations concerned with the disappearance of these remnants of North Texas's pioneer history. It was donated to the City of Fort Worth in 1965 and opened to the public in 1966. As a living history museum, it provides authentic experiences appropriate to the pioneer era. Here docent Ella Patton demonstrates an essential skill—candle-making. (Log Cabin Village.)

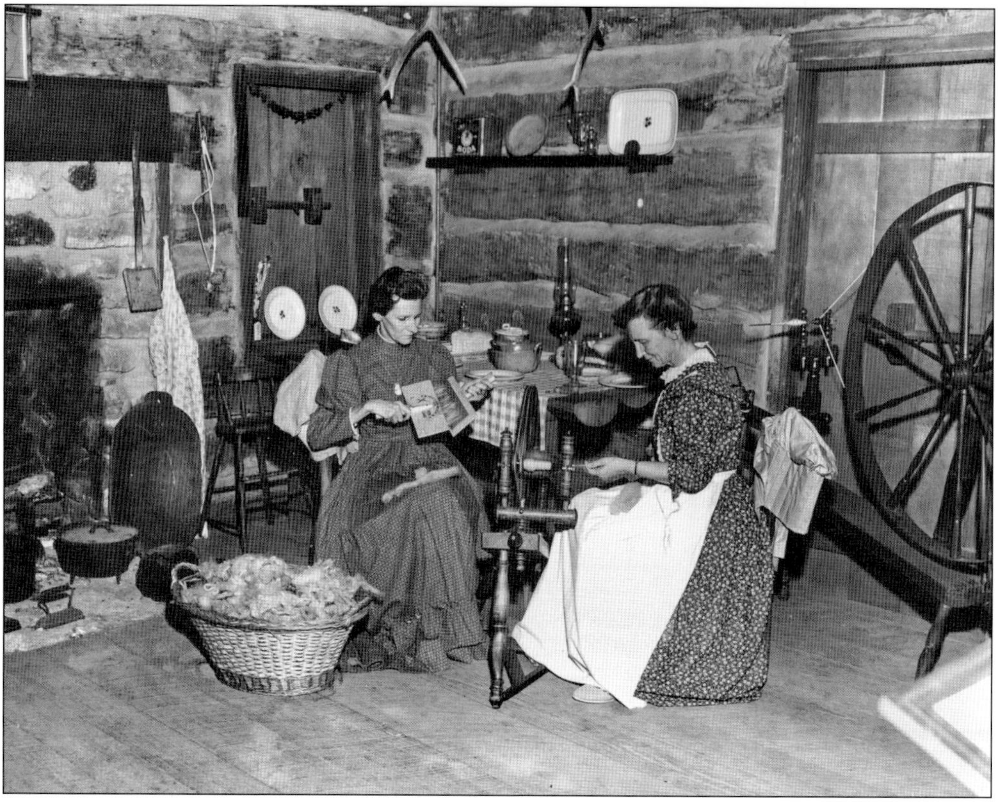

The Log Cabin Village's structures are furnished with authentic artifacts illustrating 19th-century life on the Texas frontier. The Parker Cabin, a dogtrot log house, was built around 1848 in Birdville, northeast of Fort Worth. It is the oldest structure in Tarrant County and briefly was the home of Cynthia Ann Parker, who was captured and raised by Comanches and became the mother of Comanche chief Quanah Parker. (Photograph by Daniel Zurovetz; Log Cabin Village.)

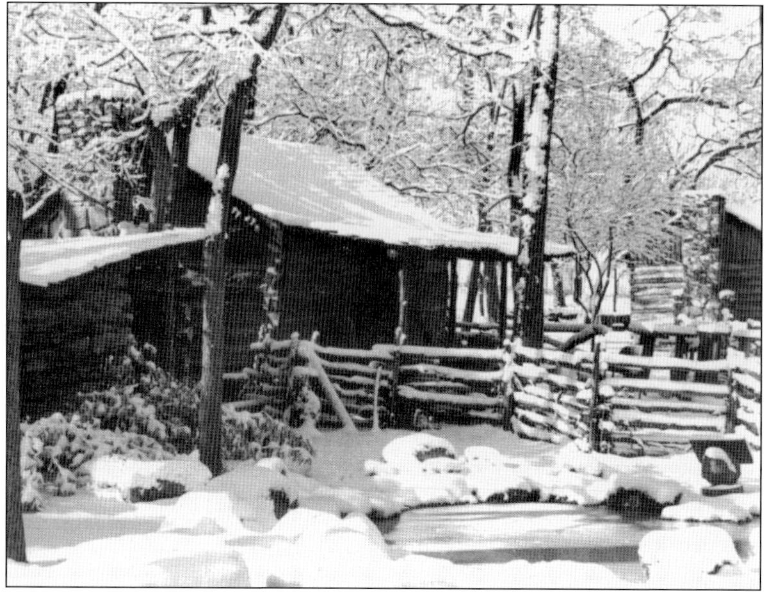

The Seela Cabin was built in the 1860s in Parker County, Texas. Everything in and around this single-pen log cabin may be touched for a hands-on learning experience. As shown in this photograph, the Log Cabin Village is located within a dense cover of trees, adding to the museum's sensory experience. (Log Cabin Village.)

The Shaw Cabin and Gristmill is one of the few working gristmills in Texas. Although the *c.* 1854 cabin from Parker County, Texas, was not originally constructed as a gristmill, the milling equipment inside of it dates to the mid-1860s. Milling operations were important to 19th-century Texans, and this mill's authentic millstones continue to produce freshly ground cornmeal. (Log Cabin Village.)

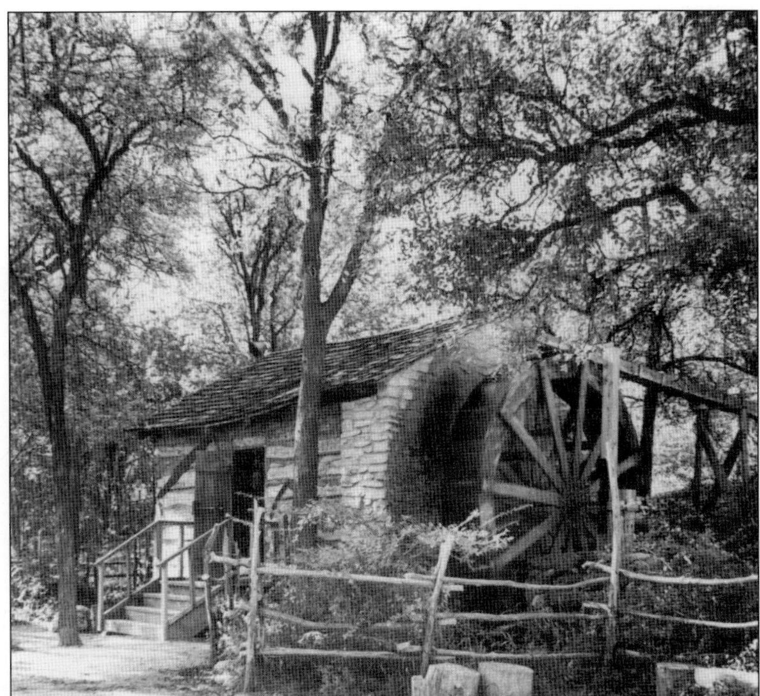

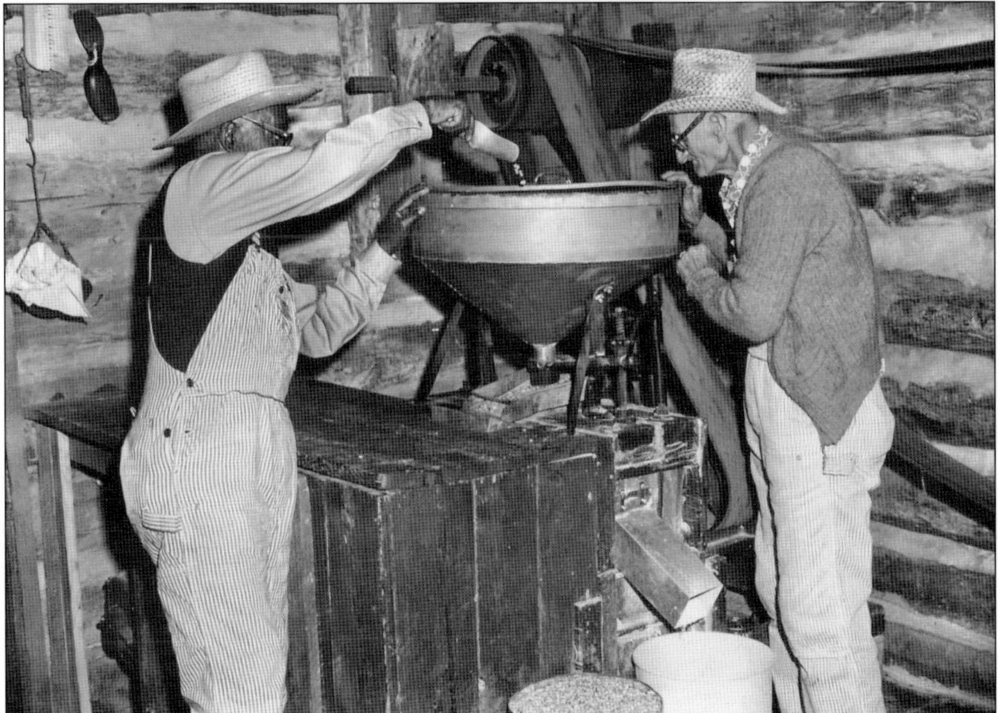

The gristmill equipment in the Shaw Cabin came from a small mill owned by the Smith family of Moline, Texas. It was in constant use for 70 years until 1930, when the mill stopped operating. In 1970, the City of Fort Worth purchased the equipment and installed it in the Shaw Cabin. (Photograph by Daniel Zurovetz; Fort Worth Fire Department.)

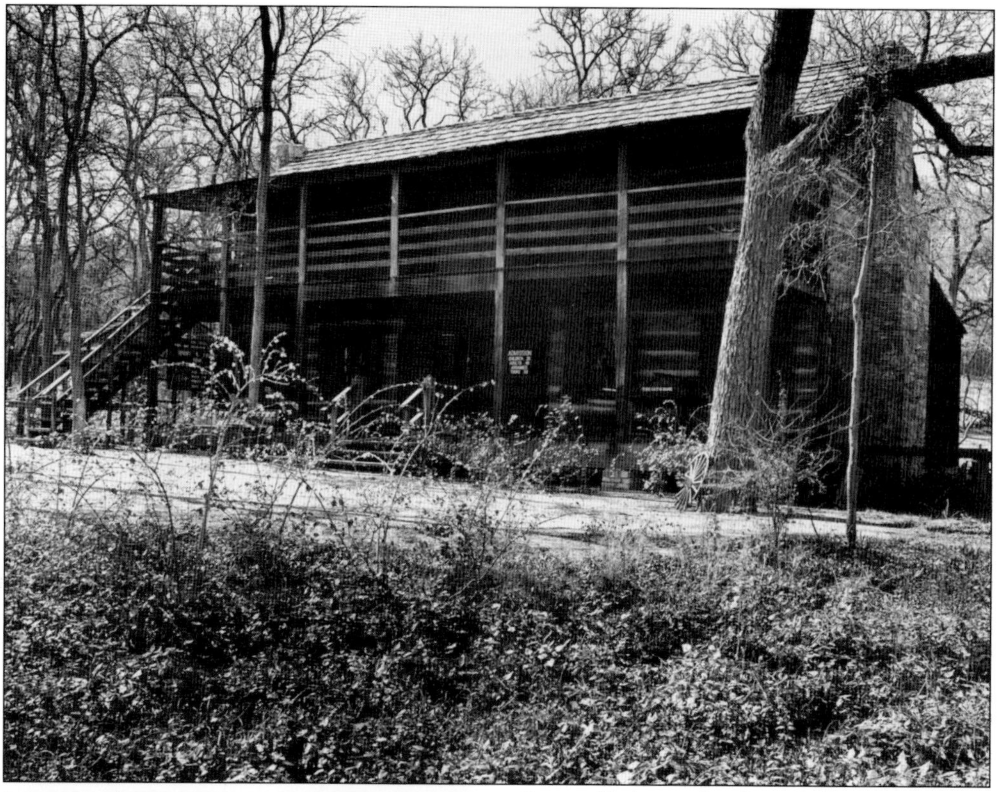

Originally located in Port Sullivan, Texas, the Foster Cabin is one of the few surviving plantation houses in Texas. It was constructed around 1853 by slave labor. Its parlor is furnished with artifacts from the Foster family. The cabin also serves as the location of the Log Cabin Village's museum store and staff offices. (Photograph by Daniel Zurovetz; Fort Worth Fire Department.)

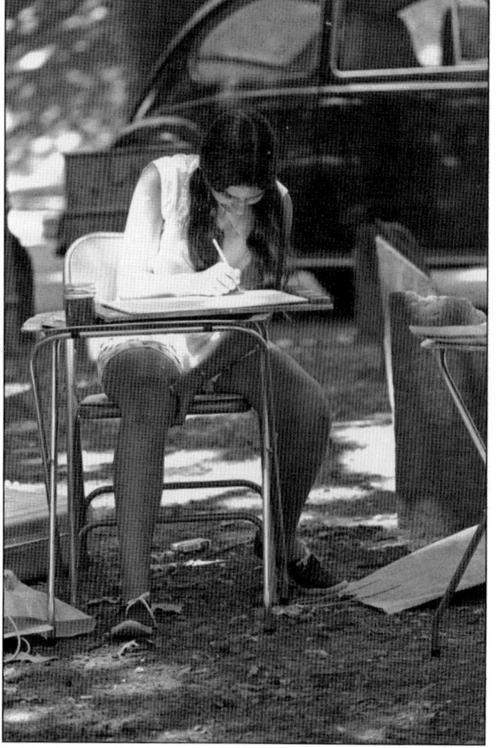

Artists have long sought out parks as places of inspiration. Mamie Moore Sanders, an 83-year-old artist, taught a painting class every Friday morning at the Duck Pond in Trinity Park during the summer of 1969. The students sometimes referred to themselves as the Duck Pond Doodlers. One of her youngest students, Christina Garcia, is pictured here. (FWSTC/SCUTA.)

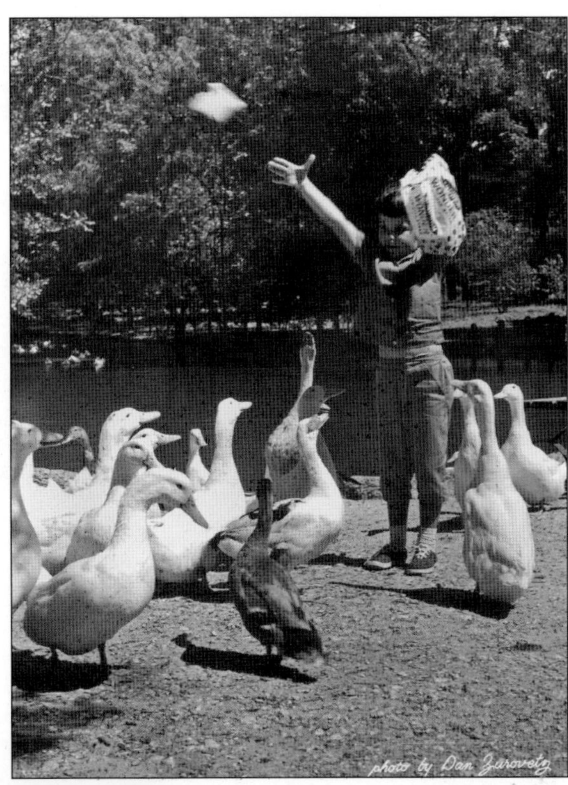

The Trinity Park Duck Pond has long been a popular place for families to gather and feed the ducks. Anyone with a loaf of bread quickly catches the attention of the resident fowl, as demonstrated by the photograph at right. Motorists traveling along Trinity Park Drive are still warned to be on the lookout for web-footed wanderers crossing the road by a similar-looking sign. Today, as the 17th largest city in the United States, there are still places in Fort Worth where animals have the right-of-way. These include Exchange Avenue in the Stockyards National Historic District, where longhorns are paraded twice daily, and the ducks in Trinity Park. (Photographs by Daniel Zurovetz; both, Ann Zurovetz.)

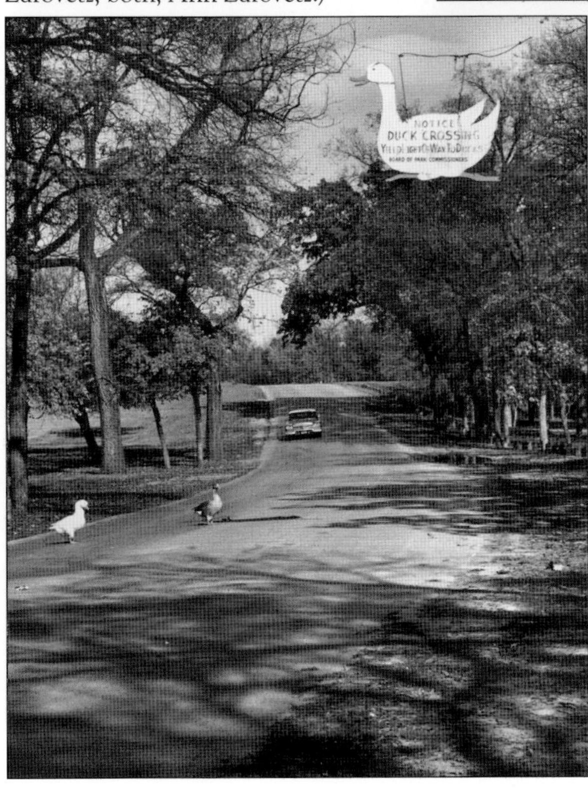

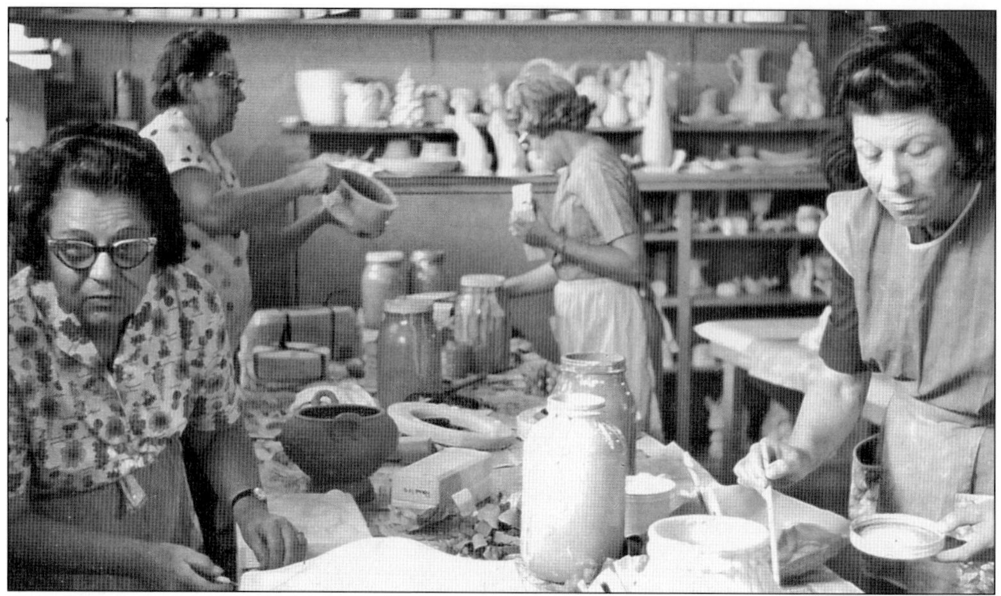

Recreation centers offered arts and crafts classes, including this ceramic class taught by Auereen Oxley at the R. D. Evans Recreation Center. These women were preparing items for the park and recreation department's exhibit at a Home Show in May 1966. Pictured from left to right are Mary Hughes, Mrs. Charlie Longguth, ? Lamos, and Betty Graves. (R. D. Evans Community Center.)

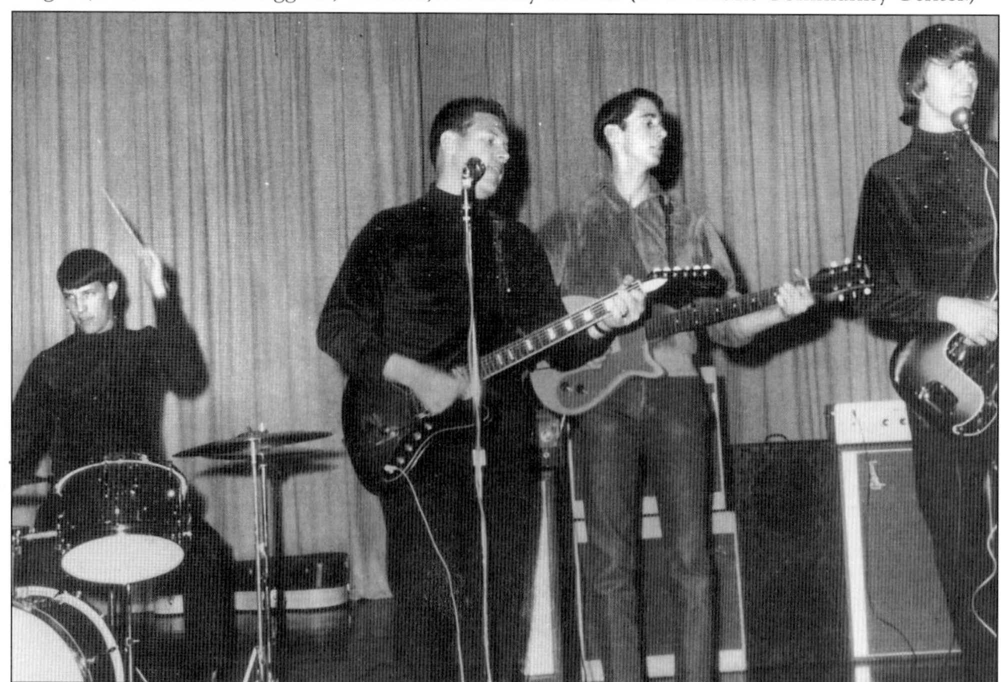

Gym-Jams kept the R. D. Evans Recreation Center rocking during the mid-1960s. On the first and third Fridays, bands such as the Marqueys, Entries, Jack and the Rippers, and Four Minus One performed to appreciative teen audiences. Shown here are members of the Sonics: from left to right, Jimmy Stephens, Bill Goodale, Terry Haney, and Johnny Brooks. (R. D. Evans Community Center.)

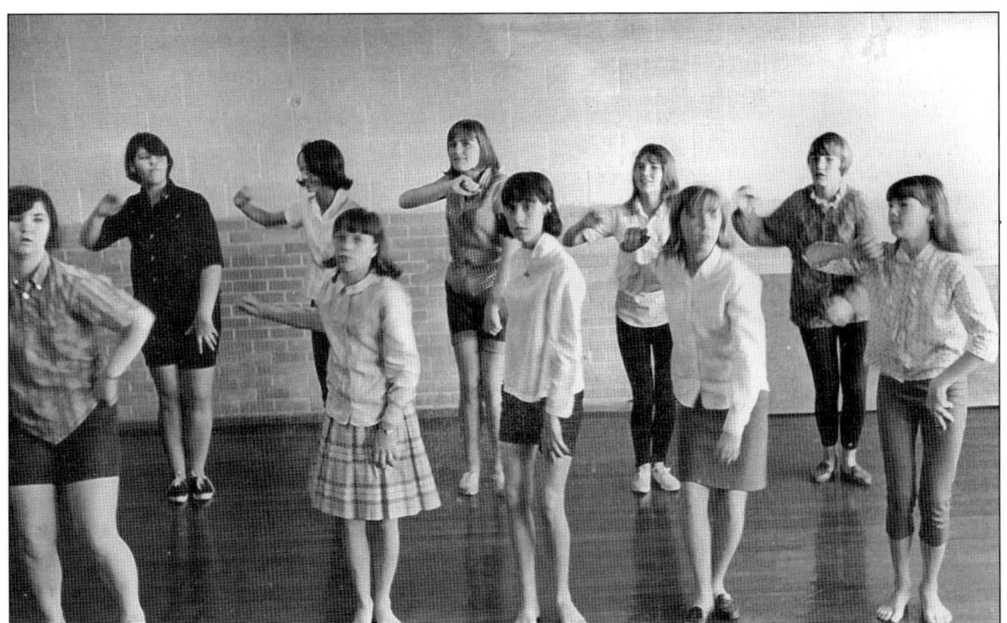

More than 200 girls competed for a chance to perform as Go-Go Girls at the R. D. Evans Gym-Jams. After weeks of tryouts, 14 girls were selected in March 1966 to perform with the featured bands. The girls practiced each Wednesday and Friday at the recreation center. (R. D. Evans Community Center.)

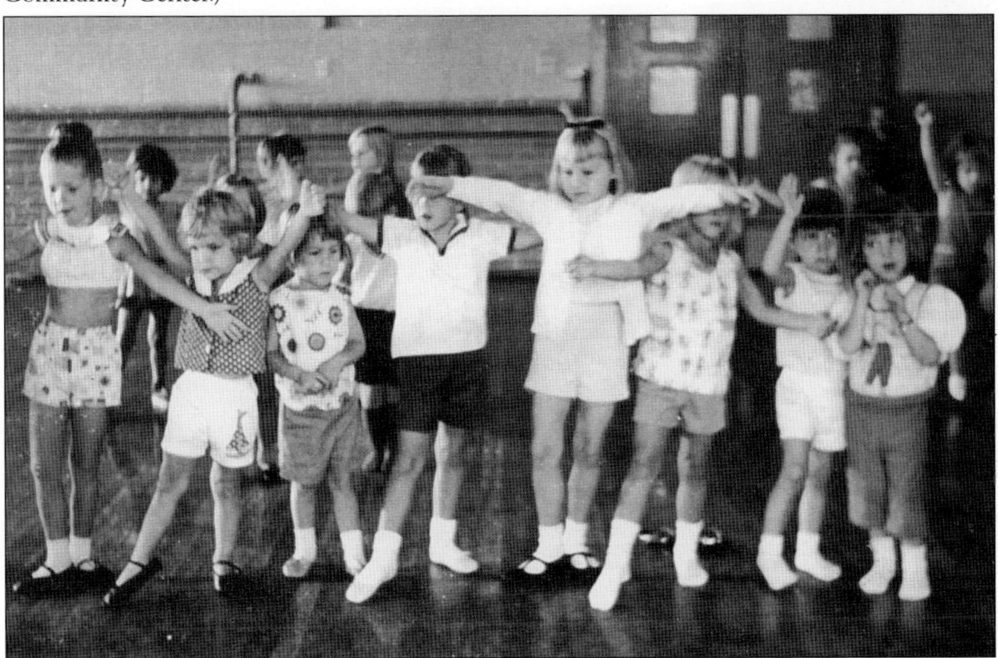

From baton twirling for preschoolers to ladies' "trimnastics" and ballroom and square dancing for teens and adults, recreation centers offered classes that kept Fort Worthians of all ages moving. This photograph from October 1965 shows members of the Thursday morning preschool ballet class as they practice their moves at the R. D. Evans Recreation Center. (R. D. Evans Community Center.)

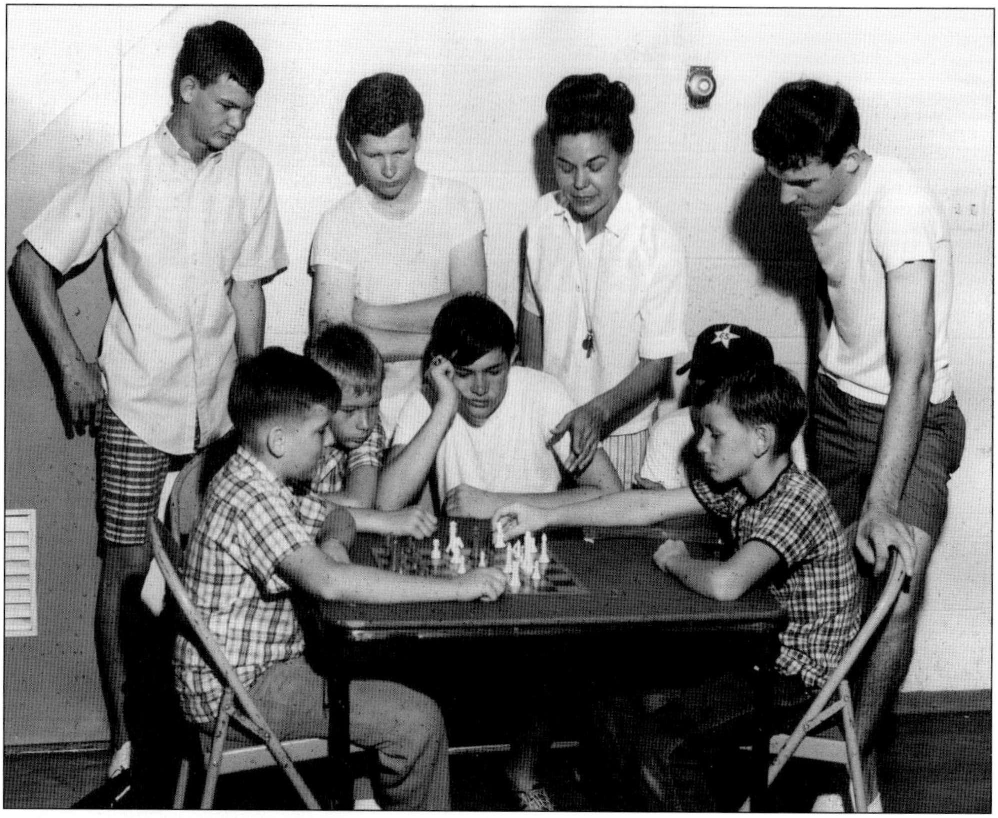

Recreation centers offered opportunities to exercise the mind as well as the body. On an early summer day in June 1966, serious young chess players received guidance in game strategies from a recreation director as older boys looked on. (Fort Worth Fire Department.)

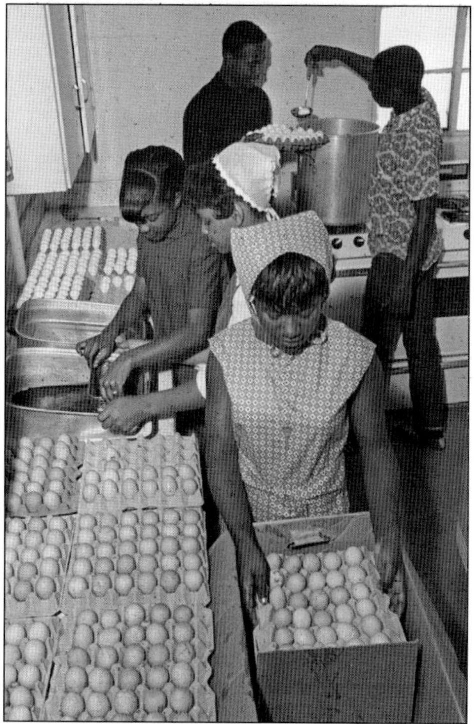

In the spring of 1968, student volunteers at the Harmon Recreation Center made dozens of Easter eggs to hide in Lake Como and Sycamore Parks. Pictured (from front to rear) are Patricia Smothers, Roy Doris Freeman, Barbara Martin, Donald Graham, and Robert Whigam. The Harmon Recreation Center still largely served the African American community at this time. (FWSTC/SCUTA.)

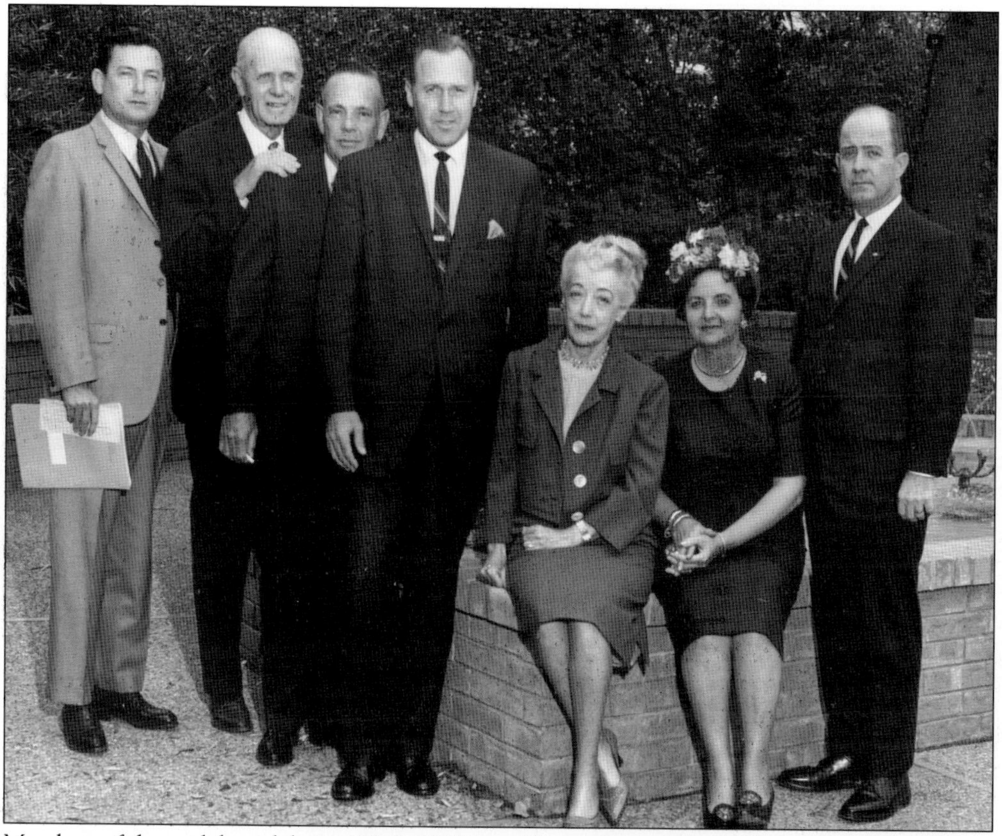

Members of the park board during 1965–1967 were, from left to right, Bobby Malone, Jess Tarlton, Alan Wilson, Dr. Bobby Brown (chairman), Mary Kittel, Rita Stewart, and Charles Ringlar. During this board's tenure, a major controversy arose over the firing of a popular zoo director in 1967. (Bobby Malone.)

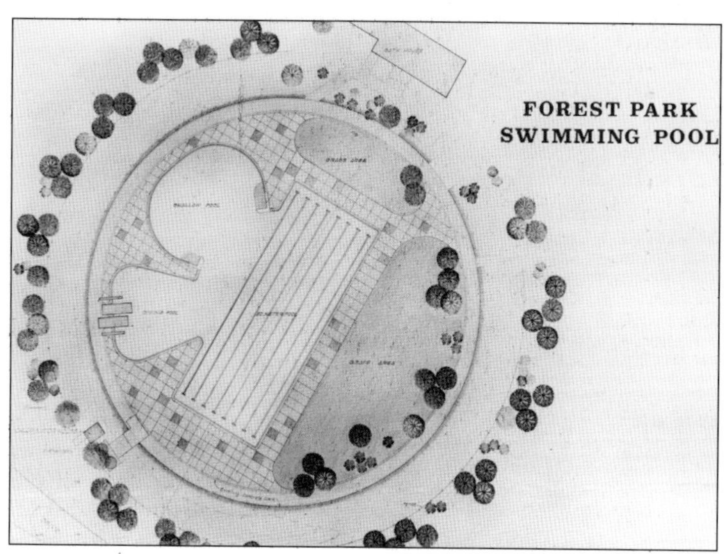

In 1966, engineers prepared plans and specifications for a new swimming pool for Forest Park. Designed with an Olympic-size pool with a diving pool and shallow pool radiating off of it, the new pool was set within the circumference of the former pool. The new design addressed some of the safety issues associated with the 1922 pool. (Fort Worth Fire Department.)

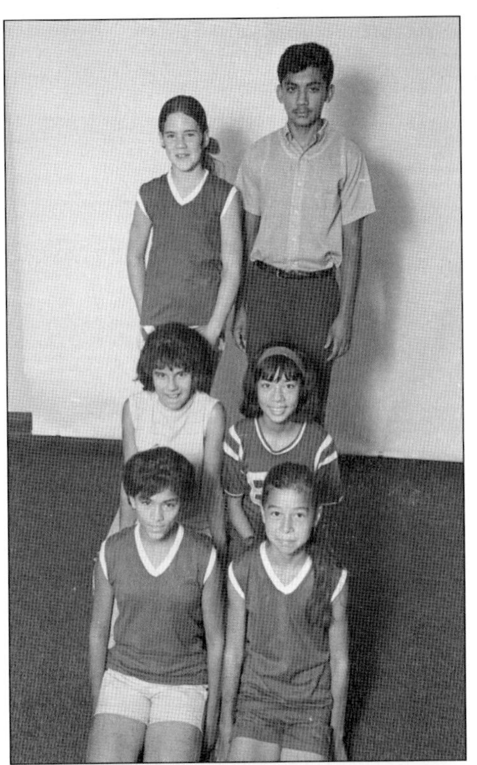

These winners of the recreation department's annual summer track program represented Fort Worth in the Texas Amateur Athletic Federation (TAAF) met in Denton, Texas, in 1969. From left to right are (first row) Mary Ramirez and Delia Garcia; (second row) Cathy Frazier and Taanya Trantham; (third row) Frances Fulfer and Jesse Castellon. (FWSTC/SCUTA.)

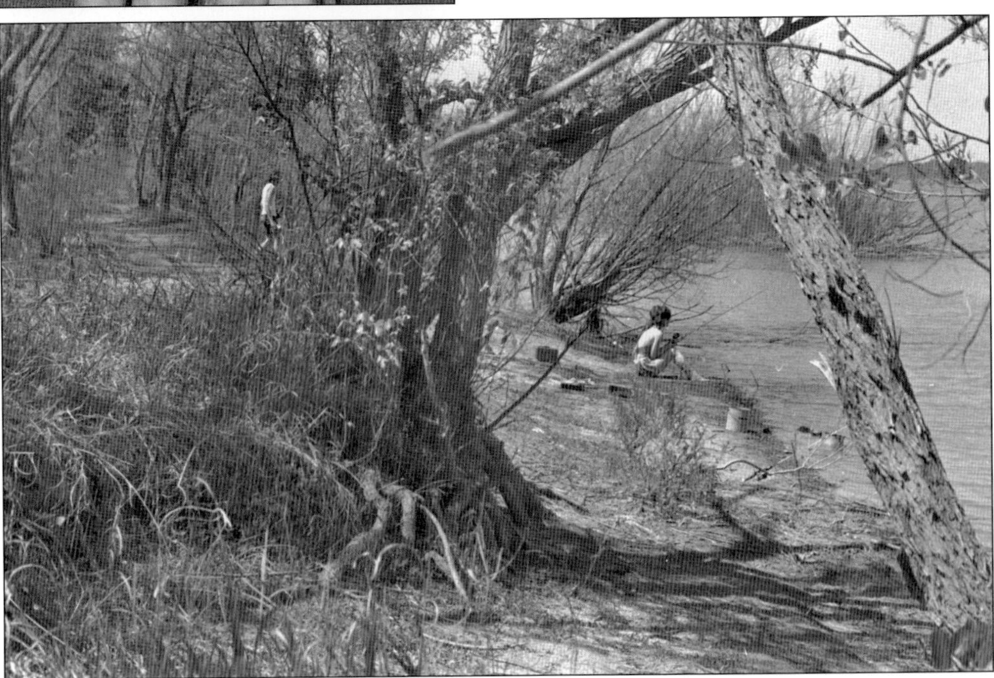

In 1964, the Fort Worth Audubon Society, allied organizations, and individuals concerned with the disappearance of native habitat in Fort Worth approached the park department about setting aside Greer Island in upper Lake Worth as a nature preserve. The request was granted with nearly 400 acres being designated as the Greer Island Nature Center and Refuge. (FWSTC/SCUTA.)

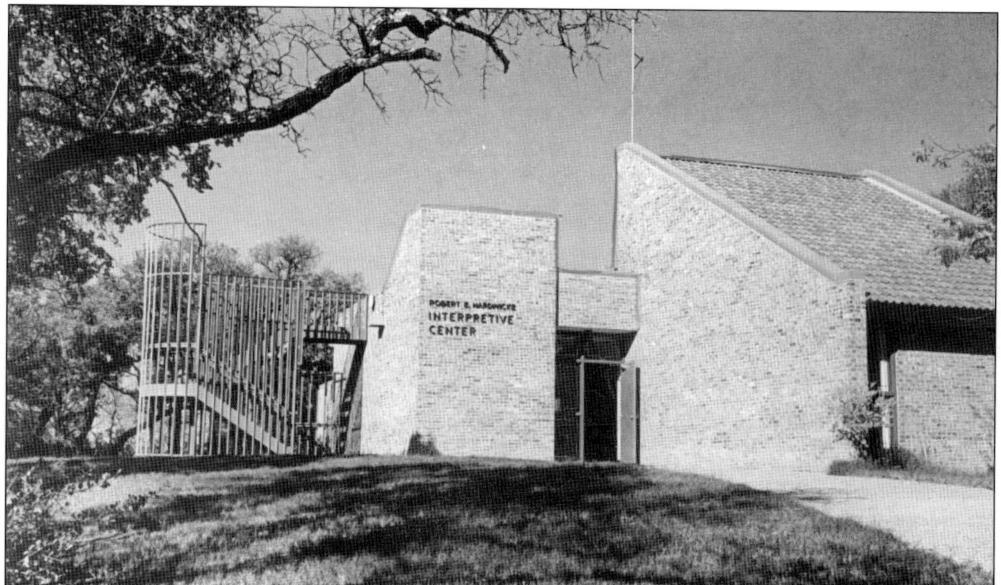

The Robert E. Hardwicke Interpretive Center at the Greer Island Nature Center and Refuge was dedicated in September 1971. Built in part with funds from the U.S. Bureau of Outdoor Recreation, the building was named in Hardwicke's memory to acknowledge his contributions to the conservation movement in Fort Worth and the establishment of the refuge. (FWSTC/SCUTA.)

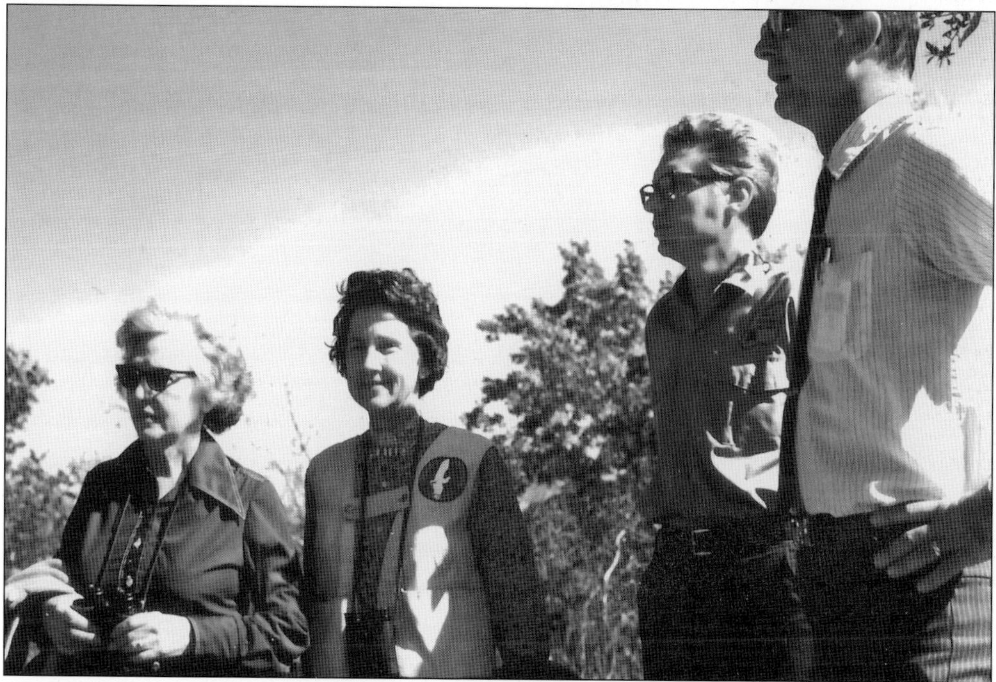

Over the years, the refuge, now known as the Fort Worth Nature Center and Refuge, has grown to more than 3,600 acres, making it one of the largest municipal-owned nature centers in the country. Its National Recreation Trail was the first such trail designated in Texas. Early advocates included, from left to right, Jessie Maye Smith, Margaret Parker, Harold Arnold, and Ted Hofsiss. (Fort Worth Nature Center and Refuge.)

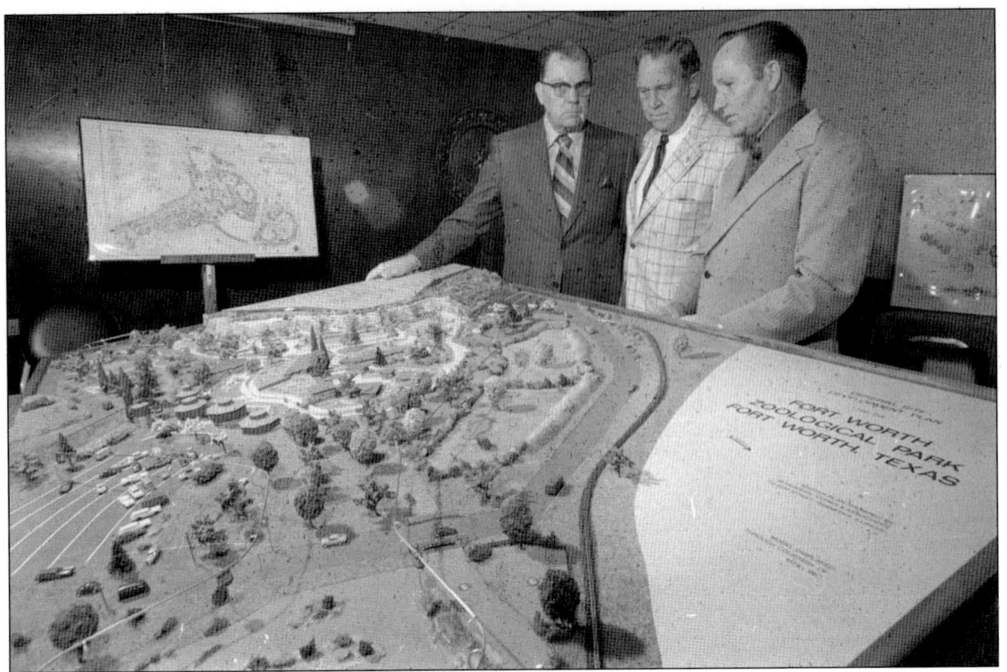

A new master plan, meant to modernize the zoo, was unveiled in September 1971. The plans included expansion of the grounds, the creation of naturalized habitats that would allow many of the animals to roam more freely, and the initiation of an entrance fee. Discussing the plan are, from left to right, Mayor Pro Tem Ted C. Peters; Harry Tennison, president of the Fort Worth Zoological Association; and Elvie Turner, zoo director. (FWSTC/SCUTA.)

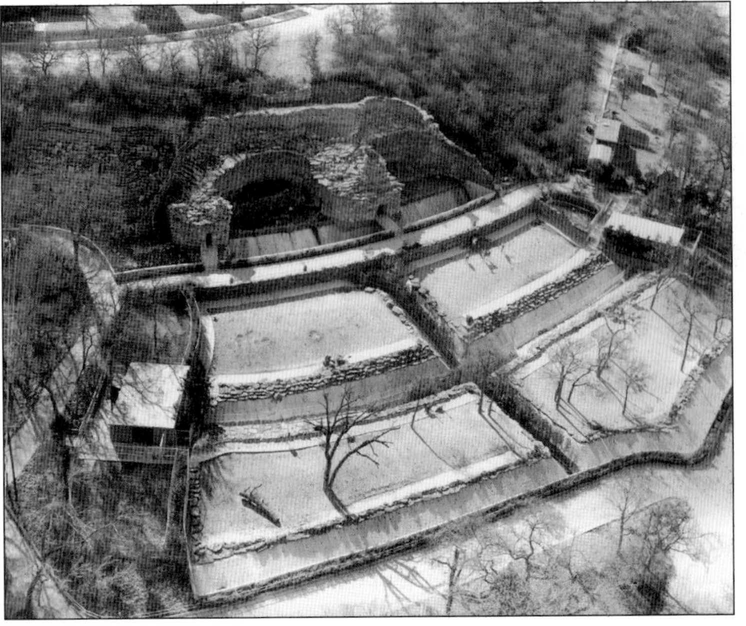

This aerial photograph from 1974 reveals how the enclosure for the lions was built into the side of the bluff that surrounds the zoo. Moats, walls, and fences separated different species from each other and zoo patrons. With a few modifications and more vegetation, this area still houses the lions, and hoof stock inhabit the four quadrants. (Photograph by Daniel Zurovetz; Fort Worth Fire Department.)

Mike, the gorilla, and his partner, Sue, were popular residents of the zoo from 1964 to 1985. This photograph of Mike from around 1970 shows him in an outdated enclosure. In 1979, Mike led the way into the Great Ape House, built specifically for larger primates such as chimpanzees, orangutans, and gorillas. (Fort Worth Zoo.)

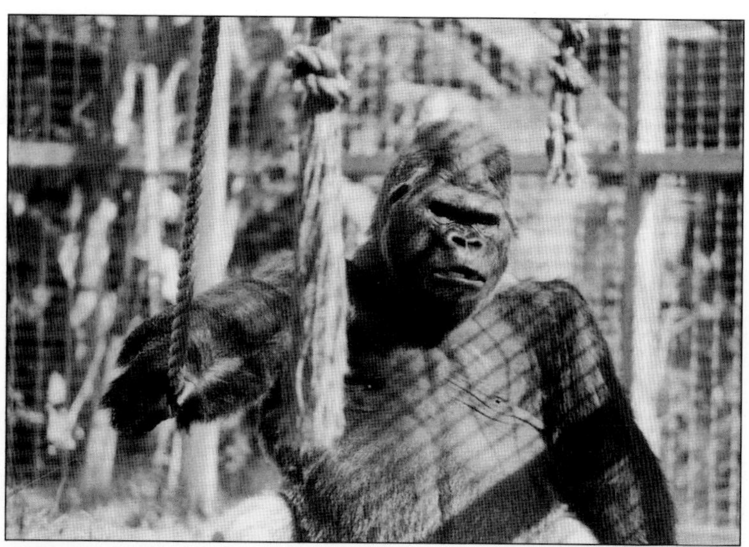

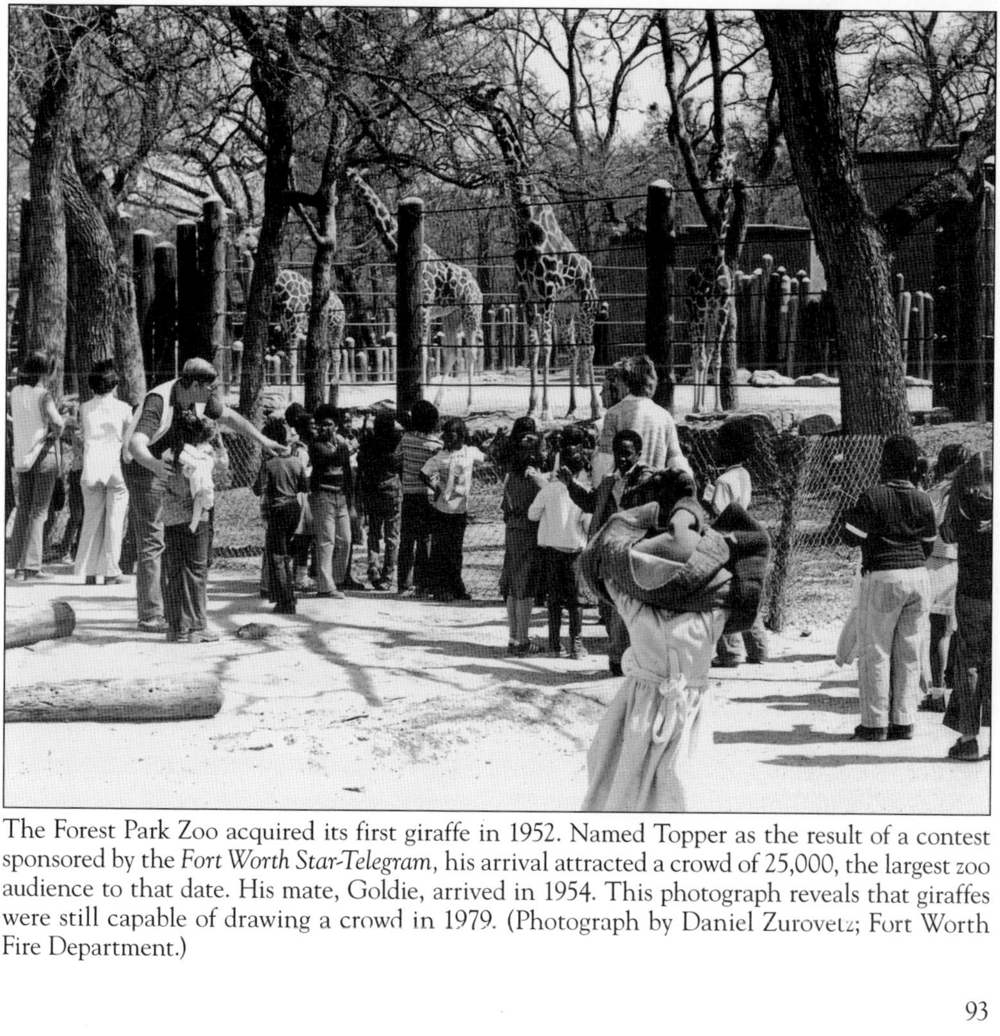

The Forest Park Zoo acquired its first giraffe in 1952. Named Topper as the result of a contest sponsored by the *Fort Worth Star-Telegram*, his arrival attracted a crowd of 25,000, the largest zoo audience to that date. His mate, Goldie, arrived in 1954. This photograph reveals that giraffes were still capable of drawing a crowd in 1979. (Photograph by Daniel Zurovetz; Fort Worth Fire Department.)

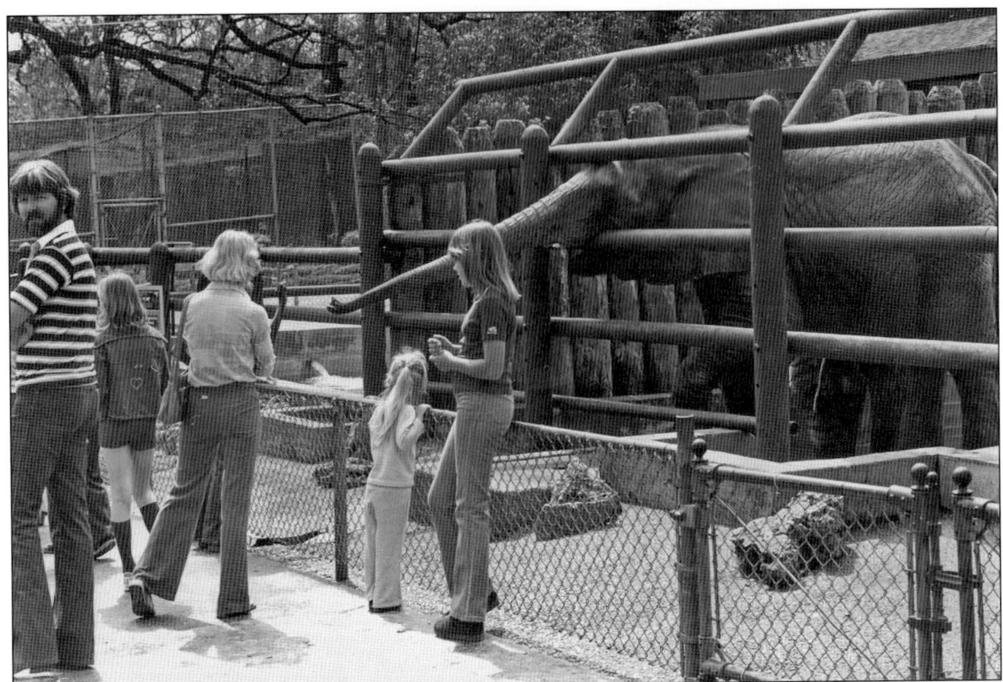

An elephant tries its best to reach a treat offered by a young zoo visitor in this photograph from 1979. Later alterations removed the metal fence, and today there are no visual barriers between the elephants and zoo patrons. (Photograph by Daniel Zurovetz; Fort Worth Fire Department.)

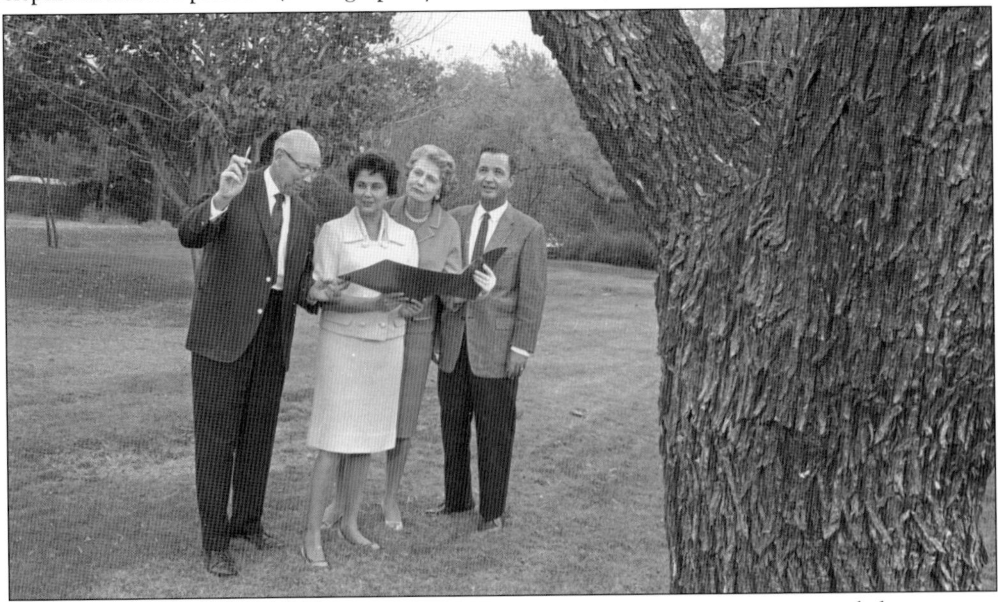

Scott Fikes (left), the park department superintendent of horticulture, envisioned the creation of an "oriental" garden within the Fort Worth Botanic Garden as early as 1958. Discussing the future garden with Fikes in November 1966 are Fort Worth Garden Club officers Jane Cranz (second from left) and Winette Jordan (third from left), and park director Charles Campbell. Through the club, the Fort Worth Botanical Society was organized to help sustain and develop the garden. (FWSTC/SCUTA.)

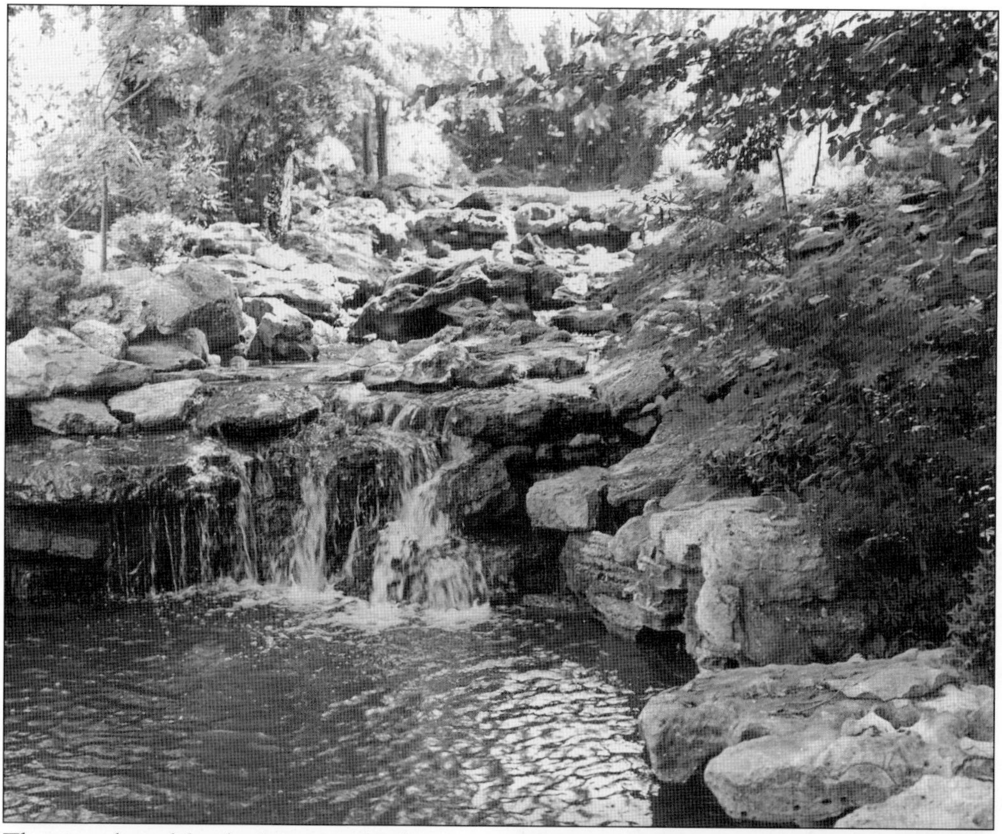

The site selected for the Japanese Garden was a former gravel pit. After the land was purchased, students from Louisiana State University drew initial concepts for the garden. Dr. Kingsley Wu of Texas Women's University was hired to prepare the final plans. Great care was taken to preserve the site's rugged terrain. (Photograph by Daniel Zurovetz; Fort Worth Fire Department.)

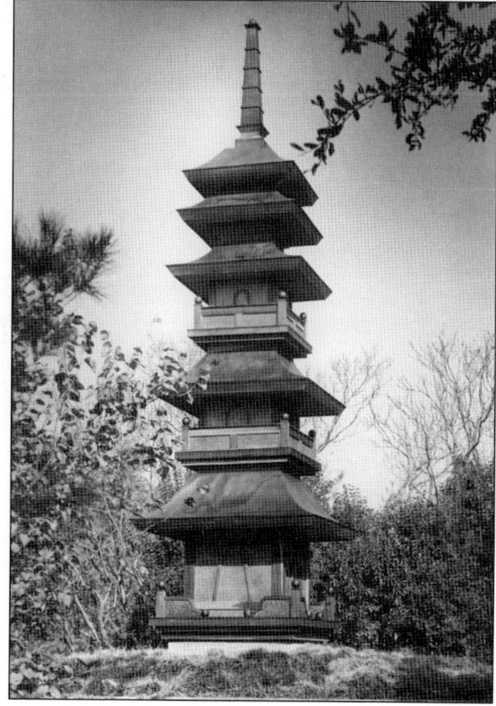

In Japan, a pagoda is traditionally used as a treasure house for the storage of family possessions. This striking version was designed by Albert Komatsu and Associates and was constructed by park labor. It is located on the south end of the garden near the exit and serves as the symbol for the garden. (FWBG.)

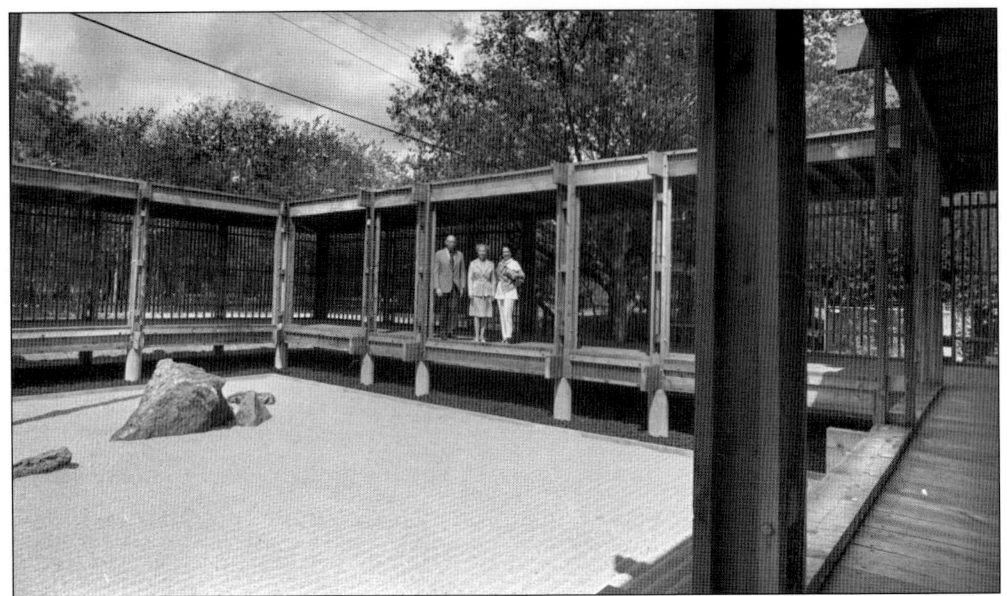

Completed in 1970, the Meditation Garden was based on the Ryoan-ji temple garden in Kyoto, Japan. The large stones in the center of the garden represented land, and the raked crush rocks represented water. It was the first major structure completed in the Japanese Garden. Pictured from left to right are Scott Fikes and Fort Worth Garden Club members Mary Louise Michie and Deborah Beggs Moncrief. (FWSTC/SCUTA.)

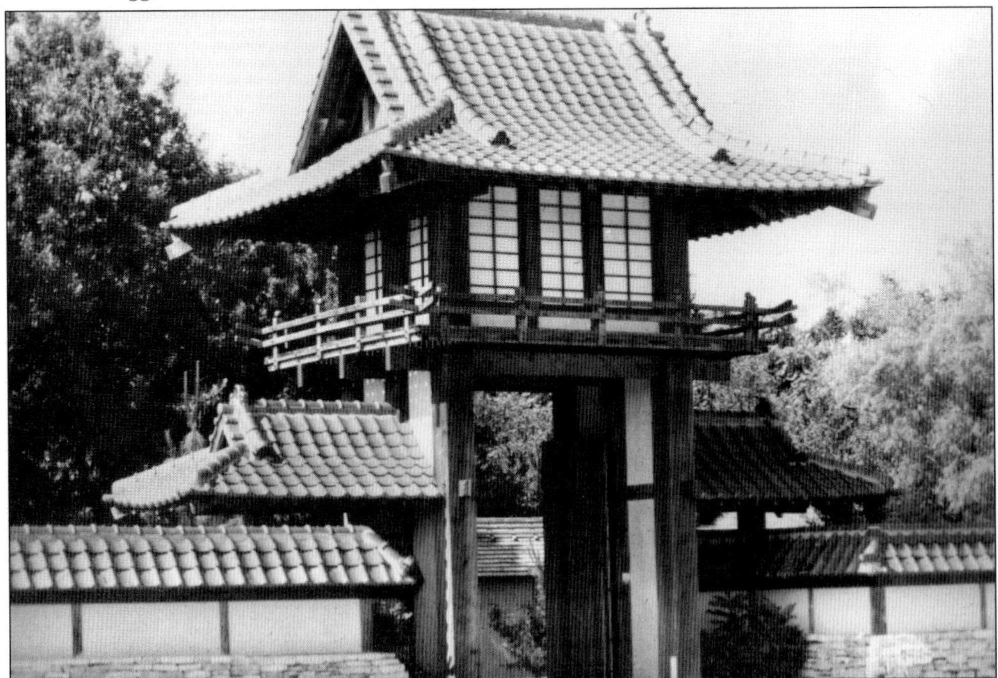

The garden was officially opened to the public on March 29, 1973. As funds became available, new structures have been added over the years. This handsome gate is the formal entrance to the Japanese Garden and was dedicated in 1976. It was designed by local architect Albert Komatsu. (FWSTC/SCUTA.)

The entrance gate was dedicated on October 28, 1976, in honor of Scott Fikes, longtime horticulture superintendent who had retired the previous year. Fikes (left) is shown holding a rendering of the gate. Seated next to him are Albert Komatsu, the designer of the gate, and Mayor Clif Overcash. (FWSTC/SCUTA.)

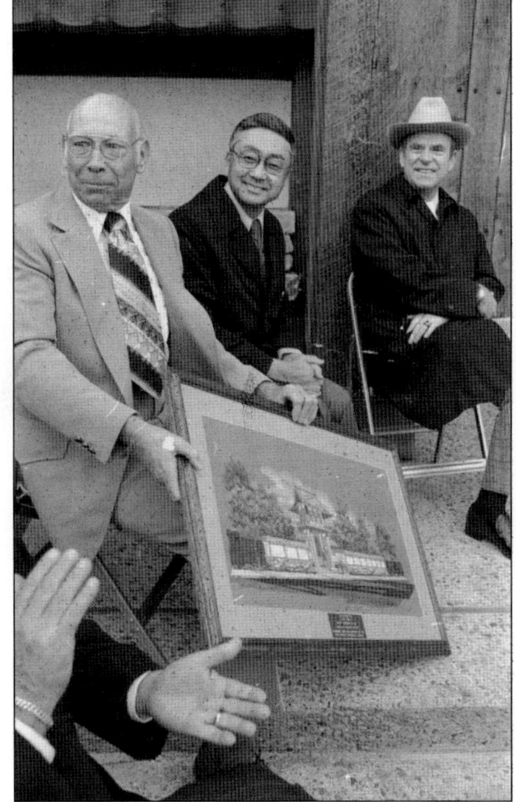

Located in far east Fort Worth, Oakland Lake Park was acquired in 1927. This view, likely from the 1970s, depicts improvements made in previous decades. The stone terrace was designed by Hare and Hare and was constructed as a WPA project. The stone shelter was designed by local architect Robert P. Woltz Jr. and was completed in 1953. (PACS.)

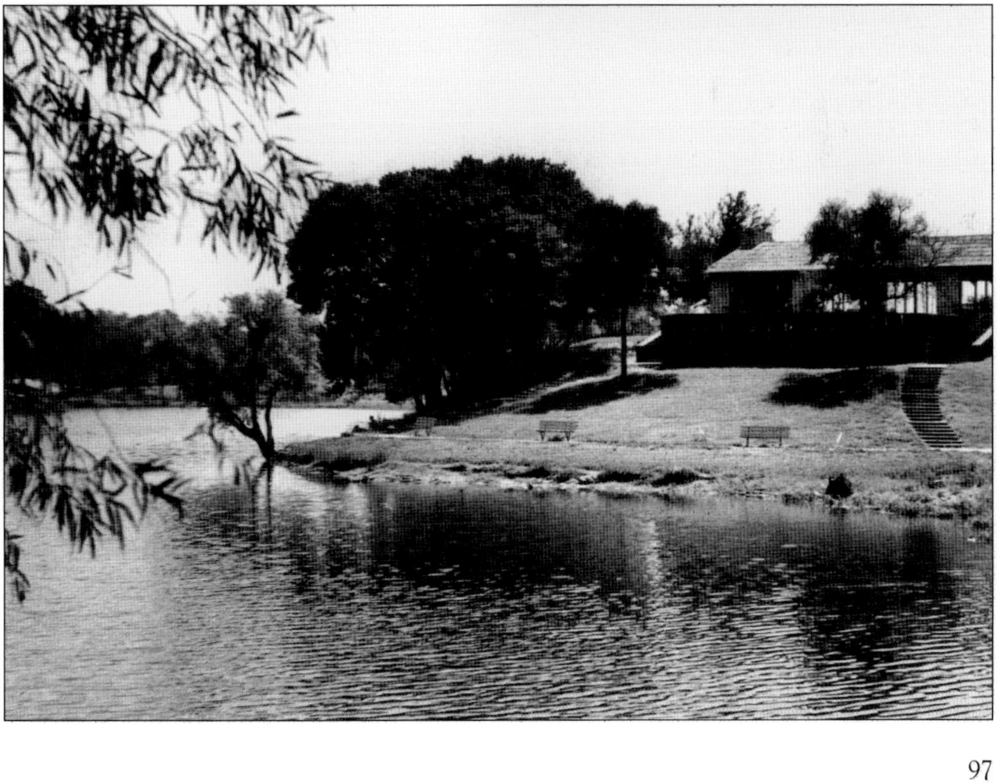

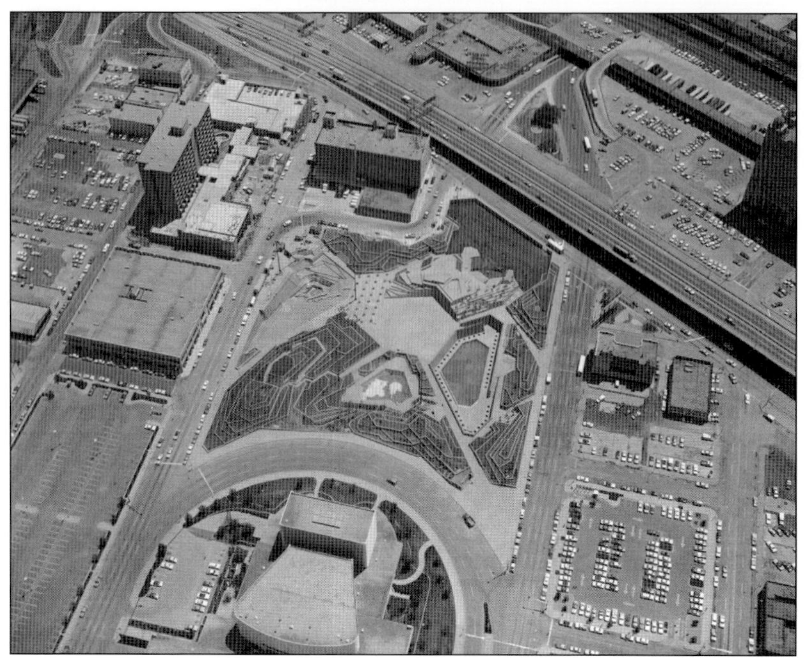

The Fort Worth Water Gardens is a modernist masterpiece designed by Philip Johnson and John Burgee near the southern end of downtown. The garden, given by the Amon G. Carter Foundation and operated by the park department, is an urban landscape with a concrete mountain, waterfalls, and pools. The above aerial photograph depicts the garden as it was nearing completion. The garden's major features are (clockwise from the upper left corner of center block) the Active Water Pool, the Mountain and Lawn/Stage behind it, the Wet Wall and Quiet Water Pool, and the Aerated Water Pool. In the photograph below, architect Philip Johnson addresses the crowd at the garden's dedication on October 19, 1974. (Above, W. D. Smith Commercial Photography Collection, Special Collections, the University of Texas at Arlington Library, Arlington, Texas; below, FWSTC/SCUTA.)

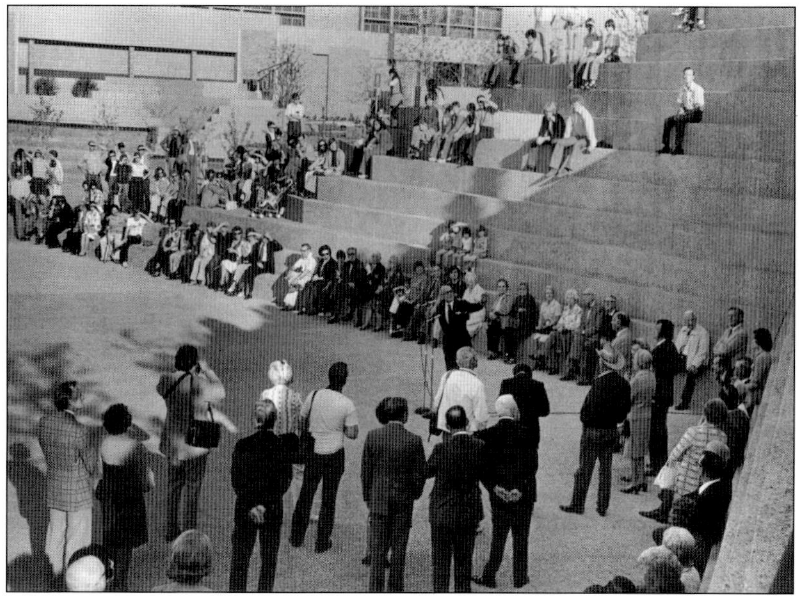

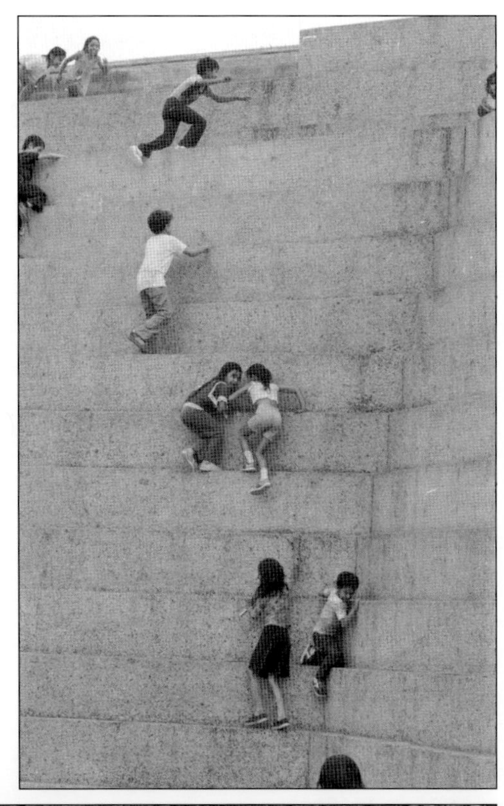

Second-grade students from Carroll Peak Elementary School celebrated the end of the 1976–1977 school year with a field trip to downtown Fort Worth, first having lunch at Burnett Park and then playing at the Fort Worth Water Gardens. The children are shown climbing the concrete "mountain" at the south end of the garden, which rises 20 feet above the ground. (FWSTC/SCUTA.)

Members of the park and recreation board in 1976 included, from left to right, Albert Chew, Mary Swink, Roger C. Hunsaker, Juanita Zepeda, chairman Jan Fersing, Linda Guminski, and Joe Paul Jones. During this year, events celebrating the nation's bicentennial were held in numerous parks, including Heritage, Forest, and Trinity Parks. (Photograph by Daniel Zurovetz; Fort Worth Fire Department.)

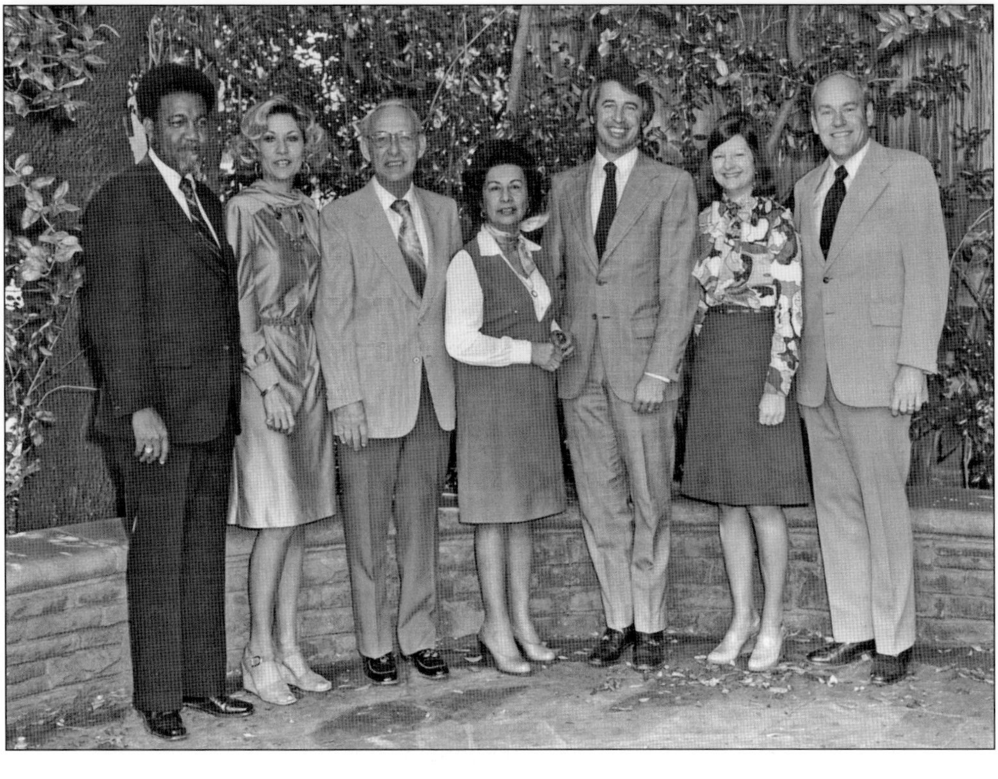

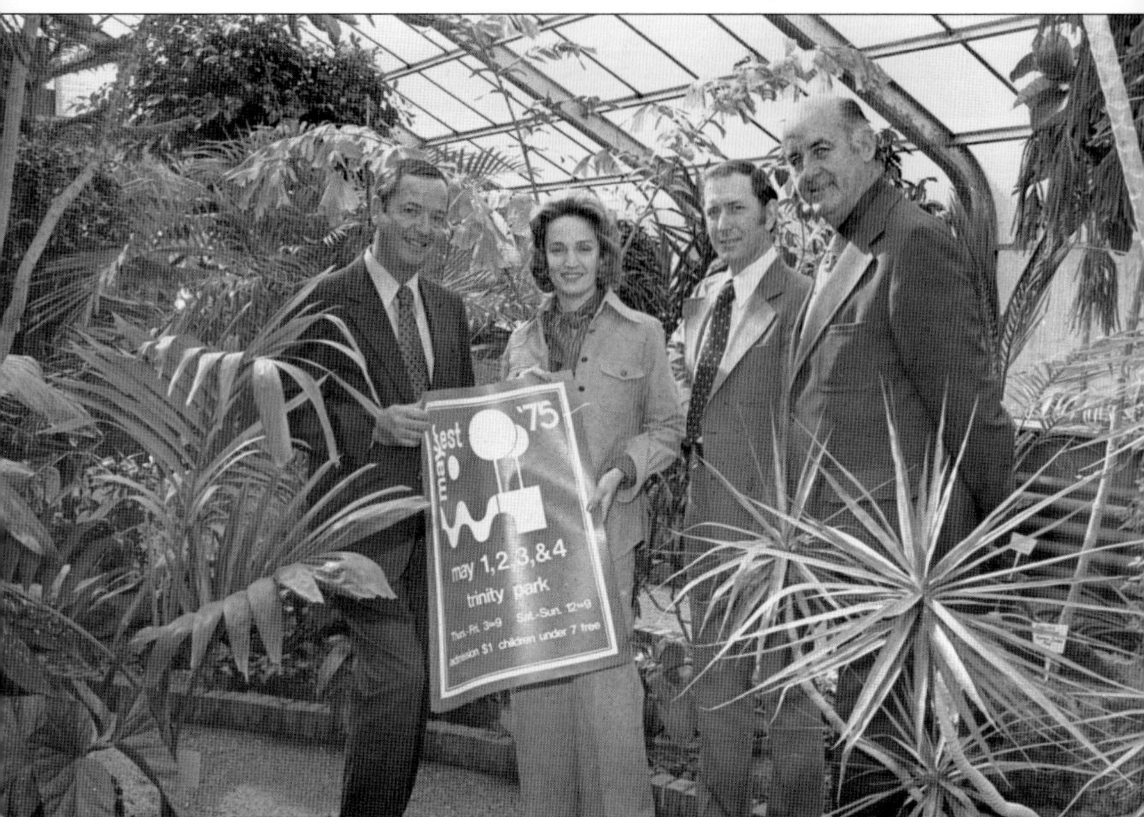

Mayfest, a four-day celebration of the Trinity River and its significance to the region, was first held in 1973. The sponsoring organizations were the Junior League of Fort Worth, the Forth Worth Park and Recreation Department, the Streams and Valleys Committee, and the Tarrant Regional Water District. It became a separate nonprofit organization in 1987. Planners for the event in 1975 included, from left to right, Charles Campbell, director, Forth Worth Park and Recreation Department; Lynda Roodhouse, general chairman; David Nivens, superintendent of park operations for the Forth Worth Park and Recreation Department; and county fire marshal Mason Langford. The group is pictured inside the greenhouse at the Fort Worth Botanic Garden. Today the event is still held in Trinity Park and attracts more than 200,000 visitors annually. Designated activity areas with family-centered events appeal to a variety of interests, and six stages provide continual entertainment. Profits from the event are returned to the community through various projects. (FWSTC/SCUTA.)

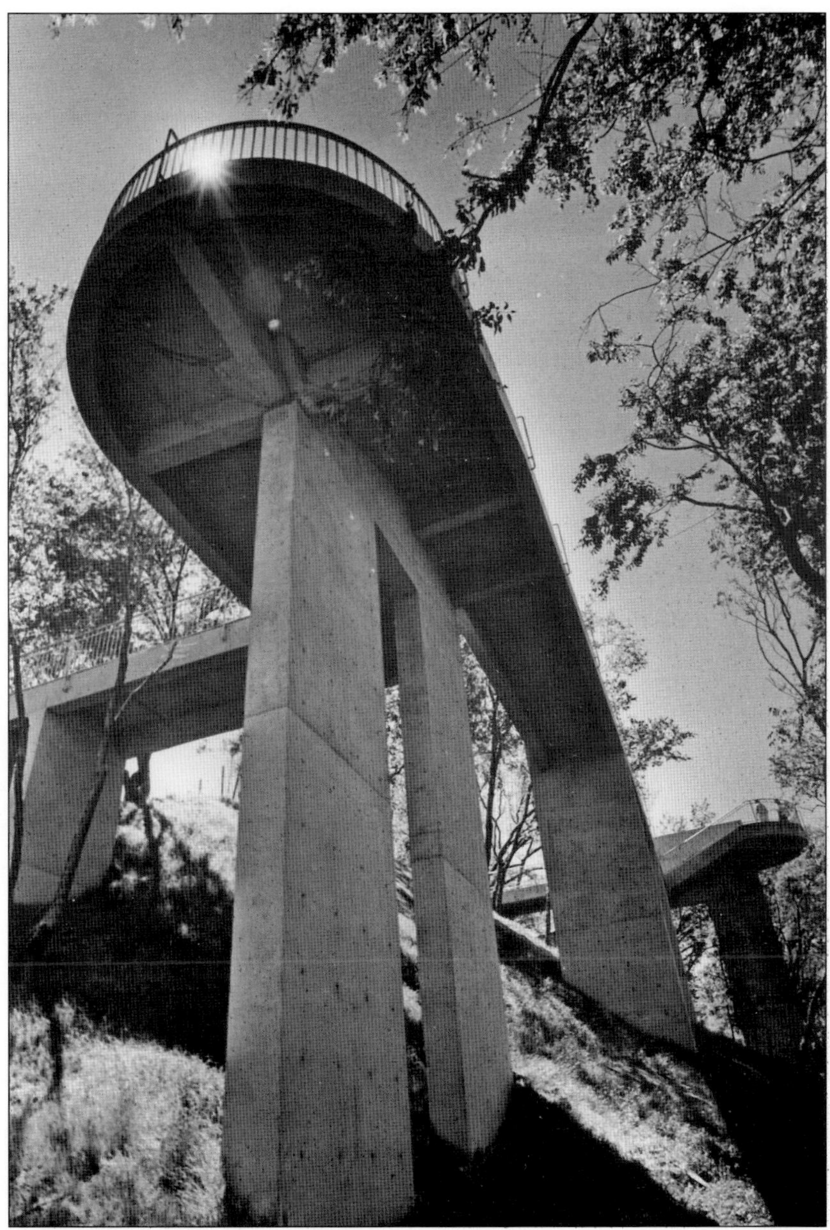

For decades, planners and city leaders had envisioned the creation of a park on the bluff above the Trinity River, the site of the city's namesake military post. That dream finally came to fruition through the efforts of such organizations and individuals as the Streams and Valleys Committee, the Amon G. Carter Foundation, Ruth Carter Johnson, the Sid Richardson Foundation, Charles D. Tandy, the Texas Electric Service Company, the U.S. Department of the Interior, the Texas Parks and Wildlife Department, the City of Fort Worth's Parks and Recreation Department, Tarrant County, and the Tarrant County Water Control District No. 1. Lawrence Halprin's design for the Heritage Park Plaza celebrated the city's past and the river that gave it life. The plaza consisted of a series of rooms connected by moving water. The rooms encouraged quiet contemplation, and projecting overlooks provided stunning views of the river. The ground for the plaza was broken in November 1977, and it was formally dedicated on April 18, 1980. (FWSTC/SCUTA.)

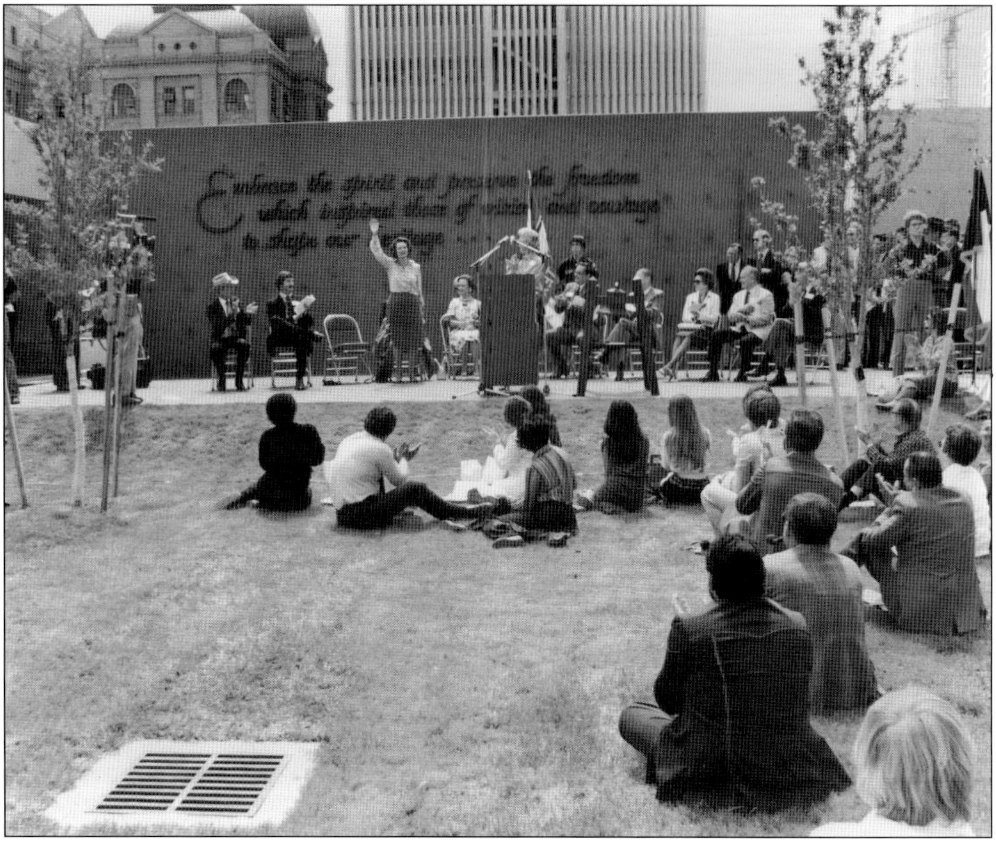

Among the dignitaries attending the Heritage Park Plaza's dedication were Gov. Bill Clements, Mayor Woodie Woods, county judge Mike Moncrief, and Nancy Bass of the Sid Richardson Foundation. At the podium is Ruth Carter Johnson of the Amon G. Carter Foundation. Waving to the crowd is former First Lady Lady Bird Johnson. The inscription on the wall reads, "Embrace the spirit and preserve the freedom which inspired those of vision and courage to shape our heritage." (PACS.)

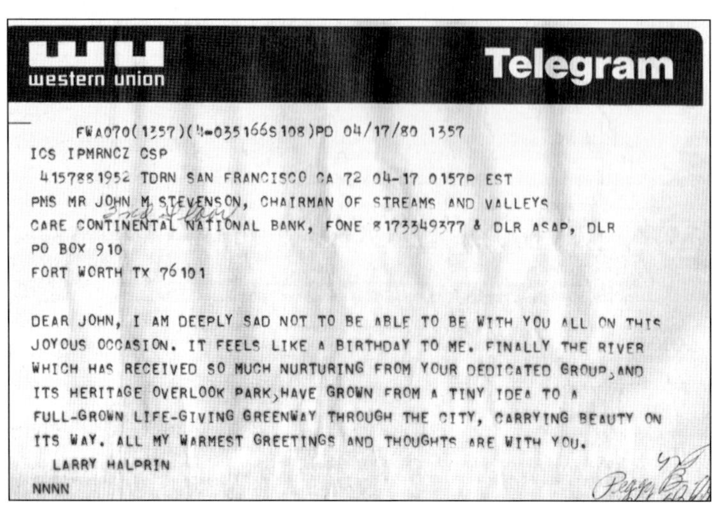

western union

Telegram

FWA070(1357)(4-035166S108)PD 04/17/80 1357
ICS IPMRNCZ CSP
4157881952 TDRN SAN FRANCISCO CA 72 04-17 0157P EST
PMS MR JOHN M STEVENSON, CHAIRMAN OF STREAMS AND VALLEYS
CARE CONTINENTAL NATIONAL BANK, FONE 8173349377 & DLR ASAP, DLR
PO BOX 910
FORT WORTH TX 76101

DEAR JOHN, I AM DEEPLY SAD NOT TO BE ABLE TO BE WITH YOU ALL ON THIS JOYOUS OCCASION. IT FEELS LIKE A BIRTHDAY TO ME. FINALLY THE RIVER WHICH HAS RECEIVED SO MUCH NURTURING FROM YOUR DEDICATED GROUP, AND ITS HERITAGE OVERLOOK PARK, HAVE GROWN FROM A TINY IDEA TO A FULL-GROWN LIFE-GIVING GREENWAY THROUGH THE CITY, CARRYING BEAUTY ON ITS WAY. ALL MY WARMEST GREETINGS AND THOUGHTS ARE WITH YOU.
LARRY HALPRIN
NNNN

Landscape architect Lawrence Halprin (1916–2009) was unable to attend the dedication of the Heritage Park Plaza. In the telegram he sent to John M. Stevenson, chairman of the Streams and Valleys Committee, he expressed the sentiment of many who had long dreamed of a bluff-top park that would celebrate the Trinity River. (PACS.)

A public-private partnership between the Forth Worth Park and Recreation Department and the Berkeley Place Neighborhood Association resulted in the restoration of the landmark Forest Park gates in 1980. The neighborhood association, which borders the gates, started raising funds for the project in 1976. Additional funds were provided through a bond issue and the adjacent Mistletoe Heights neighborhood. (Robert G. Adams.)

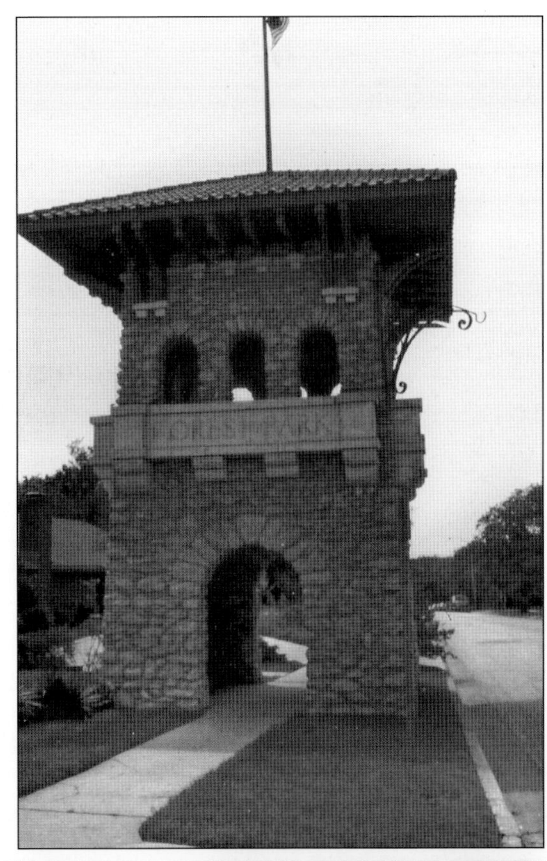

Downtown's Burk Burnett Park received a modernist makeover in 1984 through a grant provided by the Anne Burnett and Charles Tandy Foundation and city funds. Peter Walker's geometric design for the park included crisscrossing granite paths, grassy patches of lawn, and reflecting pools with candlestick fountains. (Witherspoon Associates and FWL.)

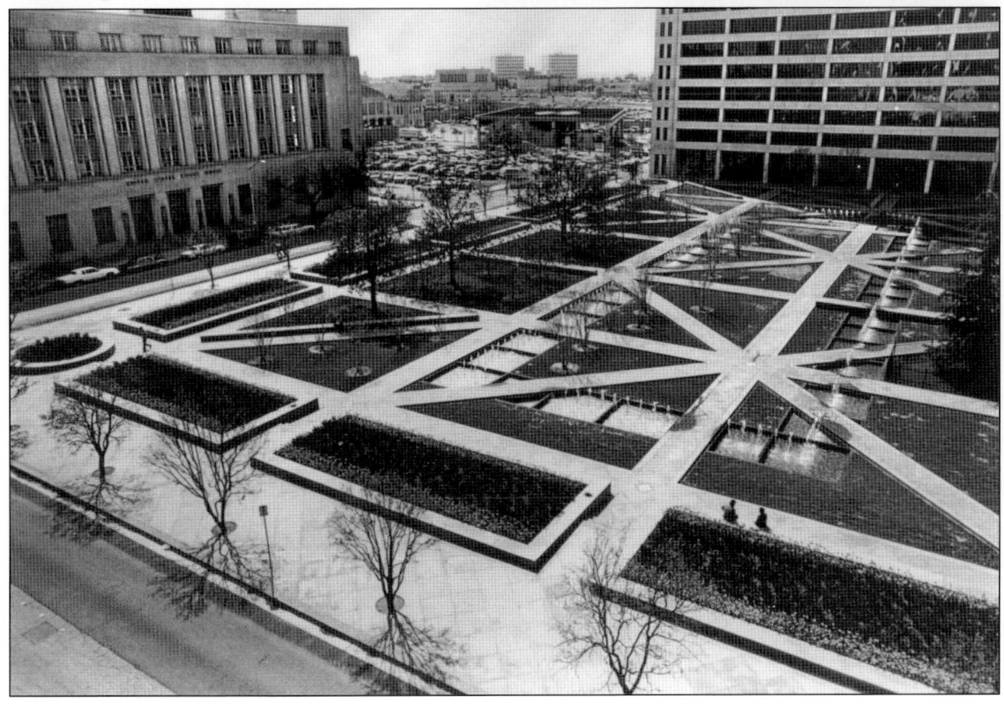

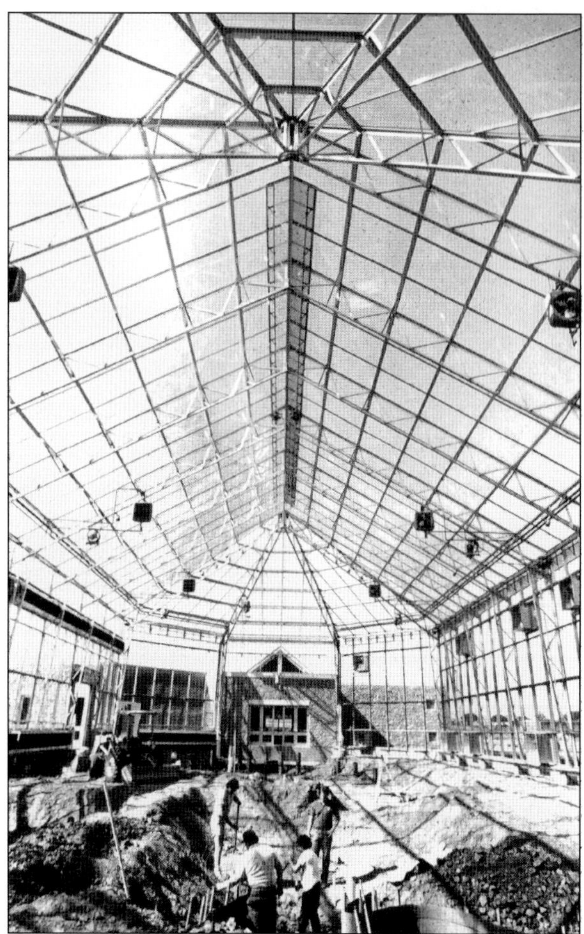

Largely through a 13-year effort of the Fort Worth Garden Club, a new garden center and conservatory was constructed in the Fort Worth Botanic Garden. Completed in 1986, the structure included a 10,000-square-foot botanical conservatory and a 17,000-square-foot education building containing the administrative offices of the botanic garden, meeting rooms, a conference room, a kitchen, and a courtyard. Tropical plants fill the conservatory. The Dorothy Leonhardt Lecture Hall was added to the north end of the building in 1988. In honor of a longtime supporter and benefactor of the botanic garden and its garden center, the garden center was renamed the Deborah Beggs Moncrief Garden Center in 2005. (Both, FWBG.)

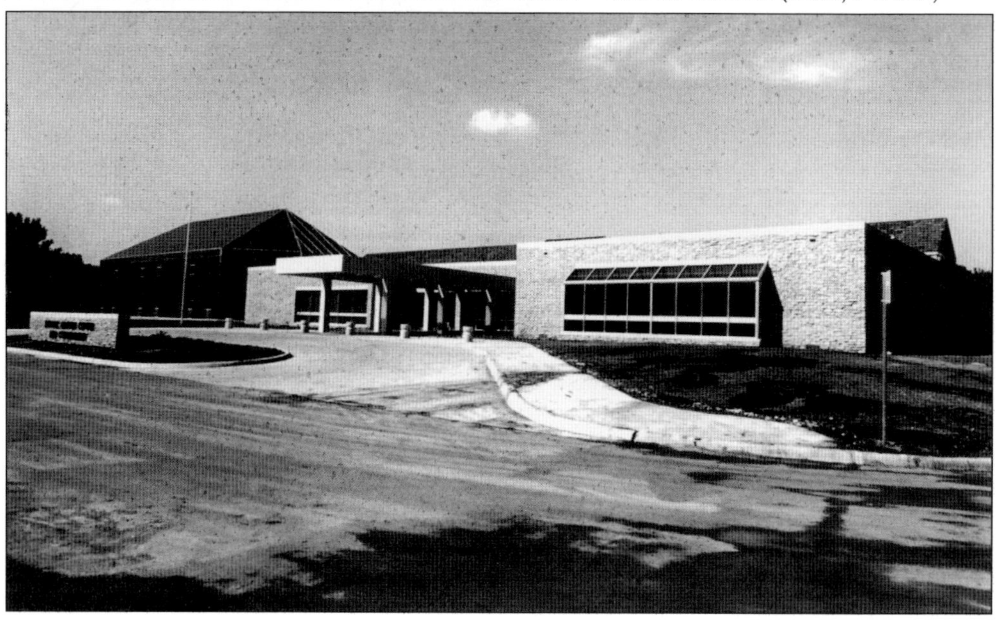

Because of its central location within the city, Forest Park is used for a variety of community events. Marathons and fun-runs are often routed though its streets, and soccer matches are a frequent occurrence. In 1987, the park was the venue for the Cowtown Balloon Round Up. (Robert G. Adams.)

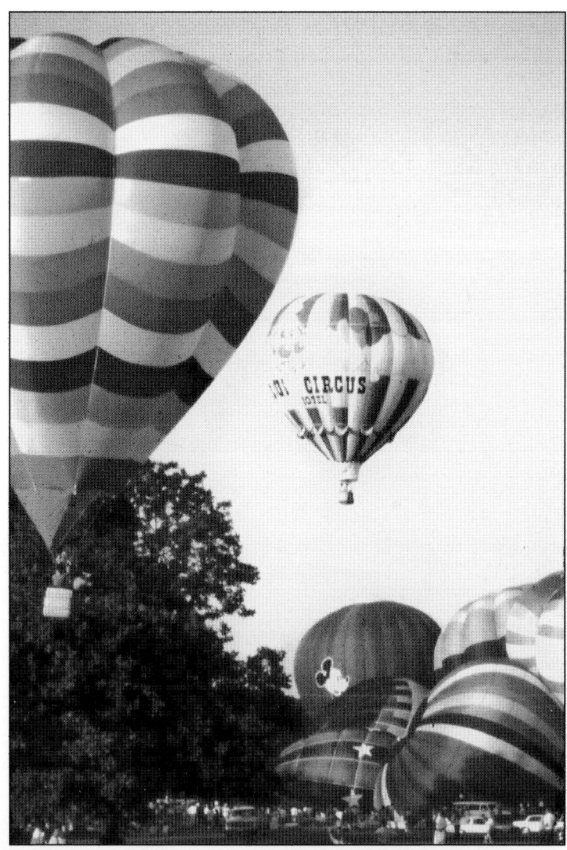

One of the larger parks on the city's north side, Buck Sansom Park, named for a prominent cattleman, was acquired in 1928 in part as a gift from the Sansom family and in part as a park board purchase. As part of an improvement program of the 1980s, it received this playground equipment. Other amenities at the park include a shelter, portable restrooms, grills, and trail features. (PACS.)

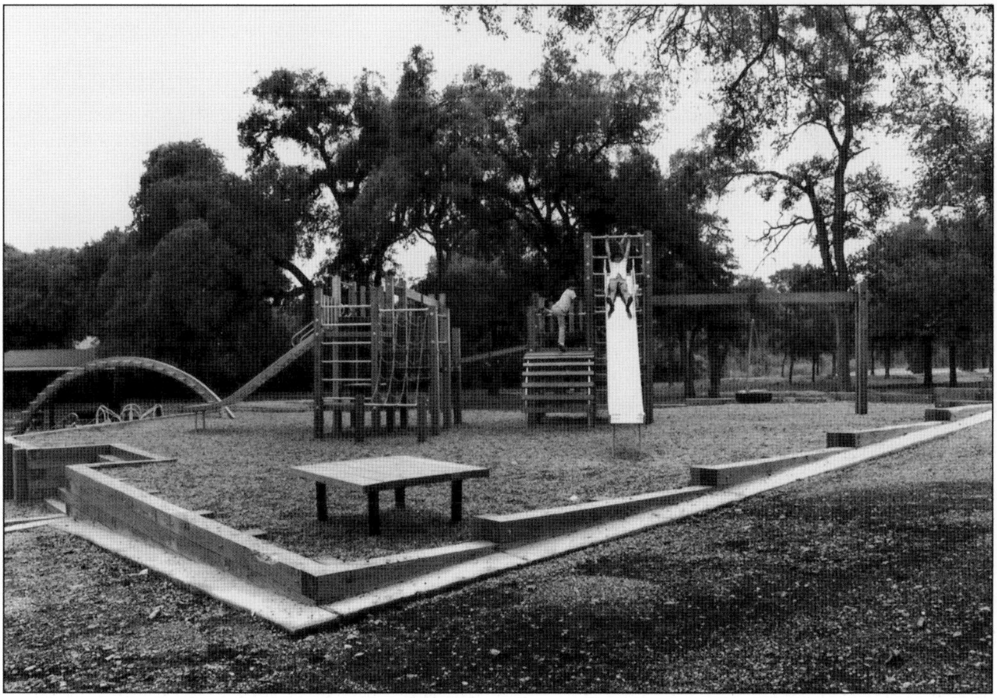

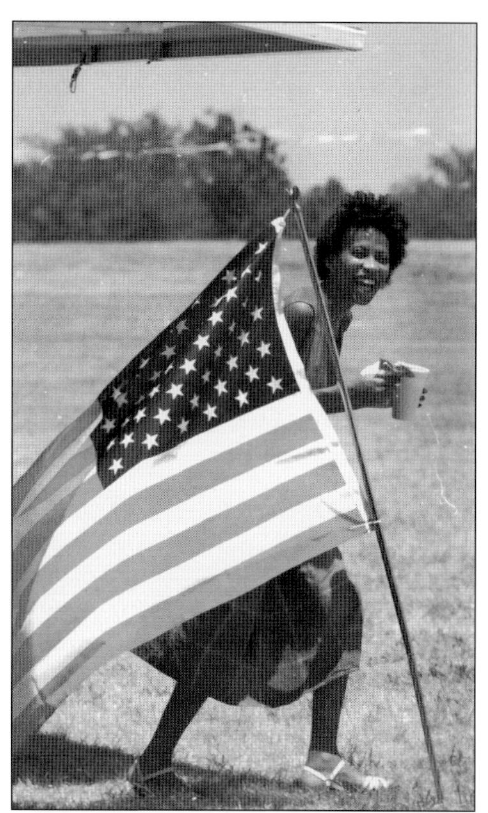

From events at Douglas Park to modern times, African Americans have used Fort Worth parks to celebrate Juneteenth, the day when Texas's slaves learned of the Emancipation Proclamation—June 19, 1865. For years, this was the only day that African Americans could visit such attractions as the zoo or the botanic garden. Here Dede Clayton celebrates Juneteenth's 125th anniversary in 1990 at Hillside Park. (FWSTC/SCUTA.)

Building on Fort Worth's "Cowtown" heritage, the mascot for the Forth Worth Parks and Community Services Department is a steer. Appropriately named "Pacs," he makes appearances at many of the department's events. Here a young visitor to the annual Mayfest celebration appears a little apprehensive over the big fellow's attempts to be friendly. (PACS.)

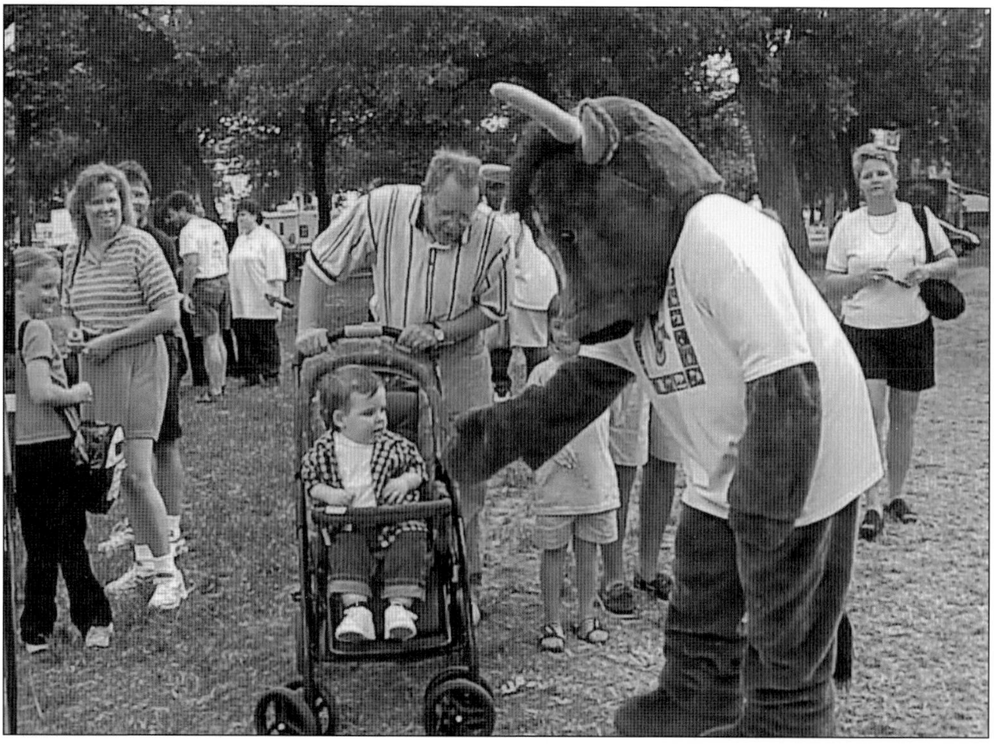

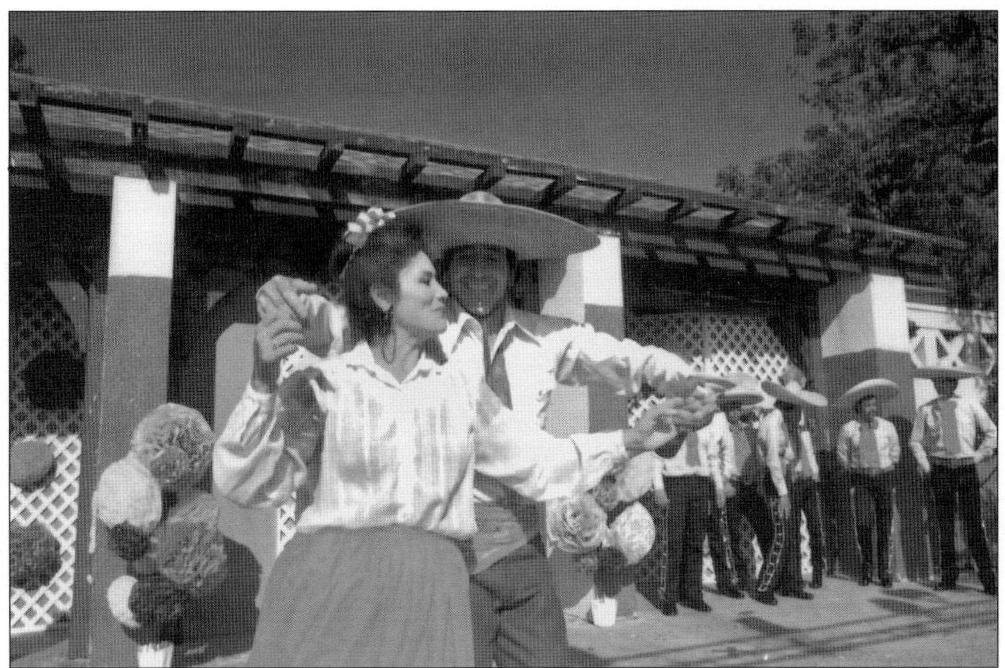

Mexican Americans in Texas and throughout the Southwest celebrate the Mexican national holiday Cinco de Mayo (May 5). This holiday commemorates Gen. Ignacio Zaragoza's victory on May 5, 1862, over the French expeditionary forces at Puebla, Mexico. Marine Park, in the heart of a large Hispanic community in Fort Worth, was the location for annual Cinco de Mayo events for a number of years. In the above photograph, taken in 1989, Francisco Franco and his wife dance with *Grupo de Dansas de Bailes Regionales*. In the photograph below from 1990, Nancy Garcia (left), Beatrice Torres (center), and an unidentified woman (right) perform *Mariachi Estrella*. (Both, FWSTC/SCUTA.)

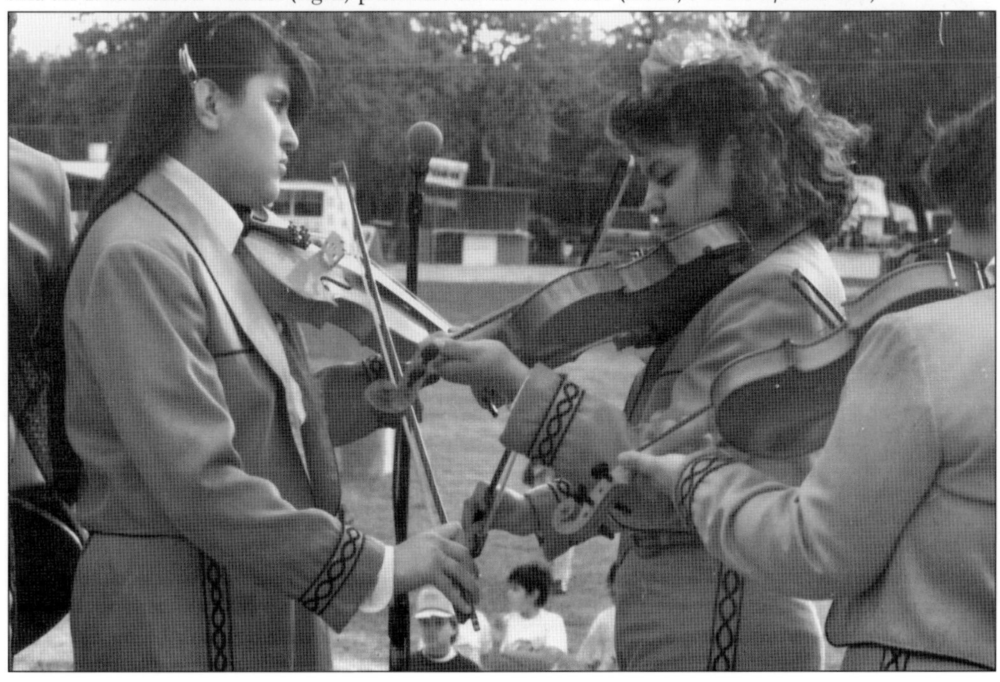

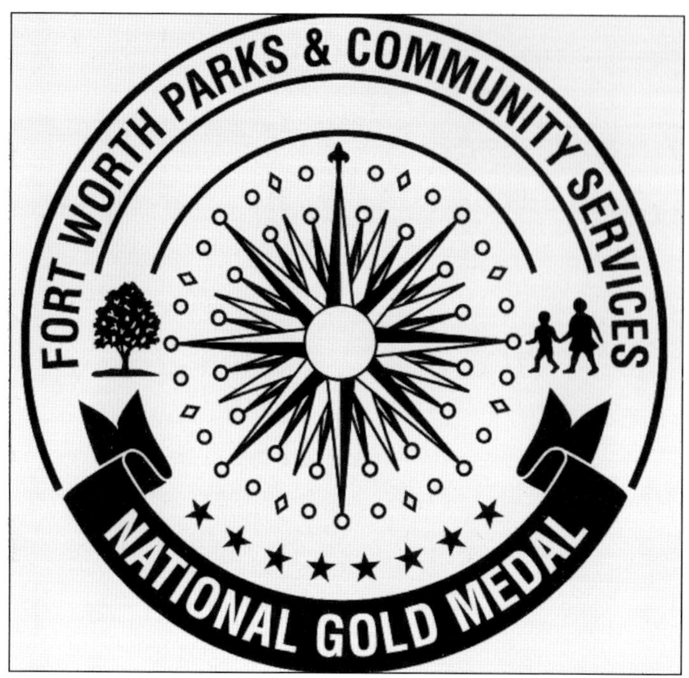

The Fort Worth Parks and Community Services Department was recognized with a National Gold Medal Award for excellence in park and recreation management in 1996. This was one of many awards received in the 1990s for individual parks, community centers, programming and interpretation, professional achievements by employees, and volunteer efforts. (PACS.)

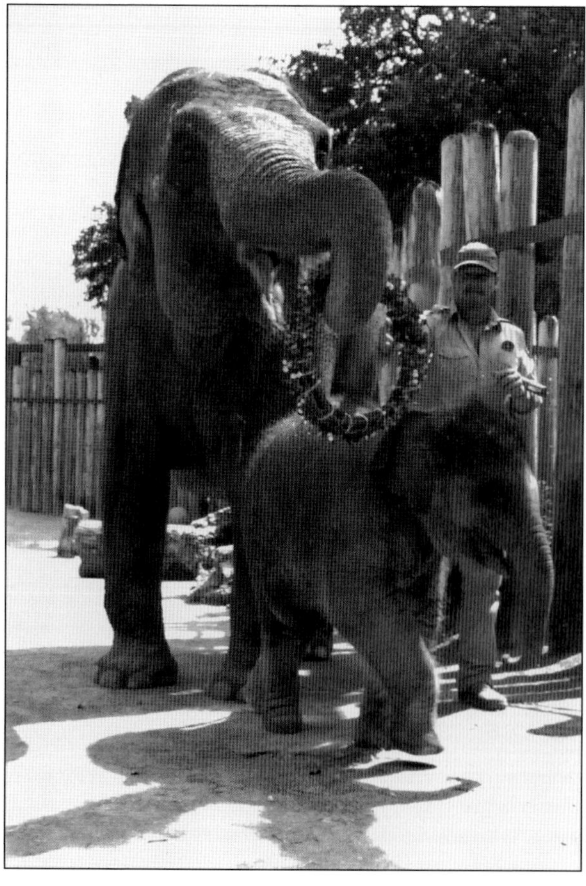

There was much rejoicing at the Fort Worth Zoo when the Asian elephant Rasha gave birth to little Bluebonnet in 1998. The successful breeding of Asian and African elephants in captivity is a concern for many zoos as they attempt to keep their elephant populations self-sustaining. Here the proud mother and baby are on parade. (Fort Worth Zoo.)

Six

A New Century 2000 to 2009

As the Fort Worth Parks and Community Services Department (PACS) enters into its second century, it finds itself addressing some of the same issues it did 100 years ago, as well as facing challenges unimagined by its founders. As always, the department is concerned with the preservation of green space and the creation of recreational opportunities for its citizens. But new technologies, environmental disasters, and responses to the needs of special communities have shaped the department's programming in profound ways.

In 2008, Fort Worth's population was 702,850, and it was ranked as the nation's 17th largest city and its fastest growing large city. Through surveys and updated or new master plans, the department is continually evaluating how best to meet the needs of the city's rapidly growing population. The creation of new parks and the enhancement of existing parks and playgrounds remain a priority. Revenue from the extraction of natural gas beneath park property as well as a voter-approved Capital Improvement Program are helping to fund many of these programs.

As the department's name implies, it also is closely involved with providing for the needs of the community at large. Through partnerships with other organizations and governmental agencies, PACS addresses issues such as hunger relief, child care assistance, gang intervention, disaster relief, and literacy and academic enrichment programs, and it provides comprehensive services to assist families in their efforts to transition out of poverty.

The goals, programs, and responsibilities of the PACS have expanded over the last century and are truly diverse. However, at its core, the same foundation binds all of its endeavors—the community of Fort Worth. Working together, the department will face the challenges and opportunities of the next 100 years.

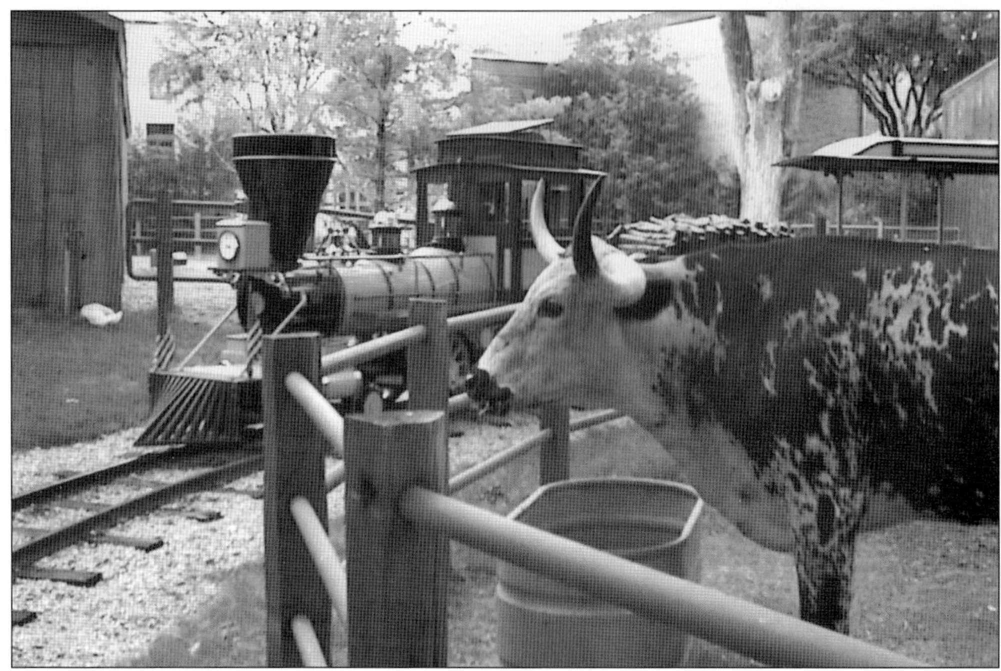

The Texas Wild! exhibit opened at the Fort Worth Zoo in 2001. Featuring interactive educational displays designed for visitors of all ages, the exhibit is zoological in nature but also part natural history museum and part amusement attraction. It explores ways in which humans and animals can coexist while highlighting Texas's diverse ecosystems and the wildlife that inhabits them. (PACS.)

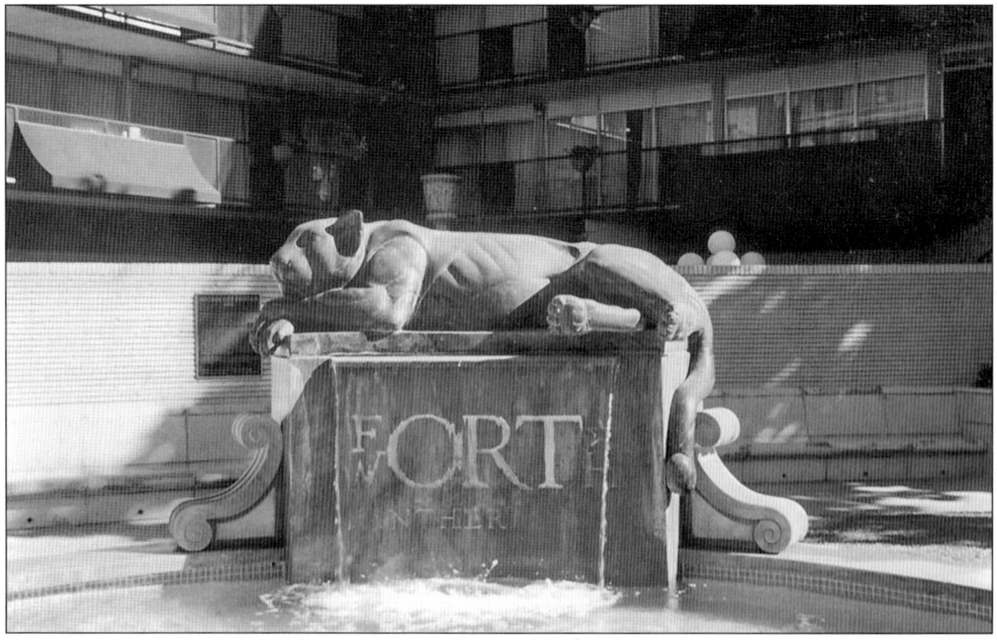

The historic Flatiron Building is adjacent to downtown's Hyde Park. In 2002, its owner, Dr. George F. Cravens, presented the city with the *Panther City Fountain* for the park. The fountain compliments the panther heads located on the Flatiron Building and gives homage to the city's nickname, "Panther City." The fountain's artist was Franco Alessandrini. (John Williams.)

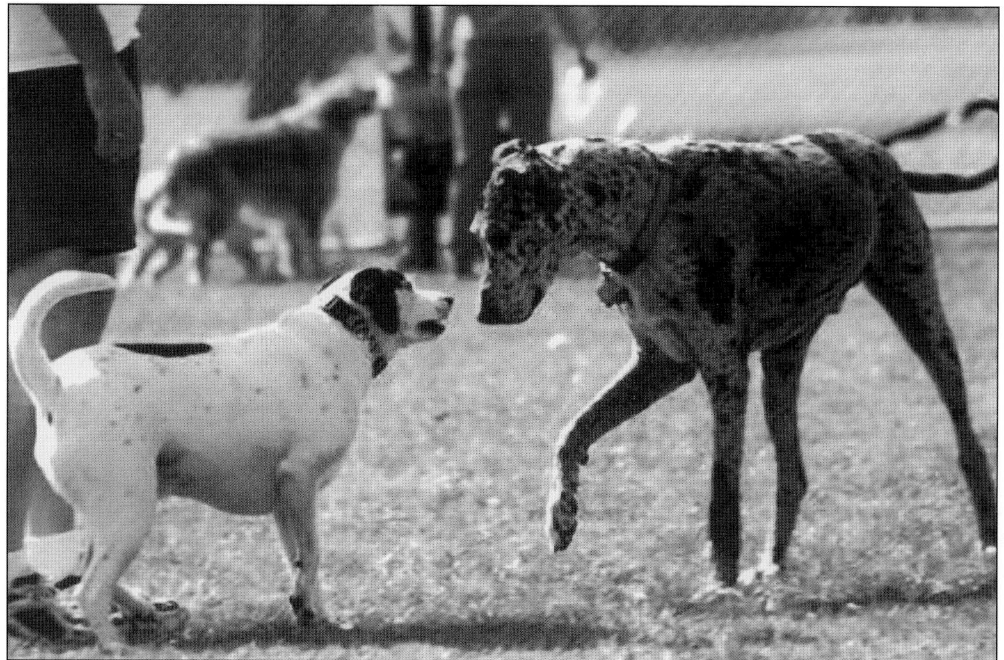

Fort Woof, Fort Worth's first off-leash dog park, opened in Gateway Park in 2003. In 2006, it was rated as the country's top dog park by *Dog Fancy* magazine. Special events such as October's Barktober Fest provide ample opportunities for socializing among dogs and their two-legged friends. (PACS.)

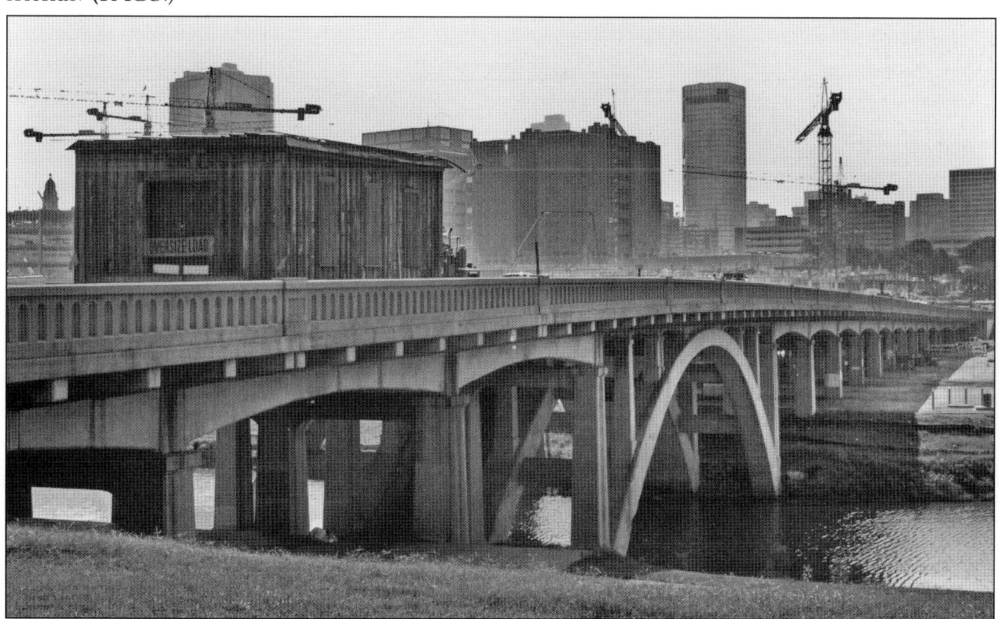

In 2003, the Marine Schoolhouse, originally constructed in 1872, was moved from parkland adjacent to the Northside Library to the Log Cabin Village. There it was restored and interpreted as an 1870s one-room school. It is open to visitors and participants in the museum's popular Pioneer School Program. This view is of the school as it was carried over the Henderson Street Bridge on its way to its new site. (City of Fort Worth Reprographics.)

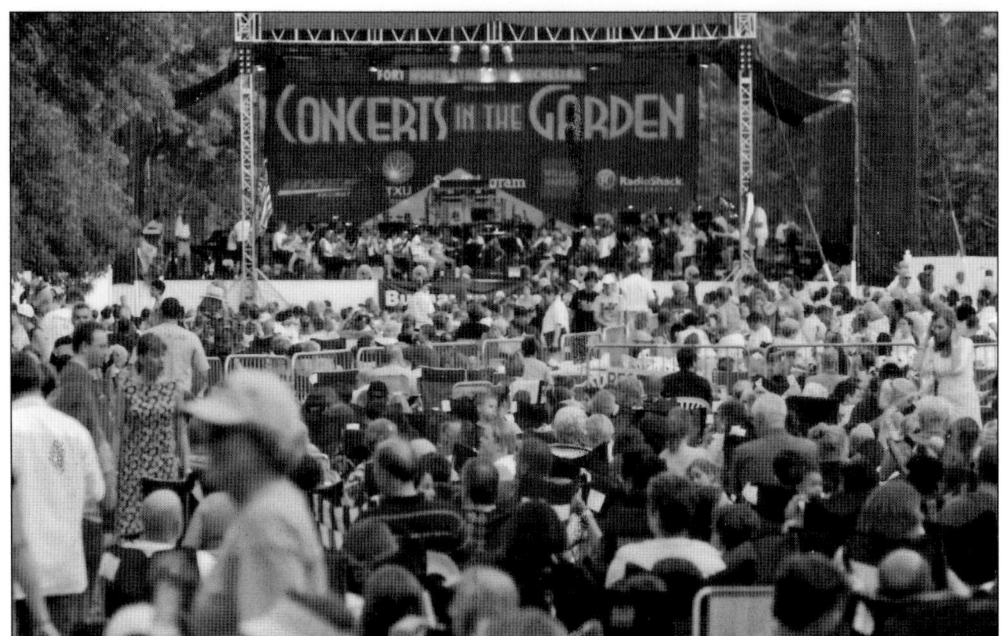

The Concerts in the Garden series has become a summertime tradition in Fort Worth. For nearly two decades, the Fort Worth Symphony Orchestra has been holding weekend concerts in the Fort Worth Botanic Garden between Memorial Day weekend and the Fourth of July. Featured performers or specially themed programs make each concert unique, and each ends with a fireworks display. (Photograph by Ron Ennis; Fort Worth Symphony Orchestra.)

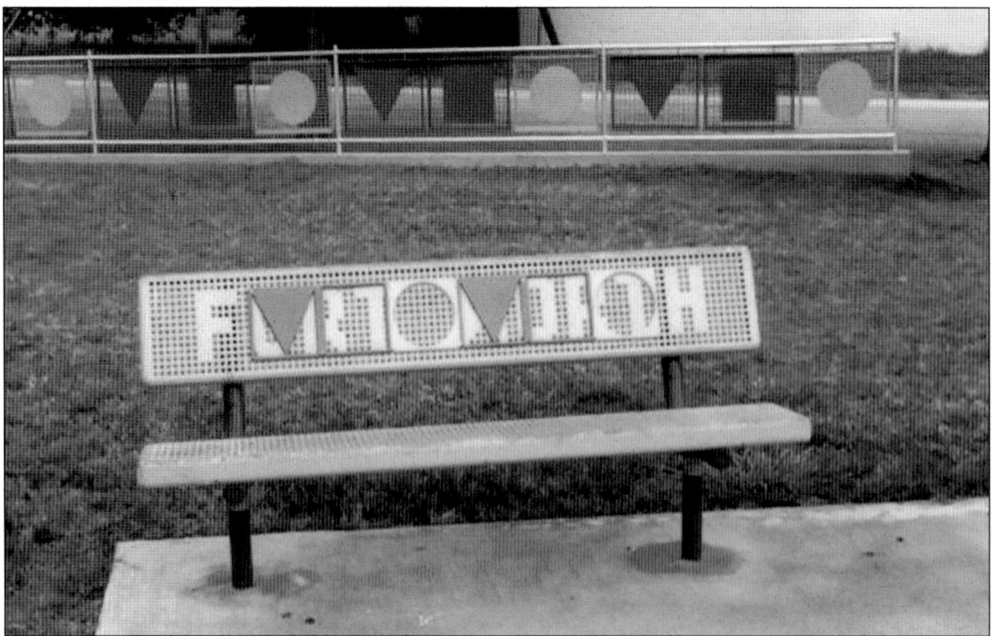

As a pilot project through Fort Worth Public Art, a team of artists designed a catalog of enhancements that could be included in PACS capital improvement projects. These included bench backs, trash receptacles, and sidewalk enhancements. The bench back and fence shown here were installed at the Como Community Center in 2008. (PACS.)

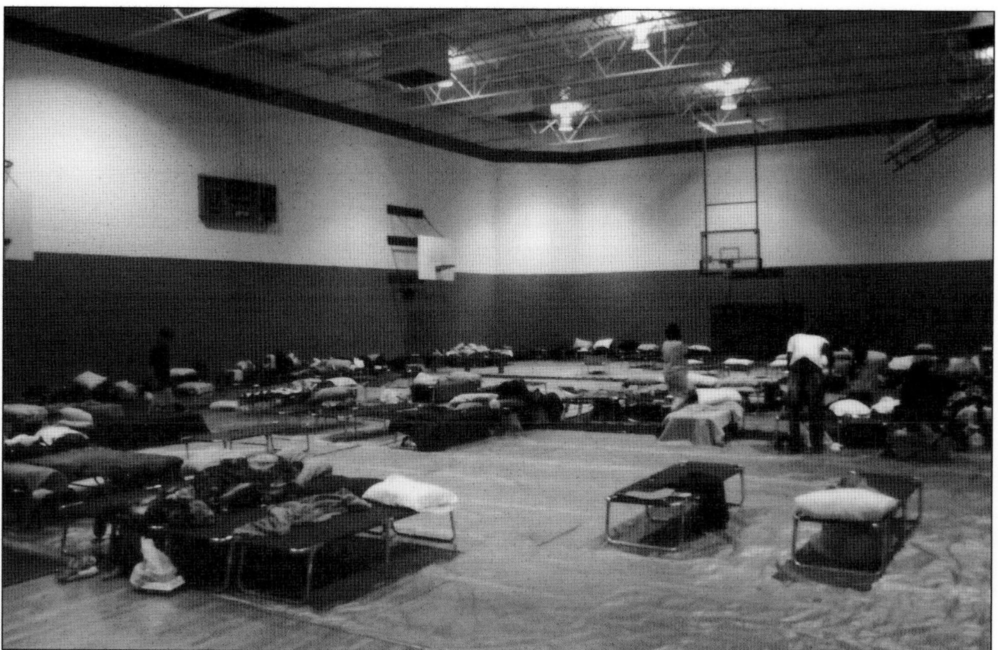

The PACS's community centers took on the role of emergency shelter for thousands fleeing Hurricanes Katrina, Rita, Gustav, and Ike. PACS led the emergency operations in sheltering evacuees. For those evacuees who chose to make Fort Worth home, case managers from the department assisted with their transition to self-sufficiency. (PACS.)

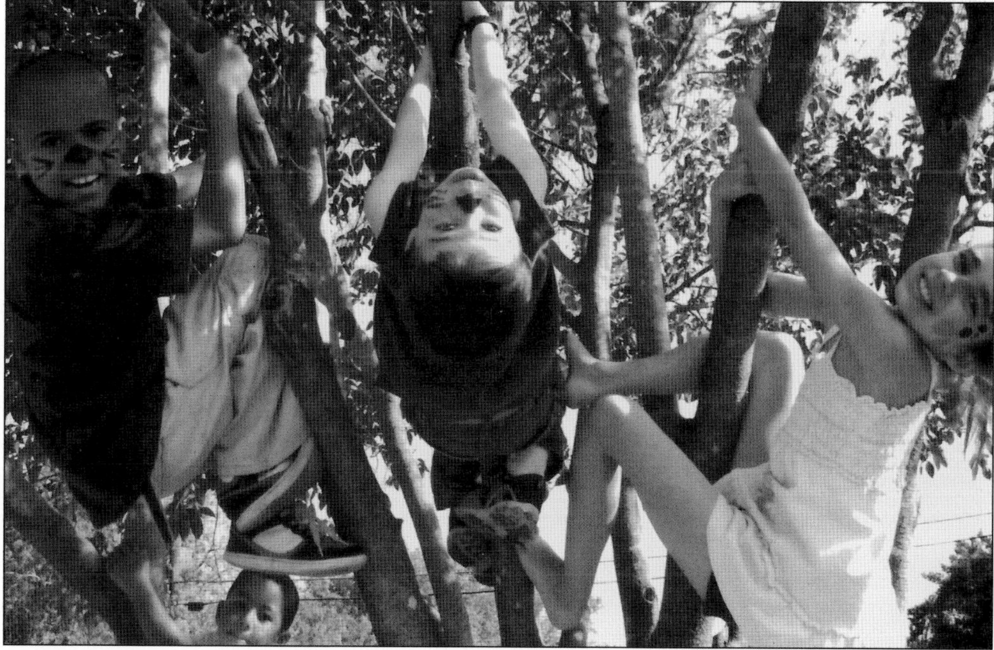

As the name suggests, the Fire Station Community Center is located in an old firehouse. The station was originally constructed in 1923. It has been serving the Fairmount and adjacent neighborhoods as a community center since 1979. These students in the center's after-school program had their faces painted and then enjoyed just hanging around. (PACS.)

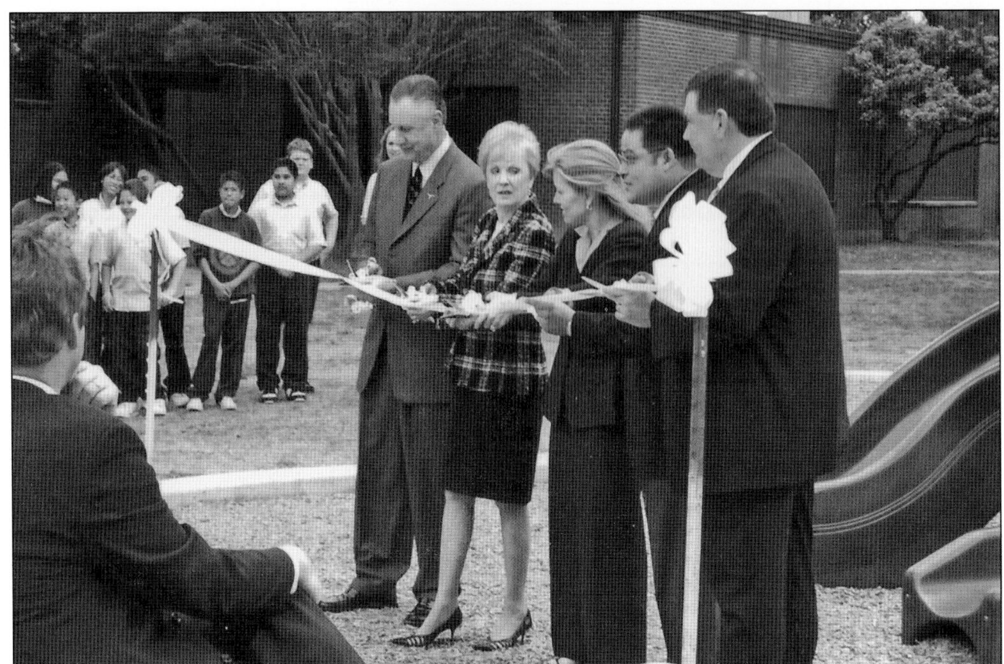

Urban Park and Recreation Recovery Act (UPARR) funds were utilized to renovate seven playgrounds in neighborhood and community parks. Dedicating a new playground at Sylvania Park in 2005 are, from left to right, Mayor Mike Moncrief; Congresswoman Kay Granger; councilmember Becky Haskin; David Vela, National Park Service; and Randle Harwood, PACS acting director. (PACS.)

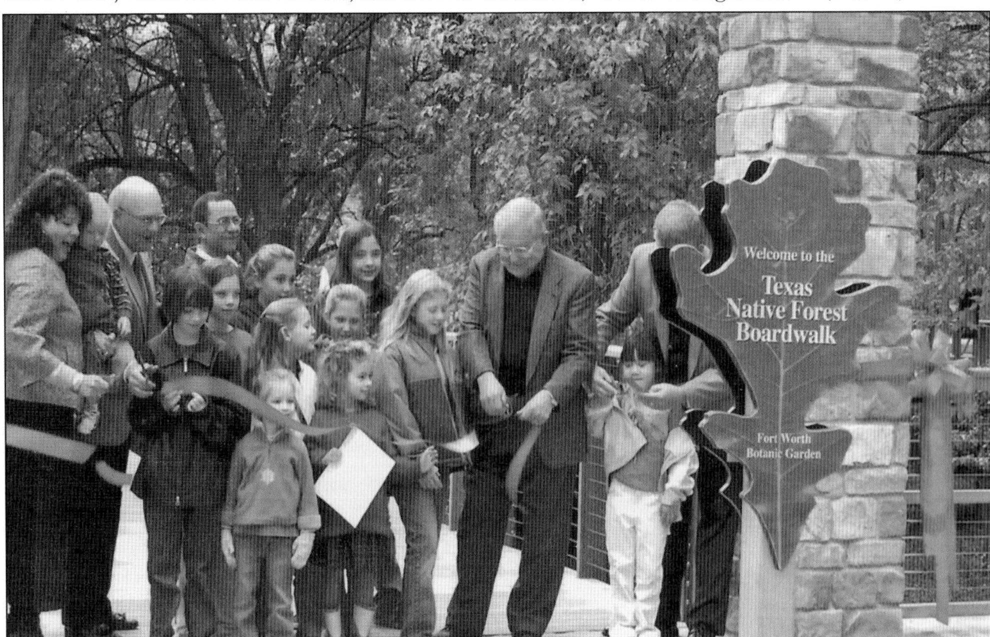

The Texas Native Forest Boardwalk opened in the Fort Worth Botanic Garden on November 4, 2006. The elevated boardwalk is an outdoor classroom designed to stimulate an interest in the stewardship and conservation of native forests. Pictured at the ribbon-cutting ceremony are PACS staff, advisory board members, and special guests. (PACS.)

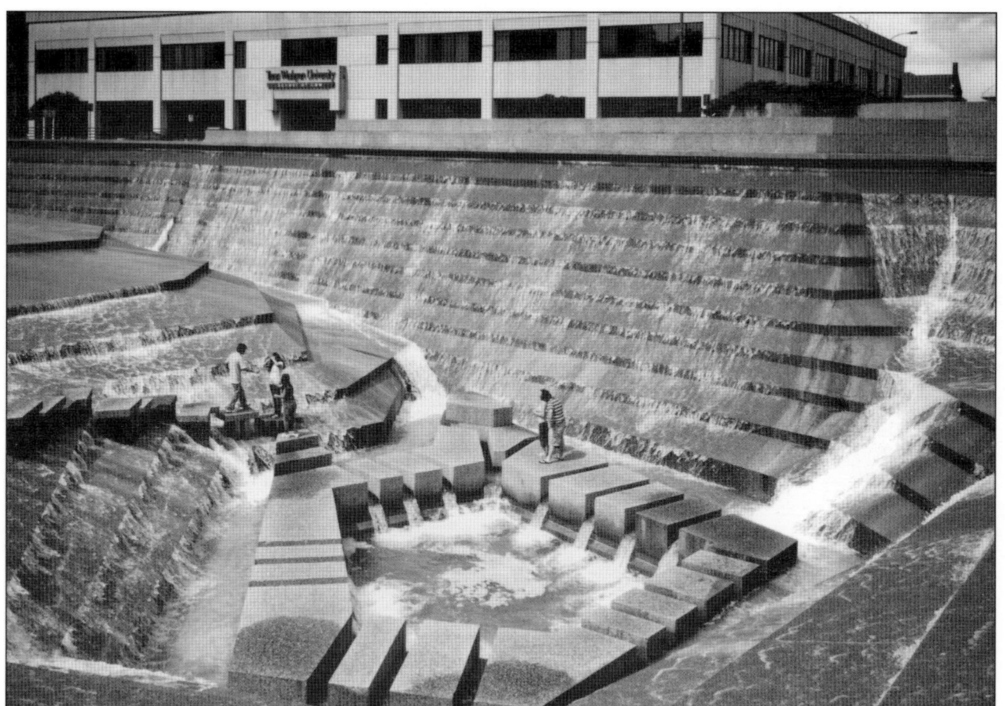

After the tragic drowning of four visitors from Chicago in 2004, the Fort Worth Water Gardens was closed to address maintenance and safety issues. It reopened in 2007 after the installation of sensitively designed barriers that did not detract from Philip Johnson's original design. In 2008, the Fort Worth Water Gardens received the Texas Society of Architects' 25-Year Award. (Kevin Buchanan, FortWorthology.com.)

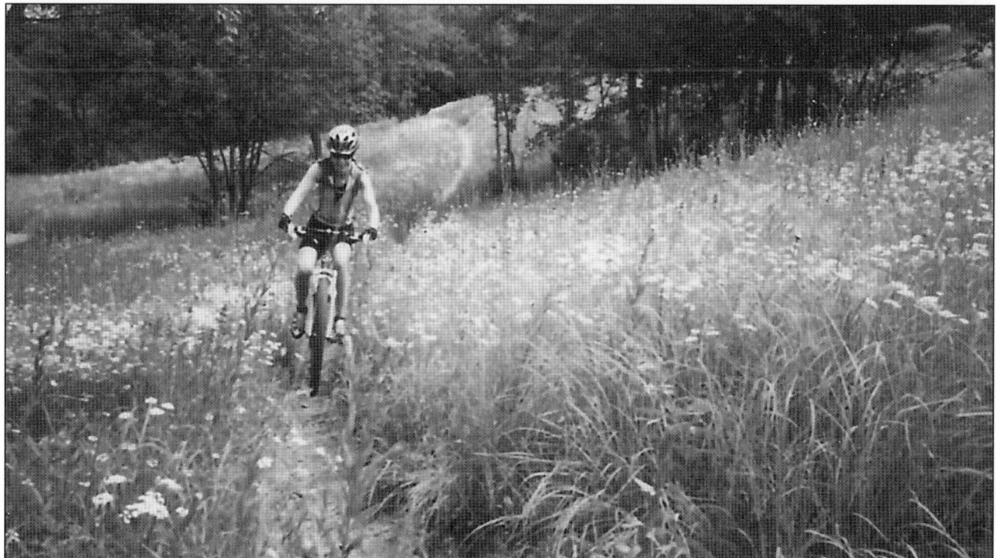

The Fort Worth Mountain Bikers' Association built, operates, and maintains biking trails in Gateway and Marion Sansom Parks. In Marion Sansom Park, where this photograph was taken, there are 7 miles of trail through fields and rugged terrain with nearly 1,100 feet of elevation change. (Fort Worth Mountain Bikers' Association.)

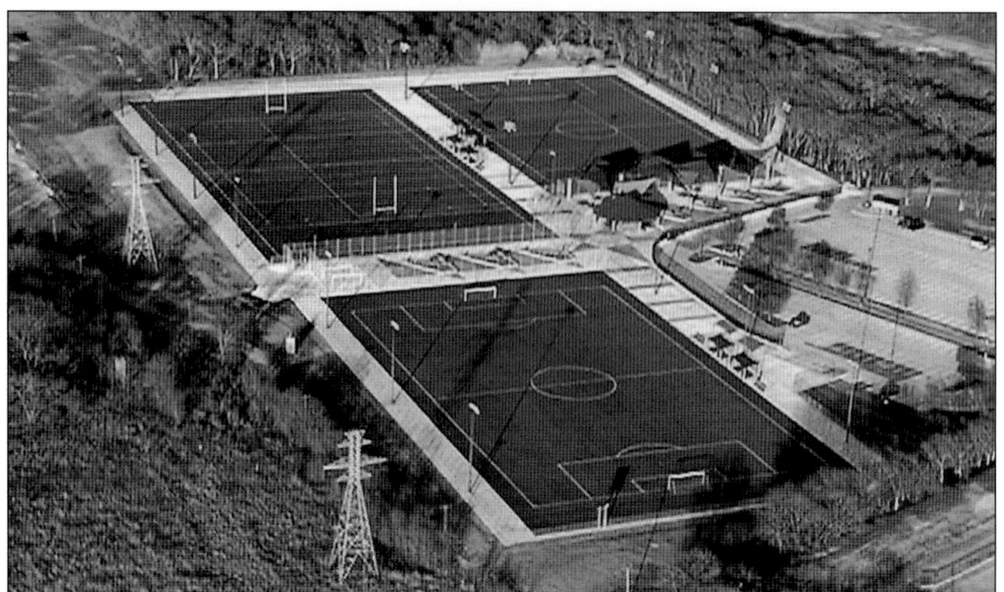

A new soccer/rugby complex was dedicated at Gateway Park in December 2006. The complex, funded by the Fort Worth Water Department, includes one rugby and two soccer fields with synthetic surfaces that will allow for unlimited play throughout the year. Also included were electronic scoreboards and covered bleacher seating. (PACS.)

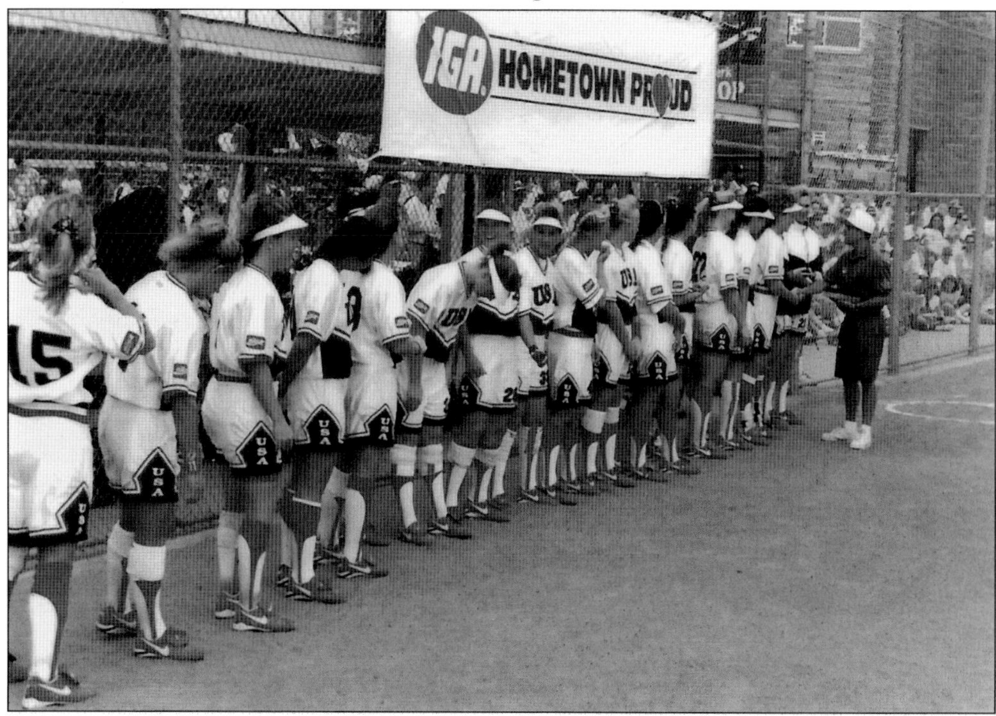

The U.S. Women's Olympic Softball Team has visited Fort Worth prior to the last four Olympics. With exhibition games against a team of area high school all-stars at Gateway Park, the Fort Worth appearances always attract record crowds. Here PACS director Richard Zavala Jr. (far right) greets players from the Olympic team. (PACS.)

The Cowboy Santas Program, Inc., is a nonprofit organization headquartered in the PACS department. The program provides toys to children ages 12 and under from low-income families during the holiday season. Volunteers from corporations, youth, and church groups, and City of Fort Worth employees make the program a success. In 2008, Cowboy Santas served nearly 4,000 families, providing toys to more than 11,600 children. (PACS.)

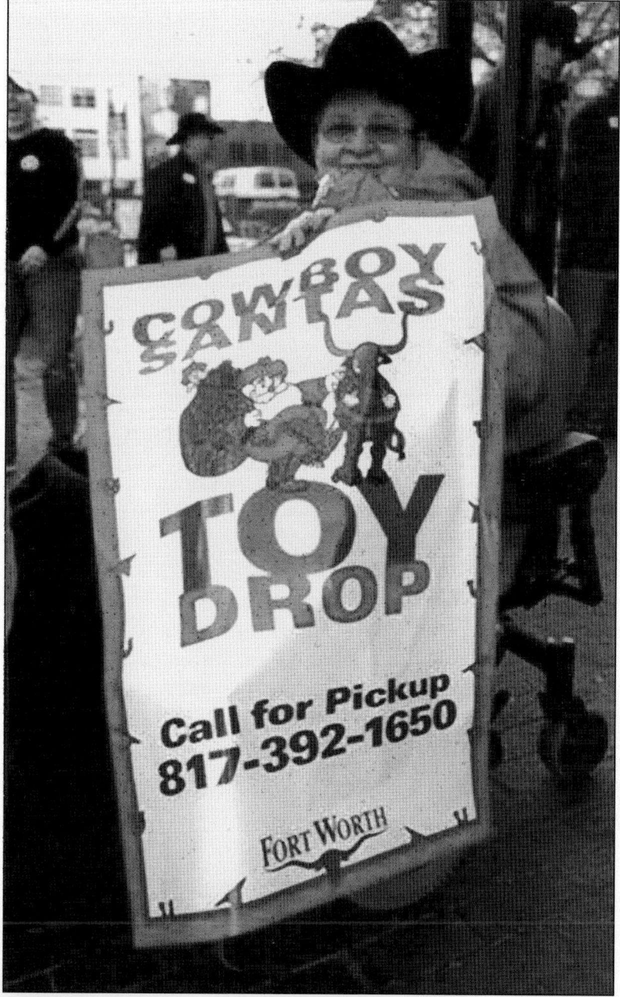

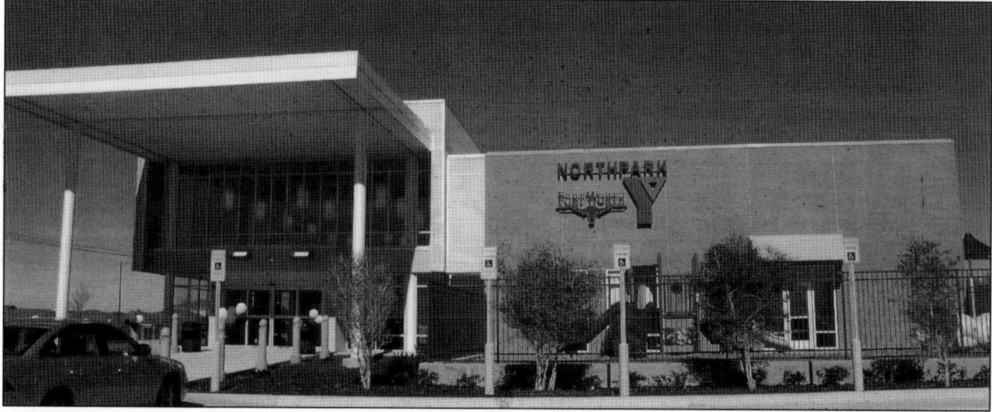

The Northpark YMCA was constructed as a joint project of the PACS and the YMCA. Each contributed $2.5 million toward the design and construction of the recreational and community facility. Located in far north Fort Worth, Northpark is helping to address the community needs of this rapidly growing area. (PACS.)

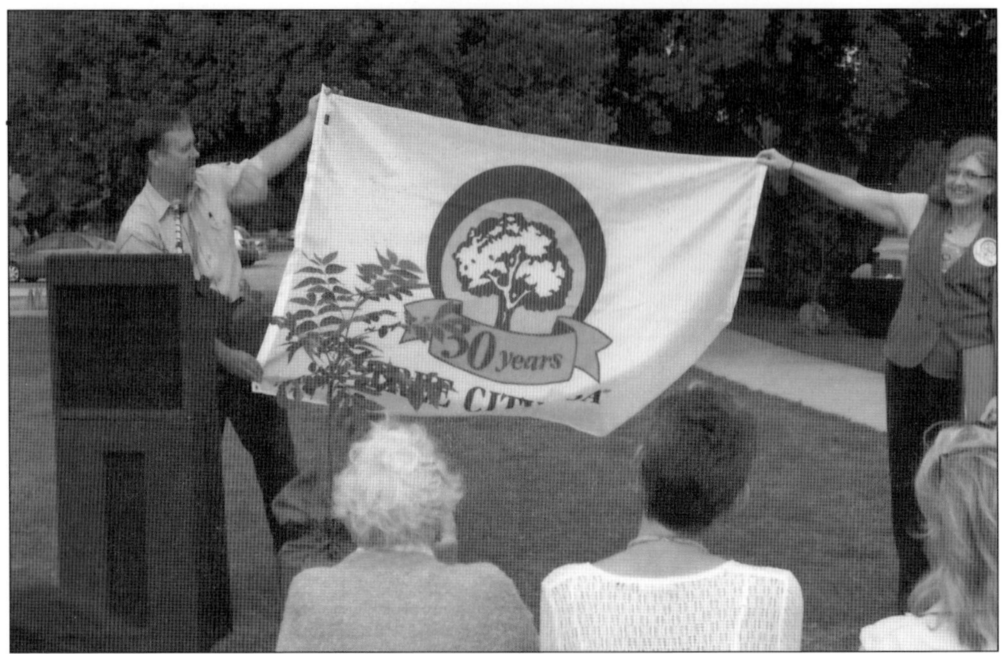

Courtney Blevins (left), regional urban forester, Texas Forest Service, presents the 30th-year Tree City USA flag to Fort Worth forester Melinda Adams under the John Peter Smith Oak Tree during the city's 2009 Arbor Day celebration. Located in the city's cultural district, the tree has been designated a Heritage Tree. The Heritage Tree program recognizes trees that have historic or cultural significance. (PACS.)

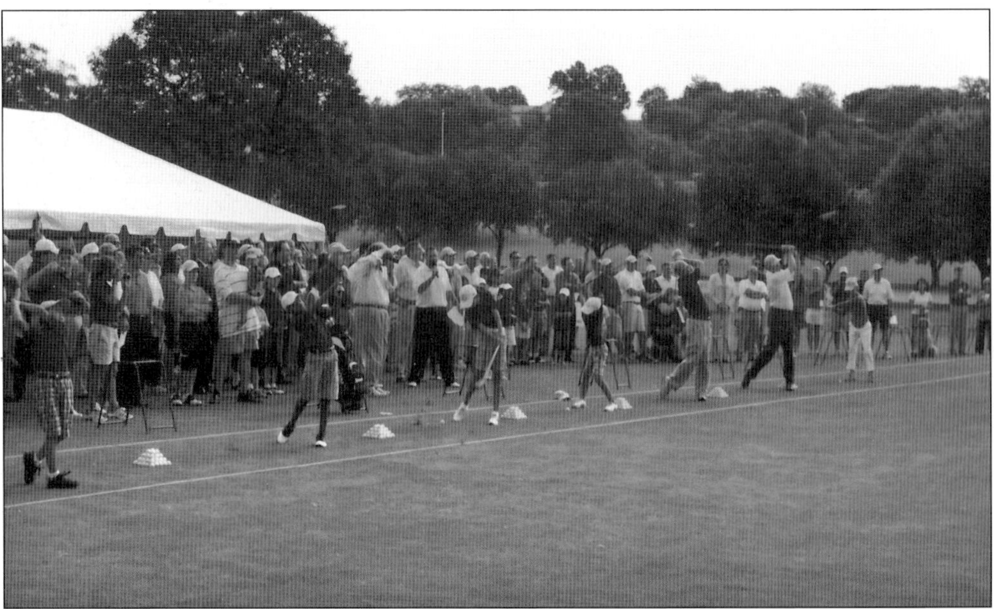

The Barnett Shale is a vast natural gas field beneath Fort Worth. Revenue from the production of natural gas below park property is being used for improvements to those parks. At the Rockwood Park Golf Course, a master plan will provide a hole-by-hole analysis of the course and assess the need for such improvements as a new clubhouse, a maintenance facility, and a practice course. (PACS.)

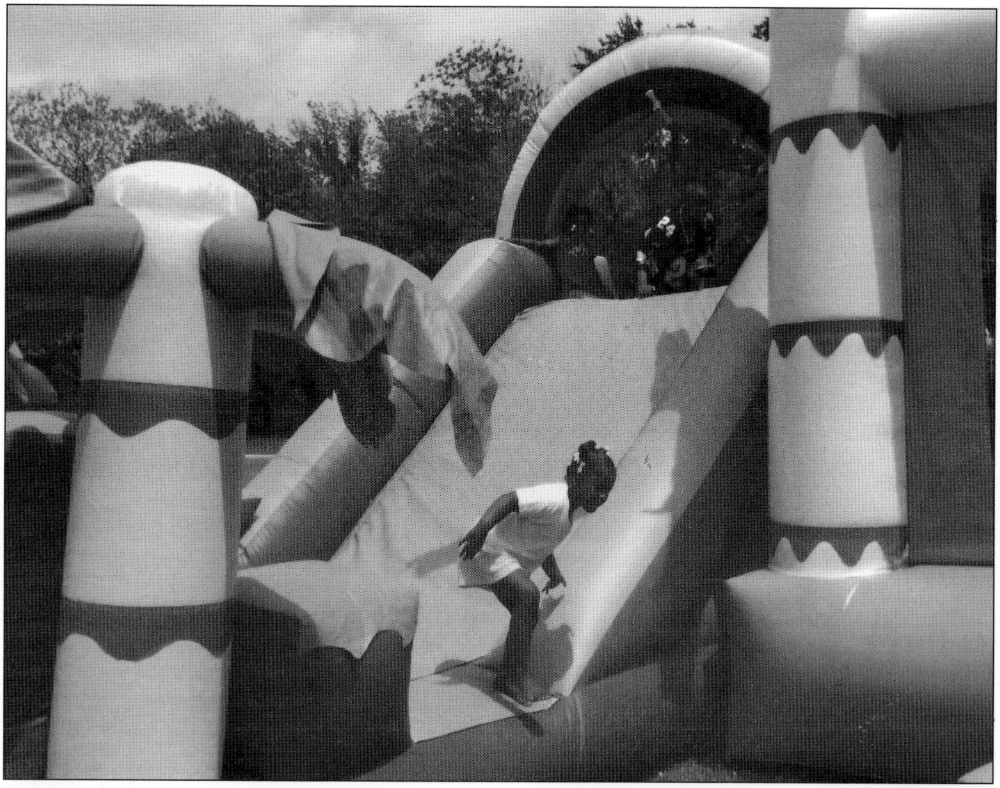

Cobb Park, first acquired in 1923, is a large park located in east Fort Worth that has remained largely unimproved. Natural gas revenue was used to fund a master plan. The plan was unveiled at a public celebration in April 2009. Here a youngster takes part in the day's festivities. (Chesapeake Energy.)

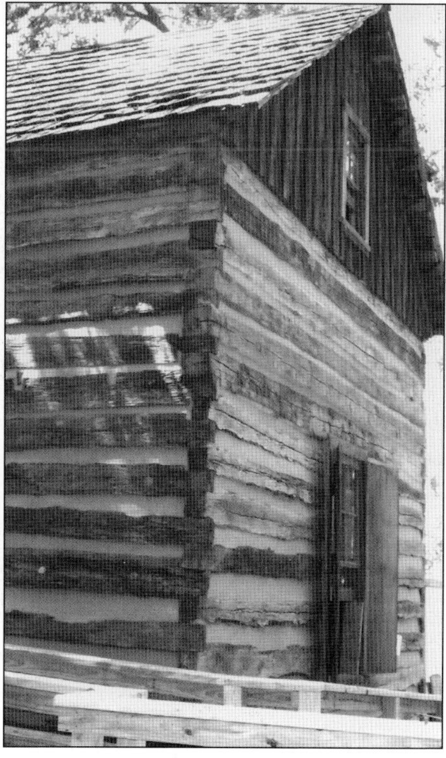

When the Log Cabin Village's Howard Cabin became structurally unsafe, Barnett Shale revenue was used to reconstruct the c. 1860 cabin. It was carefully dismantled and then reassembled on a new foundation. Original material was reused when possible. New chinking replaced Portland cement that was contributing to the cabin's deterioration. The project was completed in July 2009. (Log Cabin Village.)

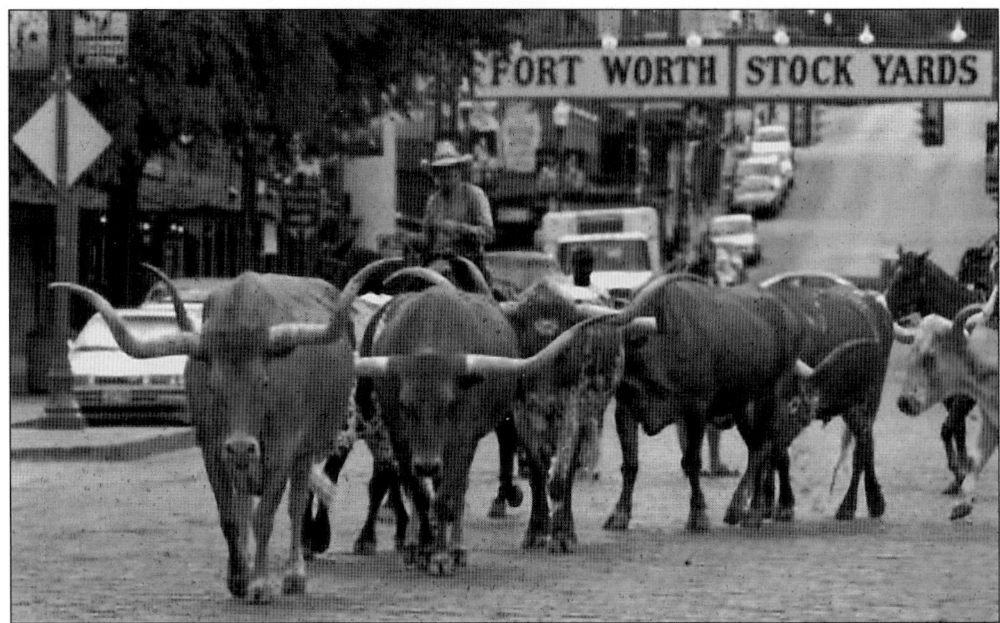

In celebration of the city's sesquicentennial in 1999, the Fort Worth Herd was created as a colorful reminder of the city's association with the cattle drives of the 19th century. Twice daily, drovers drive longhorns along East Exchange Avenue in the Fort Worth Stockyards National Historic District. Through special educational programs offered at the historic stockyards cattle pens, visitors can learn about the history of the cattle drives, see the longhorns up close, and watch the drovers demonstrate such traditional skills as riding, roping, and branding. In honor of the herd's 10th anniversary, a special drive was held on June 13, 2009. Residents were invited to bring their own horses to help drive the herd along the Trinity River and east on Exchange Avenue. (Both, PACS.)

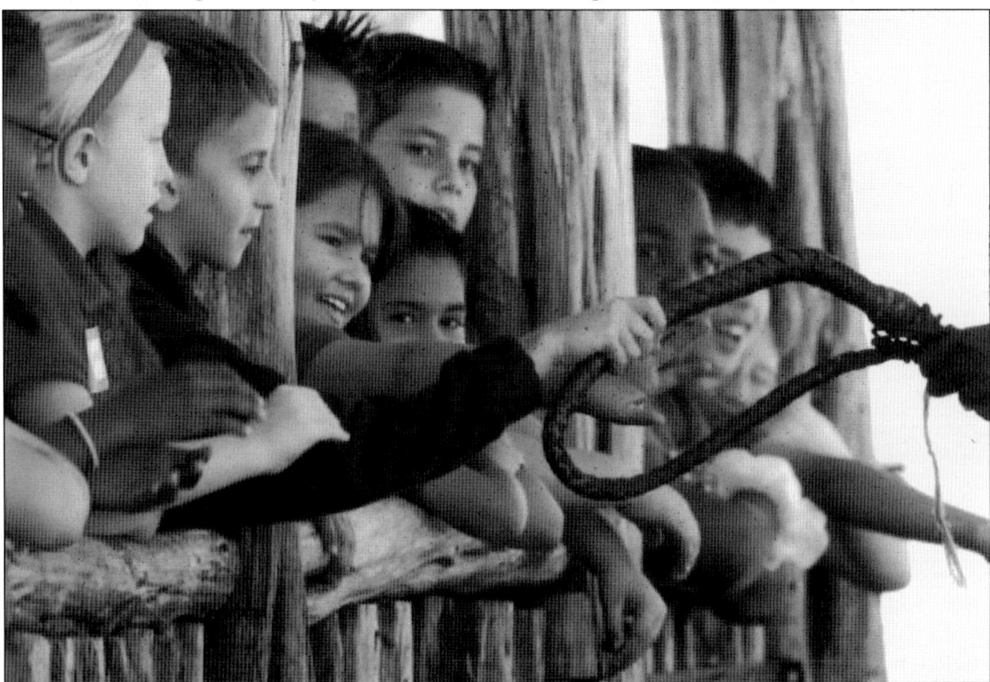

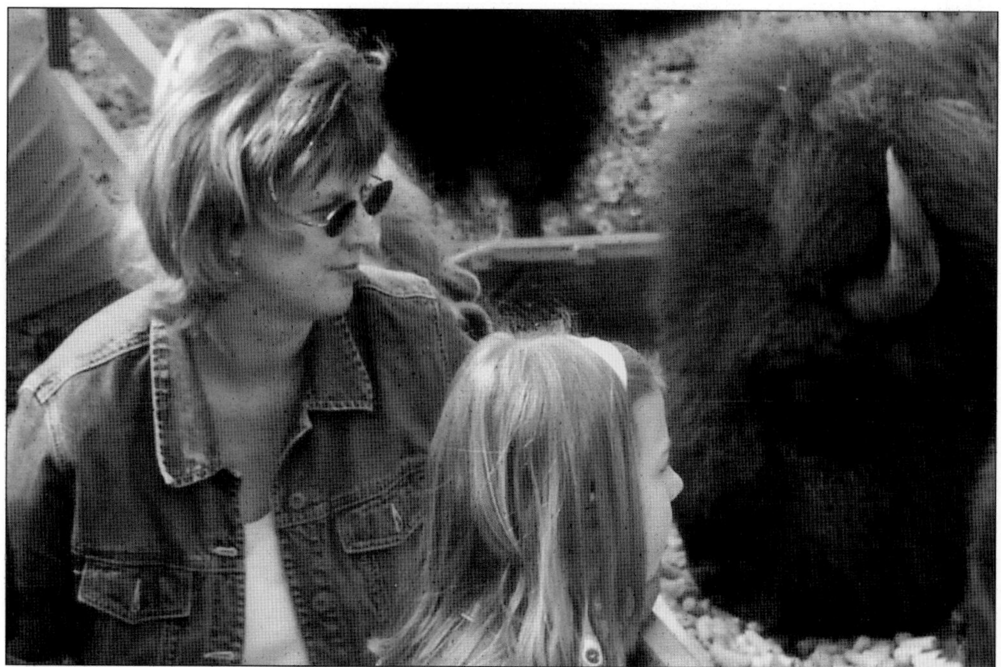

The Fort Worth Nature Center and Refuge received a Lone Star Land Steward Award from Texas Parks and Wildlife in 2009 for excellence in management of its natural and cultural resources. Prescribed burning, brush control, and rotational grazing of its bison herd are just a few of the practices that garnered it this award. (Fort Worth Nature Center and Refuge.)

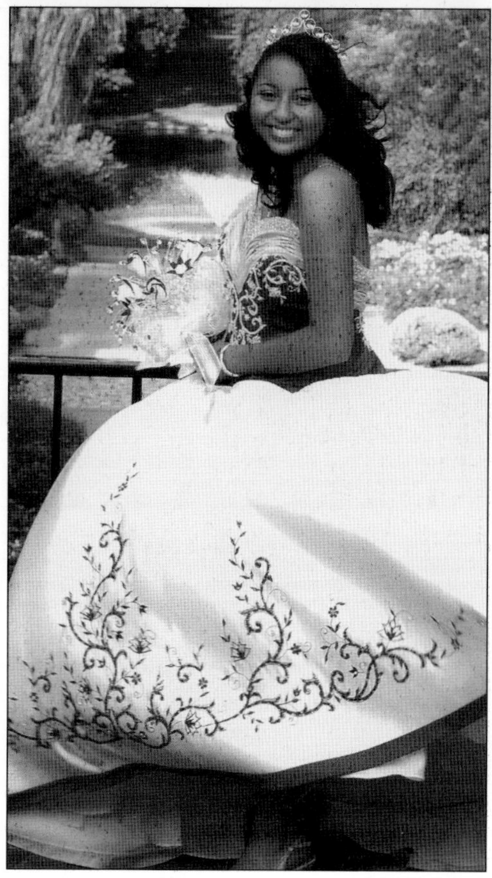

On January 29, 2009, the oldest portion of the Fort Worth Botanic Garden was listed on the National Register of Historic Places for its significance as a designed landscape. Since 1933, Fort Worthians have been coming to the garden to celebrate special occasions. Here the rose garden served as a beautiful backdrop for Natalie Marie Jimenez's Quinceañera photographs in July 2009. (Juanita Jimenez.)

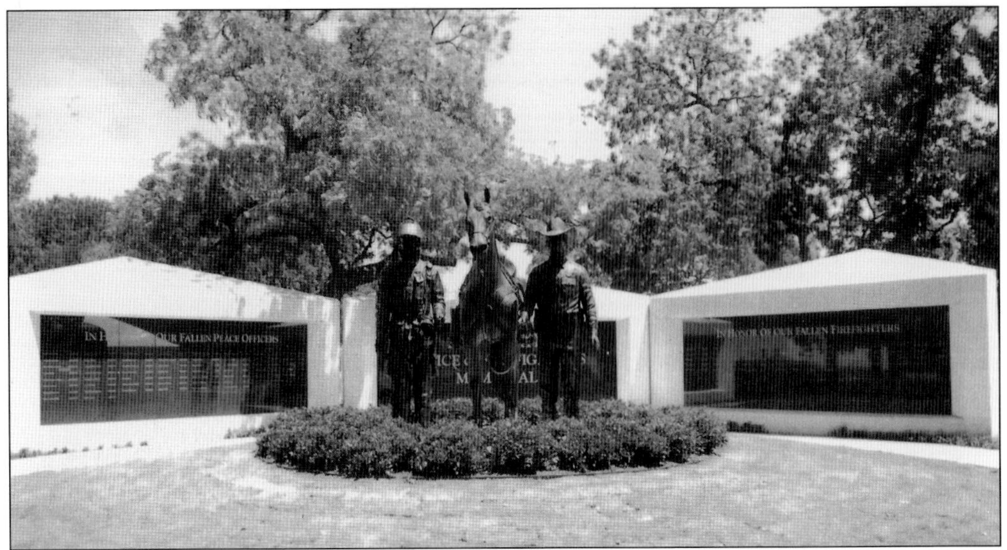

The Police and Firefighters Memorial in Trinity Park features sculptures of a firefighter and police officer flanking a riderless horse. Behind them are tablets with the names of those peace officers and firefighters who died in service to the residents of Fort Worth. The sculptor was Jack Wilson, and the architect was Randy Gideon. (Raymond Cervantes, Fort Worth Police Media Services.)

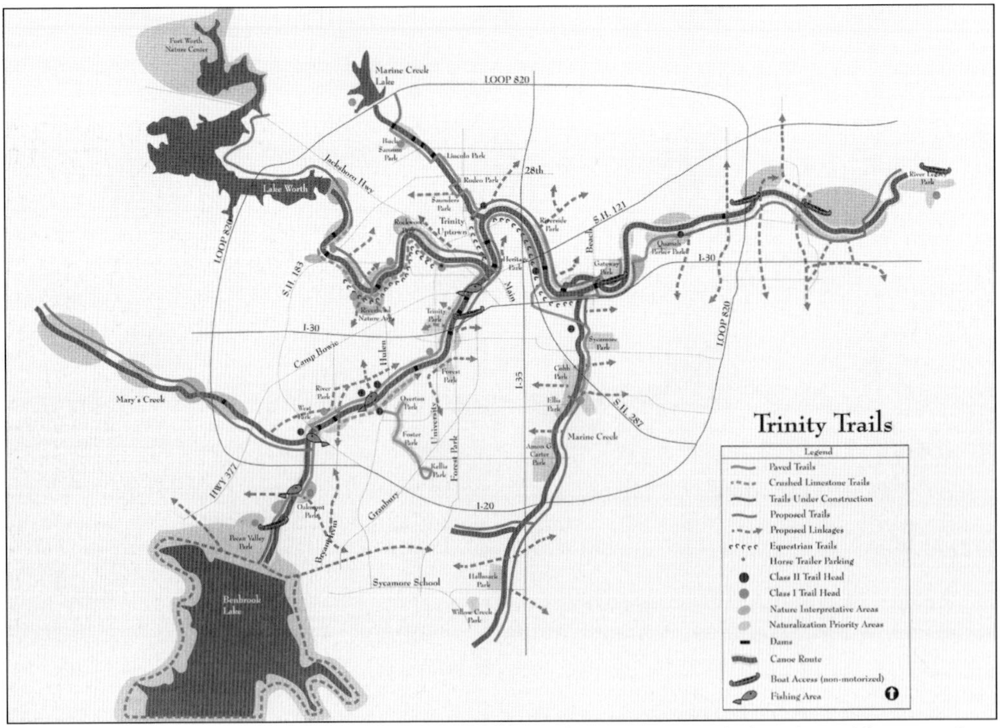

Trinity Trails

Legend
Paved Trails
Crushed Limestone Trails
Trails Under Construction
Proposed Trails
Proposed Linkages
Equestrian Trails
Horse Trailer Parking
Class II Trail Head
Class I Trail Head
Nature Interpretative Areas
Naturalization Priority Areas
Dams
Canoe Route
Boat Access (non-motorized)
Fishing Area

The Trinity River Master Plan is both an economic and environmental plan that addresses urban development, ecosystems, flood protection, recreational opportunities, and preservation of green space along the river and its tributaries. The associated Trinity Trails systems builds on the Kessler and Hare and Hare plans by beautifying the river and providing linkages to neighborhoods, downtown, and special districts. (Trinity River Vision.)

It is appropriate that the centennial logo for the PACS included a tree. The tree represents the natural environment as well as a strong department that is deeply rooted in Fort Worth's history and one that branches out to cover the city and grows with its future. (PACS.)

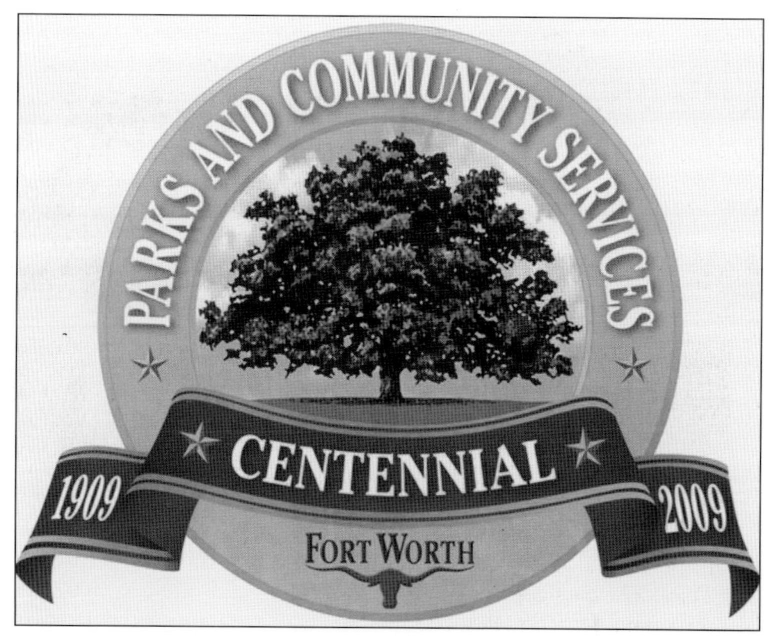

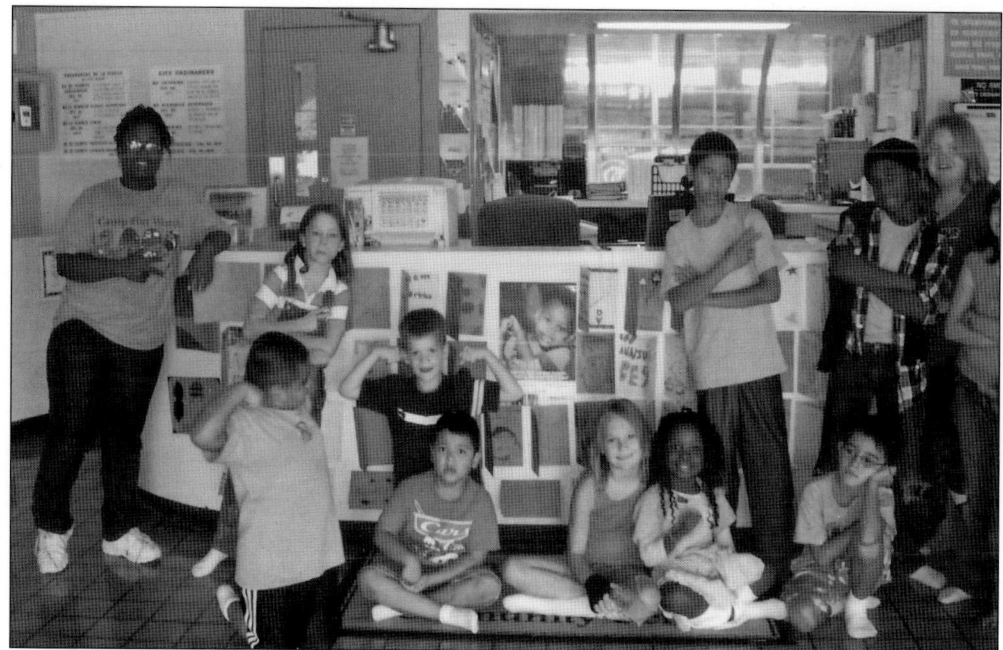

As the PACS marked its centennial in 2009, birthday celebrations were held at community centers and parks across the city. Here youngsters at the R. D. Evans Community Center pause for a photograph in front of birthday cards they made commemorating the occasion. (PACS.)

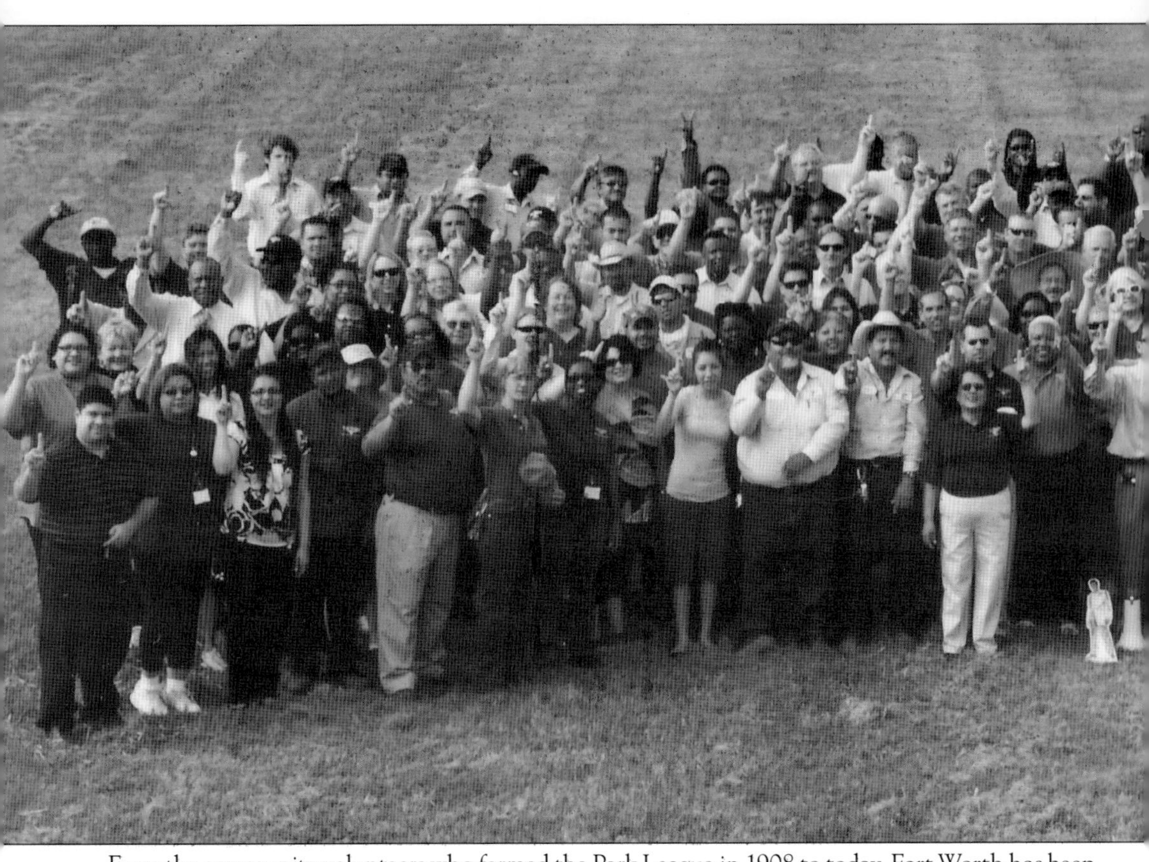

From the community volunteers who formed the Park League in 1908 to today, Fort Worth has been blessed with a citizenry dedicated to the preservation of green spaces and the creation of recreational opportunities for all. The employees of the Forth Worth Parks and Community Services are proud to be a part of this great legacy. Here they gather on the great lawn at Gateway Park to take a

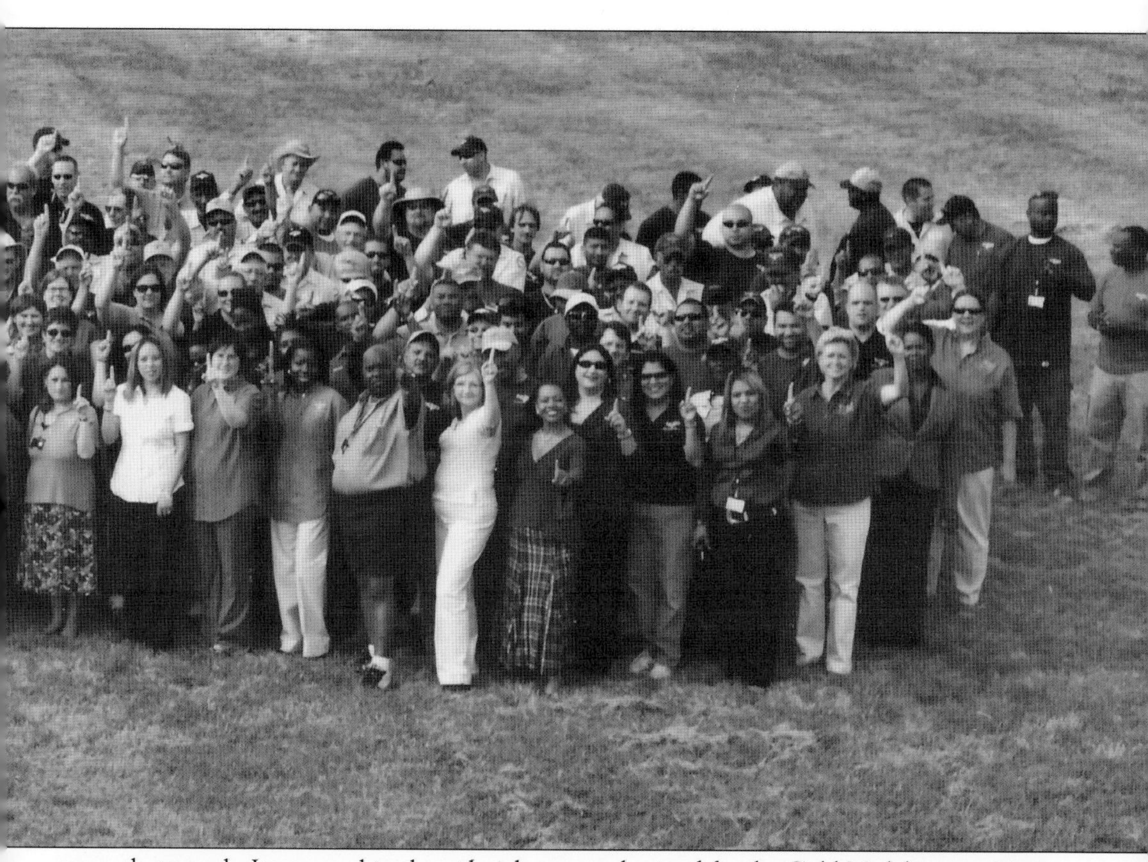

group photograph. It was used in the video that was submitted for the Gold Medal competition when Fort Worth was named one of the final four from across the nation being considered for this prestigious award for excellence in park and recreation management. (PACS.)

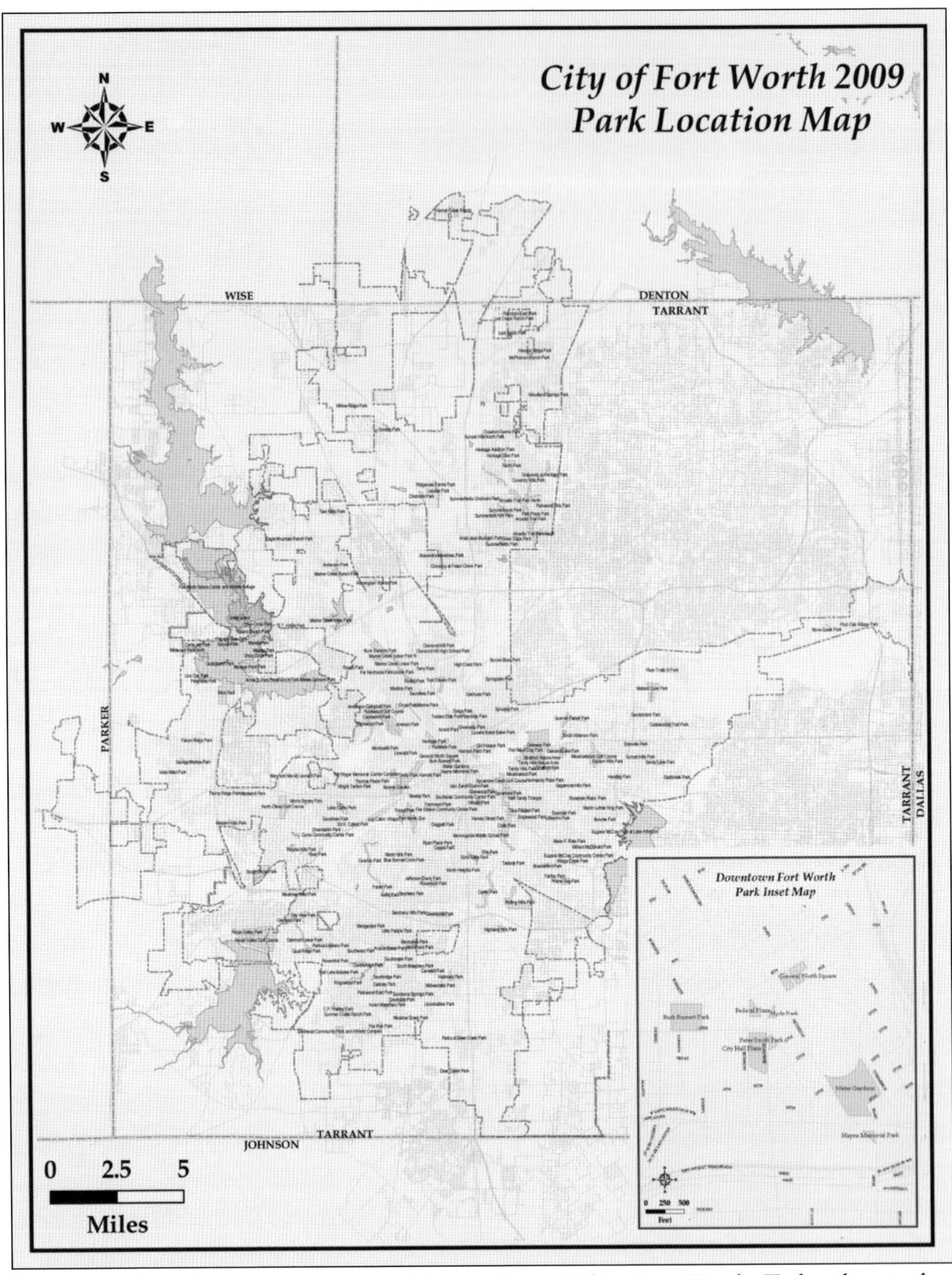

Recreational and leisure time opportunities are bountiful in Fort Worth. Today the city has 244 parks with 10,976 acres. They are found throughout the city and include one in an adjacent county. The park system includes 154 playgrounds, 61 miles of walks and trails, 46 competition softball/baseball fields, and 109 shelters. (PACS.)

Bibliography

Cashion, Ty. *A Contemporary History of Fort Worth and Tarrant County*. San Antonio, TX: Historical Publishing Network, 2006.

Evans, Marvin D. "What Recreation Means to Fort Worth." *Playground* 19 (February 1926): 601–602.

Fort Worth Star-Telegram Clippings and Photograph Collections. Arlington, TX: Special Collections, University of Texas at Arlington Libraries.

Good, Albert H. *Park and Recreation Structures*. New York: Princeton Architectural Press, 1999 [reprint of 1938 edition published by U.S. Department of the Interior, National Park Service].

Hare and Hare Collection (KC206). Western Historical Manuscript Collection. Kansas City, MO: University of Missouri–Kansas City.

Jordan, Terry G. *Log Cabin Village: A History and Guide*. Austin, TX: Texas State Historical Association, 1980.

Lake, Mary Daggett. "A Pioneer in Southwestern Garden History: The Fort Worth Botanical Garden is a Shrine in Peace and War." *Parks and Recreation* 26 (January–February 1943): 117–122.

Morrison, R. C., compiler. "United States Community Improvement Appraisal, Fort Worth, Texas, Before and After Work Relief, 1932–1938." Original copy on file at Fort Worth Botanic Garden.

Morrison, R. C. and Myrtle E. Huff. *Let's Go to the Park*. Dallas, TX: Wilkinson Printing Company, 1937.

Obert, D. D. "New Views in Fort Worth's Park System." *Fort Worth Magazine* 23 (November 1949): 21, 45.

Pearce, Paul. "The Fort Worth Zoological Park: A Sixty-Year History, 1909–1969." Fort Worth, TX: Texas Christian University, master's thesis, 1969.

Selcer, Rick. "Historic Marker Application for Douglass and McGar Parks." Copy on file at Tarrant County Archives. Fort Worth, TX: 2009.